⟷

ROMAN REPUBLICS

ROMAN REPUBLICS

HARRIET I. FLOWER

PRINCETON UNIVERSITY PRESS ❖ PRINCETON AND OXFORD

In the United Kingdom: Princeton University Press, 6 Oxford Street,
Woodstock, Oxfordshire OX20 1TW

Library of Congress Cataloging-in-Publication Data

Flower, Harriet I.
Roman republics / Harriet I. Flower.
p. cm.
Includes bibliographical references and index.
ISBN 978-0-691-14043-8 (hardcover : alk. paper)
1. Rome—Politics and government—265–30 B.C.
2. Rome—History—Republic, 265–30 B.C. I. Title.
DG231.F567 2010
937'.02—dc22   2009004551

British Library Cataloging-in-Publication Data is available

This book has been composed in Sabon

Printed on acid-free paper. ∞

press.princeton.edu

Printed in the United States of America

1 3 5 7 9 10 8 6 4 2

nostra vero aetas, cum rem publicam sicut picturam accepis-
set egregiam sed iam evanesentem vetustate, non modo eam
coloribus eisdem quibus fuerat renovare neglexit, sed ne id
quidem curavit ut formam saltem eius et extrema tamquam
lineamenta servaret.

In truth, our own generation, although it inherited the *res pu-*
blica as if it were a master painting, yet one that was now
fading as a result of age, not only failed to restore it with the
same colors that had been there before, but did not even see
to it that at least its design and as it were its basic outlines
were preserved.

Cicero *De republica* 5.2, written in the late 50s BC

CONTENTS

⊷ PREFACE ⊷

Crisis n., point or time of deciding anything, the decisive moment
or turning point.
Chambers Twentieth Century Dictionary (1973)

A vitally important or decisive stage in the progress of anything,
a turning-point, a state of affairs in which a decisive change for
better or worse is imminent, now applied esp. to times of difficulty,
insecurity and suspense in politics or commerce.
Compact Oxford English Dictionary, second edition (1991)

This book is dedicated to the memory of my father, Michael
Gerald Dealtry, who planted the first seeds of the central idea
that inspired its writing. Some years ago, when I was editing
The Cambridge Companion to the Roman Republic (Cambridge, 2004), he questioned me about the use of the word
"crisis" in the title of a chapter that described the period in
Roman republican history between 133 and 49 BC (chap. 4).
He felt that the term "crisis" was being misused, since a crisis
was by definition an acute event of short duration with a mea-
surable outcome. How could there be a crisis that went on
for over eighty years? He advised me simply to use a different
word in this chapter heading.

At first I was resistant to his suggestion, which I did not act
upon, thinking that I simply needed to explain to him more
clearly the traditional periodization and classification of the
Late Republic, which has often been described as a crisis.
Later the force of his argument came home to me, at a time
when I was working in more detail on the time of Marius and
Sulla (ca. 120–78 BC), a period that in modern discussions has
often been overshadowed by subsequent events. Meanwhile, a
decade of teaching undergraduate surveys of Roman history
has made me acutely aware of the challenges of framing and
summarizing the essentials of republican politics in terms that
are accessible to beginners.

In contemplating a different chronological approach, I began to realize (yet again) how deeply ingrained the concept of a single, long crisis had become in modern thinking, serving as a basic premise for scholars from different countries and different generations, working in very different schools of thought. A new perspective is perhaps long overdue and can be helpful in reformulating and then in addressing persistent questions about the role and rate of change in republican politics. No single scheme will, however, offer the definitive answer, and much can be gained from a variety of perspectives.

History will always consist of a shifting pattern of continuities and discontinuities depending on emphasis and evidence. The "fall" of "the Republic," and especially the analysis of it offered here, will deliberately stress discontinuity and change with a primary focus on the political sphere. I will not be concentrating on a single ancient author as a guide, nor do I provide a history of modern scholarship. I do not have a new set of data to present. Rather I offer a rereading of material that is already very familiar to students of Rome, with all the risks that such a project entails.

This essay is not meant as an attack on, or an endorsement of, any existing school of thought about ancient Rome. The scale of this short study does not allow for a full engagement with the vast modern literature, either in the text or in the footnotes, and it is not intended to be dismissive of the rich and varied work of earlier scholars.[1] In suggesting a different periodization as an approach to republican Rome my interpretation will inevitably differ from many, if not most, previous studies: it is simply offered as a single alternative to these. My purpose is to initiate a renewed discussion of Ro-

---

[1]The footnotes are designed to help the reader pursue topics by mentioning recent studies, sources of bibliography, or classic treatments. They are not meant to be comprehensive guides to the scholarship in each field. Most source references can be found in Broughton's *MRR* and Greenidge and Clay 1960 for the years 133–70. For a general discussion of the ancient sources for republican Rome, see esp. Lintott 1994. For bibliography, see volumes 8 and 9 of the second edition of *The Cambridge Ancient History*, with Bleicken 1995a, 1995b, and 2004; Christ 2000; Hölkeskamp 2004a and 2004b; von Ungern-Sternberg 2006; Rosenstein and Morstein-Marx 2006; and Bringmann 2007. The best brief overviews of the Republic are Hölkeskamp 2000b and Jehne 2006b.

man republican political culture, of its evolving nature, of the kinds of challenges it faced and overcame over time, and of the precise historical circumstances in which it succumbed to a combination of outside pressures and internal violence. This study is designed to suggest a new beginning rather than a set of definitive conclusions.

All dates are BC unless otherwise specified. All translations are my own.

Princeton, New Jersey
September 5, 2008

⟶ ACKNOWLEDGMENTS ⟵

This study has been influenced by all of my teachers and students over the more than thirty years since I discovered, first, the manifold lessons to be learned from past times, and subsequently, a special fascination for the history of the old Romans and of their remarkable city.

The initial draft of this book was written during a sabbatical leave from Princeton University in the fall semester of 2006. My investigation of republican Rome was greatly enhanced by the generous support of the university for faculty research. I am grateful to all my colleagues in the Classics Department for their consistent encouragement and for the stimulating intellectual environment they foster every day. Some of the main ideas in this study were presented as papers at Yale University, Brooklyn College, and Amherst College. I owe a debt to the audiences in each place for their valuable suggestions and lively discussions.

I would like to thank Rob Tempio, Terri O'Prey, Karen Edwards Donohue, and Dimitri Karetnikov of Princeton University Press for their help in making my manuscript into a book. I also benefitted greatly from the technical advice and support of Donna Sanclemente, technical support specialist in the Classics Department at Princeton University. Judith Chien once again lent her special expertise to the editing of my prose.

The following people have read versions of my manuscript and offered invaluable advice: Corey Brennan, Peter Brown, Jessica Clark, Michael Flower, Bob Kaster, Dan-el Padilla Peralta, Kurt Raaflaub, and Susan Satterfield. I have also learned much from discussion of individual problems with Denis Feeney and Josiah Ober. My own stubbornness has prevented me from following more of their sage advice. I am especially indebted to Ted Champlin and to Kathryn Morgan for their particular moral and practical support.

This intellectual endeavor was made possible by the daily loving encouragement of my family: Michael, Isabel, Rosalind, and Roo.

⟹ ABBREVIATIONS ⟸

Greek authors are abbreviated according to the conventions in H. G. Liddell, R. Scott, and H. S. Jones, *Greek-English Lexicon* (Oxford, 1968); Latin authors according to P.G.W. Glare, *Oxford Latin Dictionary* (Oxford, 1982).

AE	*L'Année épigraphique*
*CAH*²	*The Cambridge Ancient History*², 14 vols., Cambridge 1970–2000.
CIL	*Corpus Inscriptionum Latinarum*, multiple vols., Berlin 1893–.
FGH	F. Jacoby, *Die Fragmente der griechischen Historiker*, 14 vols., Leiden 1957–99.
II	*Inscriptiones Italiae*, 13 vols., Rome 1931–.
ILLRP	A. Degrassi, *Inscriptiones Latinae Liberae Rei Publicae*, 2 vols., Florence 1957–63.
ILS	H. Dessau, *Inscriptiones Latinae Selectae*², 5 vols., Berlin 1954–55.
LTUR	E. M. Steinby, *Lexicon Topographicum Urbis Romae*, 6 vols., Rome 1993–2000.
MRR	T.R.S. Broughton, *Magistrates of the Roman Republic*, 3 vols., New York 1951–86.
*OCD*³	S. Hornblower and A. Spawforth, *The Oxford Classical Dictionary*³, Oxford 1996.
RE	G. Wissowa, *Paulys Real-encyclopädie der classischen Altertumswissenschaft*, multiple vols., Stuttgart 1894–.
RRC	M. Crawford, *Roman Republican Coinage*, 2 vols., Cambridge 1974.

Part One

FRAMEWORK

— I —

INTRODUCTION

Periodization and the End of the Roman Republic

> By the mid-first century BC, the republican form of govern-
> ment at Rome had effectively collapsed. Out of this collapse
> there emerged, in the aftermath of civil war, first the dictator-
> ship of Caesar and then the principate of Augustus. In a swift
> and striking transformation, a political system founded upon
> principles fundamentally opposed to monarchy was replaced
> by a system monarchical in all but name.
> So far, the narrative is simple—and would not be questioned
> by any historian ancient or modern.
>   Mary Beard and Michael Crawford (1999)

The entire discussion that follows is based on the fundamental idea that periodization is essential to historical thinking and
writing. In other words, it is periodization that makes an account of the past "history," as opposed to some other form of
description, narrative, or commemoration. Periodization is,
therefore, the most basic tool of the historian and must inevitably serve as the first premise from which any further analysis of a series of events will proceed.[1] Dividing past time into

---

[1] Morris 1997, 131: "We cannot get by without periodization: it is a fundamental part of the job of doing history. But if we are to avoid fetishization of
the period into something which really does resist, deflect, and disturb clear
thought, our periodization must be a reflexive exercise. And the only way to
make it such is through historical analysis of the processes of writing history." Strauss 1997, 165: "Periodization is both the requisite framework and
the false friend of all history-writing." See Gehrke 1999 for an overview of
antiquity and its periodization.

historically meaningful segments serves the same function as the punctuation in a sentence and the paragraphing on a page. We no longer write the way the ancient Romans and Greeks did, often without punctuation marks and sometimes even without any breaks between words. Just as punctuation articulates sentences, so too does periodization shape meaning even as it builds the foundation and framework of the critical message that is being communicated. Hence this study will argue, albeit often implicitly, that periodization is of vital importance to the historian and can too easily be taken for granted. We have chosen to think of history in terms of chronological periods, whether large or small, but we must delineate these with care and deliberation, for they will inevitably determine much that follows from the basic framework for interpretation that they propose.

It would be possible to keep a yearly chronicle of the community's past events, in the same way that the Roman *pontifex maximus* had his annual bulletin of community happenings published on whitened boards outside his house near the Forum, at the center of community life.[2] Such a record of annual magistrates, floods, famines, eclipses, food prices, and local happenings would not, however, be a history in the modern sense. By its very nature it could not trace patterns across years or discuss more than the events of a single year or season at a time. Even when these pontifical records were eventually published (whether around 120 or not until the time of Augustus), in the eighty books known as the *Annales Maximi*, they would have provided what amounted to no more than the raw material for subsequent writers of history. Their spare record, limited focus, and lack of analysis made them little more than chronologically ordered lists of the types of events that were of traditional concern to successive Roman high priests and their communities.[3]

---

[2]See Frier 1999, v–xix, for an outline of the debate and a full bibliography. For the bulletins posted by the *pontifex maximus*, see Cato F 77 = Gellius 2.28.4–7; Cicero *De orat.* 2.12.51–53; and Servius ad *Aen.* 1.373 with Oakley 1997, 24–27.

[3]Beck (2007) argues for the symbolic importance of this chronological format for Roman historiography.

By contrast, the characteristic funerals of the office-holding families in Rome brought past magistrates and their achievements to life in the political space of the Forum in the middle of the city.[4] When a Roman magistrate who had held high office (as aedile, praetor, consul, or censor) died, he and all of his office-holding ancestors were represented in the funeral procession by actors wearing wax masks and the garb denoting the highest office held by each man. This parade of ancestors preceded the body of the deceased to the Forum, where the members of that venerable procession sat once more on their ivory chairs of office to listen to the funeral oration (*laudatio*) celebrating the life of the man to be buried that day. The speech also celebrated the political careers and achievements of all of the earlier office-holding family members, who were now represented and commemorated anew. This pageant of Rome's past—a vital element in republican political culture, as Polybius attests in the mid-second century—created a timeless memory world in which deceased relatives from every previous age processed and spoke and sat together.[5] Yet the spectacle of Rome's political funerals, with the accompanying rhetoric of the funeral oration that was delivered from the speaker's platform (*rostra*) in the Forum, failed to create an "historical" account of the kind that the modern historian writes.[6]

A truly "historical" account needs to move beyond an annual community chronicle or a lively pageant of a family's famous names, to consider how subsequent generations can best understand and describe the past in its complex patterns of stability and change. To designate something as "history" is to transcend its particular contemporary concerns and the immediacy of its everyday politics. History takes the longer view. This is obviously relatively easy for us to do with republican Rome, a lost world that now lies more than two thousand years behind us. However, our impressions are influenced, inspired,

---

[4]Flaig 1995; Flower 1996.
[5]Polybius' famous description of the aristocratic funeral (6.53–54) is based on his own observations made in the years before 150. Would Polybius himself have felt that the transmission of values from one generation to the next, which he highlights in both the funeral spectacle and the eulogy, had started to erode by the last years of the second century?
[6]See Kierdorf 1980 for the fragments; Flower 1996, 128–50, for discussion.

and sometimes impeded by the chronologies and concerns of the ages and thinkers that lie between us and the Romans. Every generation needs to (re)consider the past in terms of its own perspective, in a way that will make sense to a contemporary audience and advance historical analysis beyond the set of standard questions that every schoolchild must face.

Periodization in historical terms is intrinsically and inevitably anachronistic, and this fact should be openly acknowledged.[7] The Romans in antiquity did not think of their lives in terms of the phases and divisions that modern historians use. Too often, however, a chronological scheme seems to take on a life of its own. Although contemporary events continue to unfold in a pattern that is by definition easier to characterize with hindsight, historians still tend to credit the Romans with more insights than they could reasonably have had at the time. By contrast, my study sets out to construct a periodization that is based entirely on hindsight and that is explicitly characterized as such. It does not aim to address in any detail the Romans' own sense of time (*Zeitbewußtsein*) or the spirit of any given age (*Zeitgeist*).[8] Nor is this discussion intended to be a study of the historiography of the Roman Republic, either in its contemporary authors or during the imperial period.[9] All these fascinating and worthwhile subjects can be pursued elsewhere.

History is not itself a story *about* time but one that is set *in* time. In reconstructing this story, dating schemes are the essential tools of research and analysis. Having a unified dating system that can relate the past experiences of ancient cultures to our own times is as essential as using a map to describe where Rome is in the physical world. In this way, chronology has been appropriately characterized as a "time map."[10] Yet the dating

[7]See Hinds 1998 for the impact of this idea on the study of Roman poetry. Zerubavel 2003, 97: "Indeed, with the possible exception of the Big Bang, at what point any given stretch of history actually 'begins' is never quite self-evident, and there is always more than just a single point that might possibly constitute the formal beginning of a particular historical narrative."

[8]For the Romans' sense of time and history, see Feeney 2007.

[9]For the historical writing of the republican period, see Beck and Walter 2001 and 2004, for the fragments; Eigler et al. 2003, 9–38; and Walter 2004, for discussion and bibliography.

[10]Zerubavel 2003; see 82–100, for a discussion of historical discontinuity. Zerubavel notes (100) that "offering a fair historical account may very well

system we now use was not invented until the sixth century AD, and thus does not belong to classical antiquity at all.[11] It is the product of another world and of a mentality not based on the heritage and identity of the individual city-state as expressed by its own local calendar. Despite the fact that our dating system fails in its original aim to identify the exact time when Jesus was born, our unified chronology is undoubtedly highly useful and has become indispensable. Its importance is reflected in the choice by many to relabel this same system of dating as BCE (Before the Common Era) and CE (Common Era) instead of BC and AD, as if it could indeed have a universal application outside the history of Christianity. Nevertheless, the system remains in many ways an arbitrary one, however useful and ubiquitous it has become. Historians need to make use of it, while being aware of its consequences and limitations.

The unique and essentially eccentric nature of this dating system emerges in relation to the BC (BCE) period, the time frame that includes the whole span of the Roman Republic under discussion here. No other dating system has a scheme of classifying time as simply "before" a central event or zero hour, a method that consequently involves counting down toward the moment when the actual period under discussion (the Christian era) is said to start. It goes without saying that no ancient Roman could have imagined such a description of time. Moreover, our dating system takes no account of the irregularities and eventual breakdown in the Romans' own calendar, especially by the mid-40s, when Julius Caesar saw calendar reform as a matter of immediate concern even amid the many other political and military issues that he faced.[12]

Given the completely "anachronistic" way in which we now describe Roman time, it is surprising how well our dating

---

require some willingness to actually consider multiple narratives with *multiple beginnings*."

[11]For the BC/AD dating system, see Blackburn and Holford-Strevens 1999; Holford-Strevens 2005; Rüpke 2006; and Feeney 2007, 7–16.

[12]The last day of the old republican calendar came at the end of December 46, which represented for Romans the end of republican time. Michels (1967) explains the republican (pre-Julian) calendar. For Caesar's calendar reform, see Yavetz 1979, 112–15; Feeney 2007, esp. 151–56, 193–201. On the calendar in general, see Rüpke 1995 and 2006.

system works, in terms of both centuries and decades, the units that we use to classify our own history. The centennial years that stand out according to this system—such as 500, 400, 300, 200, 100 (BC)—are useful in considering change in Roman politics and culture. Similarly, the lifetime of Cicero, which falls in the era best documented by far, can even be divided up for discussion into decades, as it is in the insightful chapters in the second edition of *The Cambridge Ancient History*.[13] Consequently, it makes sense for us to use our own dating system to give shape to past time, even as we must always acknowledge that the picture we are creating is our own, not a Roman one.

The shaping of time naturally corresponds to the scale of periodization that is envisaged. Long, sweeping periods of history may seem impressive and monumental at a distance, but they tend to distort and mislead by associating a variety of times with each other in schemes that are essentially not accurate or even plausible. According to this type of very generalized periodization scheme, to use a modern example, the history of the American republic since 1776 would constitute a single historical era. In recognition of the inaccuracy of such broad definitions, the label "Late Antiquity" has recently been criticized as being subject to an unwarranted extension in both directions.[14] Eventually the definition of such a period risks

[13]Chapters by decade in *CAH²*, vol. 9: the 60s (chap. 9 = Wiseman 1994b), the 50s (chap. 10 = Wiseman 1994a), the 40s (chap. 11 = Rawson 1994b), the 30s (chap.11 = Rawson 1994a). The best-documented years in antiquity are 63 (Cicero's consulship), 59 (Caesar's consulship), 50/49 (the outbreak of civil war and Caesar's invasion), and 44/43 (the Ides of March and the following eighteen months).

[14]Giardina offers a trenchant critique of "Late Antiquity" as a period (1999, 29): "Le esigenze immediate sono dunque due: individuare i caratteri di una società tardoantica in quanto distinta in modo autonomo da quella antica e da quella medievale (oppure, in alternativa, delineare in modo coerente il suo carattere di società di trasizione); fare discendere da questa analisi morfologica le periodizzazioni non sovrapponibili delle singole strutture" ("There are, therefore, two things that are immediately necessary: to identify the individual characteristics of a society we can call "late antique" and consequently distinct in its own autonomous way both from antiquity and from the middle ages [or, alternatively, to delineate in a coherent way its character as a society in transition]; and next to deduce from this morphological analysis non-overlapping periodizations of the individual structures").

becoming virtually meaningless, if it is not based on well-articulated and accepted criteria. Similarly, the Greek "Dark Age" of about five hundred years between about 1200 and 700 has come under increasing scrutiny as regards its origins and development in scholarly discourse.[15] As a category, it may tell us more about the history of classical scholarship than it does about life in Greece. The designation of a time in ancient history as "Classical" continues to raise issues, even as it asserts the enduring value of tradition in scholarship.[16]

Consequently, any study of republican Rome should really start from the realization that the traditional span of the Republic (509 to 49, or 43, or 27), covering 450 years or more, is ultimately unwieldy and uninformative when treated as a single time period. No one would deny that the city of Rome, together with its government and its presence abroad, changed beyond recognition within this period, much more so even than in the half-millennia that preceded and followed it.[17] In this sense the "Republic," whether as a time period or a form of government, created the Rome that we study as a subject in world history. Although most other towns in central Italy did not differ much from Rome around the year 500, they have become obscure and insignificant, subjects of interest only to local historians.

The history of modern thinking about Roman republicanism is a huge topic in its own right that is not essential to the purposes of this essay.[18] The study of republican Rome was put on a new footing by Niccolò Machiavelli with his book (published in 1531) about the first decade of Livy. Like many other political theorists, Machiavelli looked to the Romans for advice on politics in his own time and did not attempt to distinguish different phases of republican history in antiquity. The influence of Polybius' history (especially Book 6), which was in circulation again in Europe from around 1415, was important

[15]Morris 1997 outlines a history of scholarship on the Greek "Dark Age."
[16]See Gehrke 2004; Porter 2006; and Walter 2006, for a variety of concepts of the "classical" in antiquity.
[17]Kolb (2002, 115–329) gives an historical account of the city in the Republic. For other introductions, see the first chapter of Zanker 1988; the essays in Giardina 2000; Patterson 2006a; Torelli 2006; and Welch 2006.
[18]See Lintott 1999a, 233–55; and Millar 2002 for discussion and bibliography.

in shaping political thought about a single Republic and was supported by the monumental lists of republican consuls found in Rome in 1546 (the *Fasti Capitolini* from the Augustan age). From the point of view of periodization, however, the most influential figure seems to have been the Italian humanist Carlo Sigonio (ca. 1524–84), who thought of republican history in terms of cycles of growth and decay.[19]

The monolithic republican chronology is especially misleading for beginners and other nonspecialists with an interest in the history of Rome. In English, "republic" can and does refer both to a political system and to the time period it occupies, in a way that can produce a somewhat circular argument and is inaccurate, given that several episodes within this period—such as the decemvirate in the fifth century, or Sulla's dictatorship in the first—are distinctly "unrepublican" in tone and feel. A simplified chronology does not, in other words, make Rome a more accessible object for a history lesson in the modern world. A useful analogy is provided by the Peloponnesian War between Athens and Sparta (431–404), which Thucydides strongly and persuasively argues was a single war lasting twenty-seven years. Most have accepted his reasoning, and this has led to standard essay questions on the causes of "the war." The conflict, however, can just as usefully be seen as several shorter wars, and this is certainly how many Greeks of the fifth and fourth centuries would have understood their political history.[20]

But how can we assign a chronological span to the Roman Republic without first knowing how to describe it? In other words, which comes first, the political analysis or the time map? In fact, the Romans themselves did not really have a vocabulary of political terms to analyze their changing civic landscape: it is this situation that has shaped subsequent, modern ways of talking about Rome. The Latin term *res publica*, from which we derive our word "republic," can mean both

[19]Lintott 1999a, 245–46: "In this way Sigonio has helped to create the standard modern periodization, whereby the Conflict of the Orders ends in 287 and the decline of the Republic begins in 133, the intervening period displaying the constitution at its best."

[20]Strauss 1997 offers an insightful analysis of Thucydides and his periodization of a single Peloponnesian War.

the political community (*politeia*) itself *and* its increasingly characteristic system of government.[21] On a basic level, *res publica* simply means "government with participation of the governed" rather than anarchy or tyranny, both understood as forms of lawlessness. With these words Romans who came after the end of the hereditary monarchy defined the new government as the "public matter." In modern terms, the phrase may seem vague, but it does contain the seeds of the political ideas that developed in Rome after the expulsion of the kings.

Res publica makes perfect sense in terms of Roman political culture and the gradual evolution of a civic community that was based on the equality of adult male citizens within an established system of law and on the ability of each citizen to participate in person in the various voting units, whether the units were based on tribes or on army divisions. Closely related to the concept of this shared political space was the very Roman idea of the citizen's stake in the community, represented by private land ownership guaranteed by the state and by the citizen landowner's corresponding service in the community's army. Equally significant was the drafting of a written law code that was publicly displayed and available to every citizen, originally in the form of the Twelve Tables of the mid-fifth century. Hence *res publica* also implies transparency, openness, and due process, rather than secrecy and individual power used behind closed doors for personal goals.[22]

---

[21]The definitions of *respublica* offered by the *OLD* (1982) appear in the following order: "1. Activities affecting the whole people, affairs of state, an item of public business; 2. The welfare of the state, the public good, the national interest, the resources of the state; 3. The body politic, the or a constitution; 4. A free state in which all citizens participate." Tacitus uses the term to refer specifically to the pre-imperial state (*Hist.* 1.50; *Ann.* 1.3 and 7).

[22]Suetonius (*Claud.* 10.3) refers to *communem libertatem* (shared political freedom) in reference to a republican form of government in the context of a debate in the senate in AD 41. Walter (2004, 328) gives an insightful description of how politics appeared to Cicero: "einem stets prekären System, in dem es keine wirksamen institutionellen Sicherungen gegen das Versagen von Institutionen und Personen und damit auch keine wirkliche Sicherheit durch Verfaßtheit gab, in dem aber zugleich das immer neue Knüpfen von Bindungen und Ausgleichen von Interessen Auswege versprach" ("a constantly precarious system, which did not have any effective institutional safeguards against failures of institutions or of individuals; consequently a system without

The term *res publica* also suggests the unity of all citizens in a shared civic community that transcends the social divisions of class, neighborhood, or family. Such a community is fundamentally at odds with the whole concept of political parties that divide citizens into permanent factions or allegiance groups. In practice, however, the system that expressed these ideas developed slowly after the end of the monarchy. It is characteristic of Roman politics that it did not produce either individual lawgivers or prophets who implemented republican revolutions at specific times, as so often happened in Greek cities and other ancient Mediterranean communities.[23] Moreover, Rome's founding fathers—such as Romulus, Numa, or Servius Tullius, to whom so much is attributed—all lived before a republican system was instituted. Political development tended to come slowly and as a result of complex, now mostly obscure, negotiations of power between different groups in society. All of the above considerations are vital to an understanding of Roman political life; they do not, however, help us with the immediate issue of delineating a time map. If it is a delicate matter to define the Roman Republic in precise political terms, its periodization is equally fraught with difficulty, and in closely related ways.

Thus chronological articulation is the first order of the day, and the only way toward a more accurate and less superficial way of talking about Rome after the end of the monarchy. In other words, even if the Romans did not have a generally accepted and detailed chronological scheme for these five hundred years, we need one for our own use. This issue is of a very different nature from the chronology of the "imperial" period, which is naturally articulated by the reigns of emperors and of their families or rivals. According to a recent and very effective argument, the "triumviral period," the years between the death of Julius Caesar on the Ides of March 44 and the Battle of Actium in 31, which made Octavian sole ruler of the Roman world, should be seen as a separate period in its own

---

any real security created by constitutional means. Yet it was at the same time a system that always held out the promise of escape routes through new allegiances and balances between different interests").

[23]See Gotter 1996, 233–66, esp. 246–50.

right.[24] Recognizing the political and social factors that made these "triumviral" years a time of transition between Caesar's dictatorship and the emergence of a more formalized system of one-man rule designed by the man who took the name of Augustus is a real step forward in terms of historical analysis. Too often "the Republic" has been defined simply as "not a system of one-man rule." This may have made some sense for Romans who could not predict how events would unfold, but it does not meet the criteria of modern historical research or political analysis.

Within any periodization of republican Rome, the final phase, or "Late Republic," is particularly important, and consequently received special attention from later writers, notably Plutarch and Appian, both writing in the second century AD. Needless to say, the loss of Livy has forced us to rely on later writers. Everyone who looks back to republican Rome is influenced by the knowledge that this political community did not survive and was replaced by its antithesis, an emperor, and, therefore, by an "imperial period," a new time that was permanently marked by the divisions of individual reigns and dynasties. Our whole picture of what republican politics in Rome consisted of is shaped by when and how we think it came to an end, by our sense of its failure (whether deserved or tragic, overdue or sudden and unexpected). Its ending contributes to a definition of its essential characteristics, as they had evolved over so many generations.

The following dates have been suggested as being most significant in defining a decisive political watershed and the end of the Republic. The year 49 is the earliest that has been widely discussed, the year that marks Caesar's invasion of Italy when he crossed the Rubicon River and started a civil war against the armies of Pompey and of his enemies in the senate. If we accept this date, then we must argue that there was a functioning republic in place immediately before, and that Caesar appears to bear a large responsibility for its fall and especially for his own subsequent failure to restore any type of republican government after the end of the war.[25] By contrast, other

---

[24]Osgood 2006 (cf. Syme 1939 and Sumi 2005).

[25]Jehne (2005) discusses the importance of Caesar's crossing of the Rubicon. Mackay (2004, 154) describes Pharsalus on August 9, 48, as the "death blow of the Republic," but also says (176) that "[t]he outbreak of the civil

historians would choose Caesar's assassination in 44 as the turning point, as if his dictatorship was still part of "republican" politics.[26] Such a choice presumes that Caesar's ultimate political intentions remain unclear and that he did not establish a new system. By choosing the death of Caesar as the end of the republican period, however, we would seem to make the same mistake that the "Liberators" made. They thought that Caesar's death would see the immediate and spontaneous reemergence of a republic, which in the event did not happen. Somewhat more logical is the choice of the end of the year 43, when a triumvirate had emerged after Caesar's death and Brutus and Cassius' cause, if we can indeed identify it as "republican," had been defeated.[27] Again, we seem to be accepting the propaganda of the Liberators, men who behaved more like warlords than like republicans, old or new. Alternatively, the Republic is sometimes extended to the Battle of Actium in 31 (when Antony was finally defeated and Octavian was left with sole power), or even to 27 (when Octavian took the name of Augustus and established a new system with himself as leading man, or *princeps*, within a restored *res publica*).[28]

What should be clear from the start is that any periodization that extends the Republic to the moment when a new system of government seems to emerge is a scheme more descriptive of what comes next rather than of what came before. A period of transition between a functioning republic and a new system with a single ruler is strongly suggested by the bulk of the ancient evidence and can be helpful in appreciating some of the difficulties of that transition for those who

---

war in 49 BC marked the demise of the dysfunctional political system of the Republic."

[26]Gotter (2000) has the Republic begin and end with a Brutus, the later one being the first man to put his head on a Roman coin during his own lifetime. Jehne (2001, 114) associates the end of the Republic with Caesar's adoption of the title of perpetual dictator on February 2, 44. At 119 he has Caesar end the Republic, but the Liberators give it no chance to be restored.

[27]Gotter (1996, 241) puts the end of the Republic at Philippi.

[28]For a concise overview of the settlement of 27, see Eck 2007, 46–58. Zanker entitles the third chapter of his 1988 book "The Great Turning Point" and starts it with the honors for Octavian after Actium, but with most emphasis on 27. The whole question is reexamined in an interesting way by Morstein-Marx and Rosenstein (2006, 625–26).

lived through it. Roman history has not been well served by a simplistic and sharply drawn dichotomy between "republic" and "empire" as chronological terms.

Meanwhile, the sometimes-tortuous details of the lengthy debate over the various merits of different end dates for the Republic should not cause us to lose sight of what is at stake, a choice that goes well beyond the minutiae of scholarly quibbling. We need to define a shape and dimension for Roman history, if we are to be able to move on to further discussion of matters of substance and meaning. Our whole picture of what republican politics consisted of in Rome depends on when and how we think it came to an end. The parameters that we choose in our definition of republican failure inevitably determine which actors take part in the drama and under which varied historical conditions. The end of the Republic has cast a long shadow over what came before, and has encouraged various teleological ways of talking about earlier Roman politics. This study sets out to address the disintegration of republican politics and practices as a topic of special importance in any overall consideration of republican political culture.

By employing several timelines one could avoid the tyranny of any single one of them. Periodization in Roman history could be based on considerations of religion (as in the case of the BC/AD system), of economic and technological change, or of the expansion of Rome's overseas domination. Many Roman historians have used Rome's external wars as the basic compass of their study, whether for specific reasons or simply by default.[29] There is much to be gained by looking at the development of Roman republican politics in terms of its overseas ambitions, especially if hegemony and empire are seen as its most defining features. Political change, however, was not necessarily driven exclusively by foreign policy or military concerns. External conflicts provide a convenient set of dates and transitions that are not objects for dispute. Ultimately, the dates of foreign wars are significant, though they are not in

[29]See, e.g., Scullard 1980 (first published in 1935) and, more recently, Bringmann 2007. L. Annaeus Florus (later second century AD) structured his Roman history (based on Livy) around external wars and into four general periods (infancy, youth, manhood, old age). According to Lactantius (*Inst. div.* 7.15.4), the elder Seneca had used these divisions.

themselves political markers, even when internal change did accompany military action.

Similarly, the lives of leading Romans have provided a traditional way of defining different "ages," not only for historians but also in other areas, such as in constructing a framework for the history of Latin literature.[30] Yet if we define history as a story articulated by the lives of great men, even by their very birth dates, before anyone can have known what roles they would go on to play or what texts they would eventually write, we will have trouble moving beyond history as it was defined and written in the past: a story narrowly focused on famous generals and their great victories. But history is not and should not be the same as biography.[31]

Moreover, how can we write the history of a "republic" simply or principally in terms of the personal biographies of its leading men? This question becomes more urgent when those leading men are openly operating outside republican norms. Are we denying that *res publica* had any meaning in an "Age of Caesar"? If that was indeed the case, the political implications of that assertion need further exploration and qualification. How can the "Age of Caesar" precede the "Fall of the Republic"?[32] A claim has been made that while Caesar was writing his books about the Civil War the Republic, or a republic, (must still have) existed.[33] This argument can easily become circular. Yet the Republic must be more than an idea in Caesar's or anyone else's mind.

My study will set out to design a new and different periodization based specifically on the evolving political life of the

---

[30]Conte 1994 and Suerbaum 2002. Syme 1964, 274: "Periods in the development of literature are a normal device, questionable but not easy to dispense with, useful when not slavishly obeyed. It is expedient to know where to make the cut."

[31]Plutarch makes the distinction at the beginning of his biography of Alexander the Great.

[32]Ovid's words *quia res est publica Caesar* ("because Caesar is the *res publica*," *Tr.* 4.4.15) were written much later, shortly before the death of Augustus.

[33]Raditsa (1973, 434) writes of the *De bello civili*: "as long as Caesar could write this narrative, the Republic still existed." So also Batstone and Damon 2006, 32: "So the terminal date for its composition is the date after which one considers the republic dead. From Cicero onwards, that has been placed well before the Ides of March in 44."

Roman community.[34] That is not to say that such a political scheme should necessarily take precedence in some absolute hierarchy of dating systems. Political chronology can and should be useful both in complement and in contrast to other dating schemes and eras. It must, however, address the essential question of how to study what is "republican" about Rome. In addition, the new time map described in this study is designed as an attempt to critique, articulate, and ultimately to dissolve the concept of *a single, monolithic Republic* in Rome, and hence of a long era that had a quasi-biological beginning, middle, and end, according to an Aristotelian pattern of natural growth, maturity, and decay. A republican system of government did come to a final end at Rome, but there is no reason for us to write about it now as if it were the effect of some inevitable fate, or an integral part of the destiny of a great leader, or a mechanical change in a pattern of successive ages.

[34]Martin Jehne has recently suggested that any systematic discussion of the Roman Republic needs a model as its basis; one may equally claim that any analytical study needs a well-articulated time map. See Jehne 2006a, 3–4: "In broad terms a model is the ordering of a series of specific pieces of information by means of a hypothesis about their relationship, ignoring details that may seem as irrelevant from a given perspective." By contrast, Peter Brunt writes (1988, 89): "In practice no systematic theory can explain without remainder the complex interweaving of human activities, especially if the course of events can be altered by the apparently contingent influence of individuals. And on this premiss the historian can never provide any complete explanation of the past."

⟺ II ⟺

TOWARD A NEW PARADIGM

"Roman Republics"

> There can surely be nobody so petty or so apathetic in his
> outlook that he has no desire to discover by what means and
> under what system of government the Romans succeeded in
> less than fifty-three years [from 220 to 167 BC] in bring-
> ing under their rule almost the whole inhabited world, an
> achievement which is without parallel in human history. Nor
> from the opposite point of view can there be anyone so com-
> pletely absorbed in other subjects of contemplation or study
> that he could find any task more important than to acquire
> this knowledge?
>
> Polybius 1.1, after the mid-second century BC

$\mathbf{B}$uilding upon my preliminary remarks about periodization
in the first chapter, I will now move on to outline a new paradigm for analyzing the history of republican politics at Rome.
This study is divided into three larger parts, each one containing
three smaller sections. The first part ("Framework") deals with
models of periodization and with the contested field of early
republican politics, while the second ("Change") addresses
the topic of change in Roman politics in the second and first
centuries. Part three ("Aftermath") offers a chronological
overview from Sulla to Caesar and beyond. The seven individual sections that follow this one explore a range of arguments
in support of the new chronological scheme. Their topics include the early development of Roman republicanism (III), the
nature and frequency of peaceful political reform at Rome
(IV), the introduction and marked escalation of political

violence after the year 133 (V), the effects in Rome of outside pressures created by warfare (VI), the constitutional settlement put in place by Sulla in 81 (VII), and the rapidly changing nature of Roman politics in the crucial decades of the 70s, 60s, and 50s (VIII). I conclude with a final discussion (IX) that sketches some of the consequences of adopting the new model as a framework for viewing the story of republican Rome.

My immediate aim in this section is to make my whole argument clearer by outlining the approach at the beginning of my study, rather than building a case slowly. Hence this discussion will serve as the essential guide to everything else that follows, although many supporting arguments are to be found in later sections. Meanwhile, it bears repeating that no time map, however elegant or compelling, can ever claim to be exclusive or definitive, especially in a society as dynamic as Rome's was in the half millennium before the birth of Christ.

The alternative to a single, long period labeled as one "Republic" is clearly several republics of shorter duration and in a historical sequence. A similar pattern is familiar in French history with its multiple republics. Such a scheme of successive republics has not seriously been proposed for Rome before, probably because it does not explicitly conform to the way in which the Romans themselves spoke about their republican traditions. We must take into account, however, their lack of a theoretical vocabulary and a corresponding tradition of formal political analysis. It was very late in the day for republicanism in Rome, by any account, when Cicero turned to writing works of political theory in Latin.[1] As discussed in the introduction, the Romans themselves did not have a way of labeling their government with terms that specifically designated a republic. In addition, the lack of a definite article in Latin means that no Roman spent much time distinguishing "*a* republic" from "*the* Republic." Moreover, *res publica* was

---

[1] *De republica* (set in 129) was written between 54 and 51 (see the new OCT text in Powell 2006). *De legibus* (set in Cicero's present) was composed around 52. Both were inspired by Platonic dialogues. Cicero turned to more overtly philosophical works in the 40s, especially in the years from 46 to 44. Gotter (1996, 247) sees Cicero's political theory, especially the *De republica*, as a practical suggestion for reform. See also Lintott 1999a, 220–32, and Connolly 2007.

the term still employed to describe the government during the subsequent "imperial" period, both by emperors and by their critics.[2]

Res publica is also sometimes found in the plural in Latin (*res publicae*), which naturally means states, constitutions, or republics.[3] The most interesting example is quoted as an unusual plural by Festus from a speech of Gaius Gracchus delivered in 126, which dealt with the expulsion of Italians who were not Roman citizens from the city.[4] The context of the quotation, however, is hard to recover in detail.

The most common and accepted dating system in use at Rome was based on the names of the consuls for each year.[5] As a result, the annual designation of each year was "republican" in form and reference, but it did not construct any relative periodization for a republic. Every year was simply another year without a king and a new year in which two elected consuls were available to take office on the day appointed for that annual transition. By contrast, the historian Livy dated and titled his comprehensive history *ab urbe condita*, "from the foundation of the city (of Rome)," without any special reference to an era that was republican. He does draw attention to the custom by which a nail was supposedly driven into the wall of the temple of Jupiter Optimus Maximus on the Capitol by the *pontifex maximus* on the first of January of each year, a practice that represented the number of years since the temple's dedication, which by tradition had been in the first year of the Republic.[6] But neither he nor any other extant source

---

[2]See especially Augustus' own use of the term *respublica* in his *Res gestae*. Galinsky (1996, 58–77) argues for an Augustan attempt to restore meaning to the term *respublica*. Gowing (2005) treats the memory of the republic in imperial writers. Lintott (1999a, 233–55) discusses later authors. Cicero (*Rep.* 2.5) also uses *res publica* to refer to the regal period.

[3]Sonnenschein (1904) mostly gives examples from Cicero.

[4]Festus 362,33L = ORF[4] 48 III.22: *eae nationes cum aliis rebus per avaritiam atque stultitiam res publicas suas amiserunt* ("those states/peoples, through greed and stupidity, lost their 'republics' along with other things").

[5]Broughton's *MRR* remains the classic source book for republican politics arranged by consular year. See also Rich 1997, for the consular year in the historical works of Livy and Valerius Antias; Lintott 1999a, 9–15, for the political year; and Feeney 2007, 14–16, 22–23.

[6]Livy 7.5–9. This custom is not much referred to elsewhere.

gives any special function in ordinary civic life to this overtly republican way of numbering the years.

Consequently, Roman habits of talking about time and its passage need not necessarily constrain or compel us to speak of a single republic, whose basic definition has been hard to find and even more challenging to explain to the uninitiated. From the vantage point of hindsight, several republics make more sense; by comparison, the argument for a single political system over nearly five hundred years is much more difficult to maintain. As soon as the concept of a single republican period is introduced, it needs to be modified, because politics and the whole city changed several times over these centuries.

Moreover, if we agree to break up the unified republic into smaller units, we are also in a position to appreciate republican political culture as much more dynamic during its evolution, even within any given time segment that could be described as a discrete period. Again, the characteristic Roman focus on *mos maiorum* and continuity with the past need not mean that we have to accept their rhetoric at face value.[7] By contrast, it seems evident that the dramatic changes Roman society was undergoing produced a discourse of tradition and an insistent claim to a timeless heritage, which should in itself be regarded as a cultural artifact created for a political purpose.[8] A new chronology of multiple republics should not, however, necessarily produce (in a variation on the received pattern) a new set of rigid time divisions.[9]

If there were several republics, then there must have been several end points or transitions, followed by new republican beginnings. The effect of such a scheme should be to place less stress on a single fall and to articulate the so-called crisis of the Late Republic into a different and more nuanced pattern. Republican political life should still be seen as resilient and

[7] Hölkeskamp 1996; Linke and Stemmler 2000; Braun, Haltenhoff, and Mutschler 2000; Zecchini 2001; Haltenhoff, Heil, and Mutschler 2003; and Pina Polo 2004.

[8] As Morgan (1997) shows, Roman investment in continuities of the past meant they did not look for breaks.

[9] Corfield 2007, 183–84: "Indeed, while stage theories do well at highlighting fundamental transformations, they consistently underplay both deep continuities and the micro-changes that bridge turning points."

especially characteristic of Rome as a city-state, but as more adaptive to historical circumstances and thus less inflexible or static. There was, therefore, no single ancient Republic that became fossilized and outlived its usefulness or its historical mission.[10] Rather, a series of republics, some more stable and successful than others, reflected the intense political debate and dynamic expansion intrinsic to Roman political culture after the end of the monarchy. Far from being conservative, Romans tended to be bold in adopting new solutions and policies to meet the changing world that they were shaping by their aggressive foreign policy—a world that provided them with growing resources and wealth of all kinds, which transformed their lives and their city. Similarly, change came to republican politics in several distinct forms and at different times, not simply through the pressures of empire or the rampant growth of individualism amongst powerful generals and their client armies.

A central contention of my study is that we have tended to underestimate and misrepresent the decisive break that came with the New Republic established by Sulla in 81.[11] This argument relates first to the devastating results of violence throughout the decade we call the 80s, and second to the novelty of the political solution proposed by Sulla. A fuller and more accurate appreciation of the huge changes Sulla both witnessed and caused affects the whole pattern of the period commonly referred to as the "Late Republic." Many, if not most, earlier discussions have tended to classify the chaos of the 80s as nothing but a brief interlude followed by the reactionary restoration of a powerful senate and a republican system that looked back to a time before the agitation of the Gracchi in the 130s and 120s.[12] A more realistic assessment

[10]Von Ungern-Sternberg (1998, 607) describes the Republic as enjoying "eine auch in der Antike beispiellose Stabilität. Selbst ihre Agonie dauerte noch ein rundes Jahrhundert, von 133 bis 30 v. Chr." ("a stability that was also unprecedented in antiquity. Even its agony lasted another full century, from 133 to 30 BC").

[11]Appian (*BC* 1.98–104) distinguishes a monarchy, a democracy, and another monarchy reintroduced by Sulla.

[12]Kolb 2002, 251, on Sulla's return to a devastated city in 82: " [Sulla] verfügte als Repräsentant der senatorischen Oligarchie über ein klares politisches Ziel: die Restaurierung der Nobilitätsherrschaft, wie sie vor den Gracchen

of the terrible destruction caused by the Social and Civil wars between 91 and 81 is called for. At the same time, a more detailed picture of the revolutionary novelty of Sulla's New Republic can help to explain why it was so unstable, even from its violent beginnings. Meanwhile, the realization that there was a major political watershed in the 80s makes it much more problematic to use information provided subsequently by Cicero and his contemporaries to interpret other, very different republican times, which were actually long gone by the 60s. In other words, it is not only the situation of our sources but also our scheme of periodization that has given Cicero such pride of place as a witness to "the Republic."

At least six republics, in addition to transitional periods of various kinds, appear to be easily recognizable in the political patterns that the ancient evidence preserves. I will now enumerate and briefly characterize these republics, which can also be found in a list at the end of this section. A full elaboration of all the details that could be associated with each period is beyond the scope of the present concise study. Rather, in the sections that follow I will focus my attention on historical chronology as a helpful guide to republican politics in Rome. I hope to make the picture clearer and more accurate by openly acknowledging the places where there are significant gaps in our knowledge and evidence.

The development of Rome's earliest experiments with republican forms of government will be outlined in greater detail in section III. The fragmentary nature of our ancient sources, whether literary, epigraphical, or archaeological, makes the period before the late fourth century especially difficult to talk about in any detail. Since the focus of this study is on chronology, I will not attempt to engage in a comprehensive way with the various debates about early Rome that have been

---

bestanden hatte" ("[Sulla] had a clear political goal as representative of the senatorial oligarchy: the restoration of the political dominance of the nobility, as it had existed before the Gracchi"). So also Mackay 2004, 130: "As the self-appointed guardian of the senate, Sulla now sought to reform the constitution in order to restore the oligarchy's political control." But, on the next page, 131: "Put together, these [Sulla's] reforms drastically changed the appearance of the governmental system in Rome."

so lively in recent scholarship.[13] For the purpose of political analysis, however, some clear distinctions do emerge. Roman republicanism did not come into being at a single moment after the end of the monarchy, nor was it created by a single lawgiver or reformer. Progress was slow, and no written law code was inscribed until the middle of the fifth century (the Twelve Tables)—in other words, much later than in many Greek city-states.

We are very poorly informed about the fifth century as a whole, a century when Rome was governed by successive boards of magistrates, ranging in size from ten (the decemvirs) to four, six, or eight (tribunes with consular powers), rather than by the two consuls who became the regular executive officers after the reforms of 367/6. Above all, the civic strife and class struggle suggested by the surviving sources is completely at variance with the picture of a much more harmonious political climate after the end of the so-called Conflict of the Orders. Similarly, the claims that patricians held all the political and religious offices suggests a hereditary system of executive power quite different from the later republican political culture shared by the *nobiles*, who were elected from both patrician and plebeian families. In section III I will present arguments for two distinct republican periods before the ascendance of the *nobiles* to political domination around 300.

Through a series of political compromises and negotiated settlements, Rome's early republican experiments were transformed, over a period of about 150 years, into a completely new republican pattern, which was characterized by the ascendancy of the *nobiles*. It is the political culture developed during this third republic, which emerged in the late fourth century, that has been most closely associated with Rome's most characteristic republicanism and with her expansion to become a Mediterranean power.[14] It is also the *nobiles* who presided over the development of Latin literature (in both prose and poetry), of Roman art, and of the Latin language,

[13]See the literature cited at the beginning of section III (n. 2).
[14]For the emergence of the *nobiles*, see Hölkeskamp 1987 and 2004a; with Forsythe 2005, 276. Bleckmann 2002 discusses developments during the First Punic War. Goldmann 2002 elucidates the meaning of the term *nobilis*. For artistic developments, see Hölscher 1978, 1980, and 1990.

which is often said to reach its "classical" stage near the beginning of the first century. Unlike the republics that had come before, this new republican culture was remarkably stable and free from internal discord, at least according to our surviving ancient sources. Rome's constitution was an object of study and admiration for Polybius, who saw Rome's striking rise to world power between 220 and 168 as a product of her characteristic political and military institutions.[15] Long-term political negotiation and the development of habits of compromise and power sharing enabled the Romans to transcend a narrow hereditary oligarchy and a condition of virtually permanent *stasis*, not unlike the political strife that seemed endemic to many Greek city-states.

It would be a mistake, however, to see the political culture of the *nobiles* as static and unchanging in the third, second, and early first centuries. Rather, the political system continued to be developed and refined, with respect to the roles and numbers of its magistrates, the function of the senate, and the interactions between citizens and leaders in the voting assemblies. Consequently, a division into three republics of the *nobiles* seems indicated, with the breaks coming in 180 with the *lex Villia Annalis*, which set important rules for the shape of political careers, and in 139 with the introduction of the secret ballot by the *lex Gabinia*. Although other moments of division could be found, the establishment of standardized career patterns seems to coincide with a number of indications of political evolution that occurred in the years immediately after the senate had asserted its political dominance throughout Italy by suppressing a novel form of Bacchic initiation cult. Similarly, the introduction of the secret ballot was a political revolution that moved away from earlier consensus rituals.

To reiterate my earlier point, it makes no sense to see the republics of the *nobiles* as being a continuation of any of the earlier systems. Those systems included a special role for a closed caste of hereditary politicians, generals, and priests. By contrast, power was now shared on the basis of election to

---

[15]The period break at 180 proposed here would be an obvious interruption in Polybius' pattern of a rise over fifty years, but his analysis is based on external wars not on internal politics.

political office of any candidate who could meet the property requirements of the census (notionally held every 5 years) and who had the requisite ten years of apprenticeship as a citizen soldier. Promotion to higher office was overtly linked to merit and achievement. Elected office created the new political class known as *nobiles*. Candidates for office, like future senators, were still wealthy but came from a broader range of social backgrounds. Famous ancestors were an advantage, but talent and personal qualities were also essential factors. The fiercer the competition between elite candidates, the harder it became for any individual, family, or group of related families to control the results of elections. Magisterial power was prestigious but short in duration, and further advancement involved returning to justify oneself to one's peers in the senate and to the electorate, especially within the city. Similarly, the status of a family group depended on each generation's production of young men who could rise to the personal and financial challenges of a political and military career based on reputation, recognition, and careful management of financial resources.

The three developed republics of the *nobiles* (300–180, 180–139, and 139–88) depended on compromise and cooperation, political strategies that could create the impression of consensus even after debate had often been fierce.[16] The shared values and rules of the political game that had been agreed upon allowed intense competition between individual leaders without disturbing the basic stability of the republican system itself. In fact, the competition between the *nobiles* and would-be candidates for political careers was essential in creating the stability and dynamism of this period, often referred to rather vaguely as the "Middle Republic." During the third and second centuries, the Romans, guided by an advisory group of senators, were able to withstand the challenges of long wars with Carthage, to keep many Italians loyal to the cause of Rome, and to expand to a position of dominance in the eastern Mediterranean, easily defeating the military might of the

---

[16]Wiseman 1985; Rosenstein 1993; Hölkeskamp 2004a and 2006a. Gotter (1996, 248) interprets the tendency to define the *mos maiorum* as itself a result of the increasing loss of consensus.

various Hellenistic kingdoms. It is essential to note that at this stage in Roman history individual competition and ambition supported, rather than subverted, a stable republican form of government. At the same time, an influential and largely effective senate did not hamper individual competition for rank and renown.

The republican culture of the *nobiles* was not, therefore, a fixed system that stayed unchanged after the end of the Conflict of the Orders (that is to say, during the third and second centuries). The rules of the political game were still subject to continual fine-tuning, despite the rhetoric of adherence to traditional behavior and values. One of the clearest examples of this phenomenon is the gradual development of the political career structure known as the *cursus honorum*.[17] This scheme, consisting of a fixed order and hierarchy of offices linked to age and experience, is one of the most characteristic features of Roman republicanism. Yet it, too, developed gradually before becoming more regulated under the *lex Villia Annalis* of 180 BC. The relative importance of offices such as the praetorship and consulship was not firmly established as a result of the reforms of 367/6. Moreover, the relative number of offices affected career paths and the degree of competition for advancement. Issues of spacing and iteration continued to be debated and were influenced by changing needs. Meanwhile, the dictatorship, which had been such a useful office in the later third century, was not filled at all in the second century. Triumphs multiplied in number and became ever more splendid in the second century, even as they remained the ultimate markers of status in Roman political culture—more crucial than career patterns and the authority wielded by those former consuls who won election to the censorship, an election held only every five years.[18] An accurate appreciation of the republican culture of the *nobiles* must take these shifting nuances into account.

The fine but evolving balance between competition and cooperation became unstable in the last third of the second century,

[17]For the *cursus honorum*, see Lintott 1999a, 144–46; Beck 2005a.
[18]Itgenshorst 2005 (with CD-ROM catalogue of all known triumphs), 2006; Beard 2007.

almost fifty years after the political innovations of 180. Some of the details of this process will be discussed in the sections below. Romans met with failure and stalemate abroad in places where they had been victorious before, while citizens both at home and in the army lost confidence in the abilities and even the honesty of their traditional political leaders. Economic and social forces combined with outside pressures to overtax the citizen army of small peasants and to start gradually replacing it with a volunteer army of the poor and landless. The size of the empire and its military needs put increasing pressure on the system of annual offices with its constant changes of political leadership. The outstanding career of Marius, who was elected to the consulship seven times (surpassing all before him), appears as a decisive rift in the fabric of republican culture at the end of the second century.

A realistic assessment of the political culture of the *nobiles*, and its basis in deliberation, negotiation, and the careful creation of and dependence on images of consensus, will also lead logically to the conclusion that this system was destroyed during the 80s, under the combined pressures of war with the allies in Italy and war between citizens in Rome, conflicts that may appear to be two faces of one continuous civil war. The Social War was hard fought and won only through the rapid extension of Roman citizenship to all in Italy who were willing to accept it and rejoin the Roman side.[19] The results of such violence and loss of control played themselves out in Sulla's two marches on Rome, in the political dominance of Cinna, and ultimately in the dictatorship set up by the victorious Sulla in the aftermath of the political collapse of the existing system.[20] Both Cinna's continual consulships and Sulla's subsequent dictatorship are clear signs of the end of the previous regime. Neither side in the civil conflict of the 80s, therefore, had any illusions that an older republic had survived.

---

[19]Sherwin-White 1973 is the classic discussion.
[20]Rich 1997 provides a relevant analysis of Livy's treatment. There is a noticeable break in Livy's scheme with the Social War, about halfway through his history. As political chaos ensued in Rome, his narrative apparently became much fuller (Books 71–90) and his annalistic structure broke down. He also seems to have started to use flashbacks as a narrative technique.

A very different (sixth) republic was then set up by Sulla in 81. The break here is clear, as indicated both by the extremely violent collapse of the remaining vestiges of accepted republican practices and by the revolutionary character of Sulla's personal vision for a New Republic that would be free of the political turmoil he had witnessed throughout his adult life. Sulla's republic will be discussed in more detail in section VII below; a few of the most essential points will simply be noted here. Although he used the traditional names for the branches of government and offices, Sulla's system was fundamentally different from what had come before. His newly enlarged senate had a different character and function from any previous such body. In essence, his new constitution was based on the rule of law enforced by a system of courts, rather than on deliberation and traditional political practices, such as the open discussions of proposed legislation put forward by tribunes of the plebs before the people in the Forum (*contiones*).[21] His system of law courts and their enforcement of extensive new legal codes were to dominate the political scene that he envisioned. He changed the balance of power within the political community: between the senate and the magistrates, between magistrates and their colleagues in office, and between the executive offices and the tribunes who represented the original compromise with and recognition of the political aspirations of the plebeians and other non-patrician citizens. Many modern scholars have referred to this new vision as a "restoration" of a previous political system, but "restoration" is a complete misnomer.[22]

For our present purposes the most important feature of Sulla's republic was its instability. Civil wars did not end during Sulla's lifetime, even after his retirement from politics, and his death in 78 coincided with renewed revolt both in Italy and abroad. The 70s were fraught with armed conflict and talk of constitutional changes, which were put into effect in 75 and especially in 70, with Pompey and Crassus as consuls. In other

---

[21]Morstein-Marx 2004 provides the best introduction to the *contio*. See also Pina Polo 1996.
[22]Bleicken (2004, 71–74) calls this part of his study "Die Restauration unter Sulla." Keaveney 2007, 98–99: "He (Sulla) fought to re-establish senatorial government and used his victory to bring in laws to strengthen the republic."

words, Sulla's settlement was modified in several fundamental ways within a decade of its implementation. It did not meet with solid support, either among the citizenry at large, or even among Sulla's political heirs, of whom Pompey clearly appears as the most important. As a new system, not sanctioned by tradition but imposed through force by a dictator, Sulla's republic was basically unacceptable to many Romans. However, they did not have another model of how to approach political reform, and the divisive, partisan effects of the civil wars hampered the cooperation and compromise that could have produced a truly new start. The previous traditional republics of the *nobiles* had by now been lost, and the shadow of Sulla loomed over the generation that came after him. As a result there was no agreement about a method for restoring a workable republic, or about how such a republic should look.

The increasingly violent interventions by ordinary citizens and soldiers in the political process tended only to weaken, rather than to bolster, the remnants of the Sullan settlement.[23] In that sense, popular politics was not necessarily "republican" in tendency. An adapted form of Sulla's republic can be seen in action in the political culture of the 60s, but things had changed again radically by the end of that decade, with the formation of a dominant political alliance of Pompey, Crassus, and Caesar—the so-called First Triumvirate—shortly before the fateful consulship of Caesar himself in 59. Long-term political alliances and the manipulation of elections now became the norm rather than the exception. Meanwhile, it is notable that the restored tribunate of the plebs only contributed to more violence and to the emergence of the multiyear commands of the great generals, rather than helping to restore anything that looked like an earlier republic. The disconnect with traditional republican political culture is exemplified by the behavior of plebeian tribunes in the 60s and 50s.

Political activities throughout the 50s were not what anyone would call "republican" in tone or content.[24] Due process

[23]Violence is discussed in detail by Lintott (1999b) and Nippel (1988 and 1995). Kolb (2002, 239–43) puts the violence between 133 and 78 in a specifically urban context.
[24]Taylor 1949 remains vivid and essential. See also Wiseman 1994a and Spielvogel 1993, with a special emphasis on Cicero.

and the holding of elections were repeatedly disrupted, while gang violence was the order of the day. The political dominance of the "Big Three" (as I prefer to call Pompey, Crassus, and Caesar, who were not offically *tresviri*) created a temporary illusion of stability, but at the expense of political debate and of the rule of law. Their alliance ended abruptly with the death of Crassus at the disastrous Roman defeat at Carrhae in Syria in 53. Chaos soon followed and constitutional government had broken down completely by early 52, which saw the burning of the senate house built by Sulla and the establishment of a sole consulship held by Pompey. Hence the final fall of republican government, now represented by no more than a modified version of the Sullan constitution, should be dated to 60, with the formation of the alliance of the Big Three. The transitional period defined by this alliance ended with Crassus' death, the breakdown of political order in Rome, and the emergence of Pompey as the dominant figure in the changed political landscape.

In other words, there was no functional republic in place in 51 and 50 to negotiate the return of Caesar from Gaul, while personal considerations and ambitions seemed to dominate on all sides. As a result, Caesar's invasion can be seen as targeting a political community that had already lost its integrity and even its shape, rather than a functioning system—let alone a traditional, inherited republic of any kind. Careful attention to this chronology and its implications helps to bring out the failures of Pompey to devise a viable program of political reform that would have restored a republican way of managing the state, in 70 and 55 (as consul with Crassus), in 62 (after his return from the East), or in 52 (as sole consul). As has so often been noted before, Sulla's display of ambition and achievement outside a republican framework set the most powerful example, and it was all the more devastating in the context of a community already stripped of its traditional political culture and deeply divided between the winners and losers in the previous civil war.[25]

---

[25]Mackay (2004, 132) claims that in 49 Sulla's example would overthrow the Republic. Kolb (2002, 251–56) sees Sulla's building program as a visual prompt for others to imitate his actions.

It is crucial to stress that republican politics stopped functioning around the year 60.[26] The civil war that started in January of 49 was the result of the breakup of the subsequent political alliance between the Big Three, made inevitable by the death of Crassus, persistent chaos in Rome, and the emergence of Pompey in the position of sole consul. According to this reading, the final disintegration of republican government took place in 60/59 even though it was not signaled by immediate civil war. A clash between Pompey and Caesar developed because there was no group of leaders, either in the senate or outside it, who could mediate between the two generals or who had the authority to stop their soldiers from following them in the role of client armies. The breakdown of republican culture thus produced a pattern of warlords with client armies that may seem reminiscent of the very earliest days after the kings had been expelled.[27] Meanwhile, it should be noted that the politics of obstruction pursued in the senate by Cato, Bibulus, and other so-called conservative senators actually had no connections with the strategies of negotiation and consensus building which had often been successful in the third and second centuries.[28] The regrets over the loss of republican political culture voiced by Cicero and others were not matched by any practical legislation or by actions intended either to re-create republican traditions or to imitate older republican behaviors. This should not be surprising, however, given that the last traditional republic of the *nobiles* had disintegrated in the early 80s when most of these men were still adolescents or only children.

[26]For Asinius Pollio, see Horace *Carm.* 2.1.1–8; Josephus *AJ* 19.187; Plutarch *Pomp.* 47.4, *Caes.* 13.5. Morgan (2000) elucidates Pollio's decision to start his history with the year 60, a choice he made in the mid-30s soon after he retired from politics. Cf. Meier 1980, 267, 280. Both Galsterer (2000, 310) and Jehne (2001, 51) see Caesar's consulate in 59 as a key turning point.

[27]Cornell 1995, 143: "One of the most important features of the society of central Italy in the archaic period is the presence of *condottieri*—aristocratic warlords whose power rested on the support of armed personal dependents, who were variously styled 'clients' (*clientes*) or 'companions' (*sodales*)."

[28]For tactics, see Burckhardt 1988 and de Libero 1992. Von Ungern-Sternberg (1998, 621) argues that the obstructionist tactics of the *optimates* ensured the continuation of *popularis* politics.

It is the aim of this study to use periodization as a tool and a framework, consciously constructed from the perspective of hindsight, to help make sense of republican political life over half a millennium. The division of this long and diverse period into several republics is helpful in distinguishing between very different political practices and times, which the Romans, according to their own political discourse, did not choose to designate with specific or technical names.

The thirteen chronological periods, including six republics, proposed here are:

1. Ca. 509–494   A pre-republican transitional period immediately after the monarchy
2. 494–451/0   A proto-republic before the first written law code
3. 450–367/6   **Republic 1**: An experiment, including the consular tribunes
4. 366–300   **Republic 2**: The emergence of a republic shared by patricians and plebeians
5. 300–180   **Republic 3**: The republic of the *nobiles* 1
6. 180–139   **Republic 4**: The republic of the *nobiles* 2
7. 139–88   **Republic 5**: The republic of the *nobiles* 3
8. 88–81   A transitional period (coup of Sulla, *dominatio* of Cinna, dictatorship of Sulla)
9. 81–60   **Republic 6**: The republic of Sulla (modified in significant ways in 70)
10. 59–53   A triumvirate (Pompey, Caesar, and Crassus)
11. 52–49   A transitional period
12. 49–44   The dictatorship of Caesar (and a short transition after his murder)
13. 43–33   Another triumvirate (Octavian, Lepidus, Antony)

The principate was then established by Augustus (as Octavian now called himself) in January of 27, after a further, short transitional period (33–28) during which he defeated Antony at the Battle of Actium (31).

The concept of multiple republics, therefore, helps to highlight the relative success of some political systems and practices and the failure of others. Each republic had its own strengths and weaknesses, different from those of other systems. The varied nature of political change emerges and, at the same time, patterns of stability and instability can be traced. There was no single, long republic that carried the seeds of its own destruction in its aggressive tendency to expand and in the unbridled ambitions of its leading politicians. Periodization can help to clarify a historical context for interpreting various republics, and to show how they grew, what helped them flourish, and under what circumstances each one came to an end.

III

EARLY REPUBLICS

(Fifth and Fourth Centuries)

Libertatem et consulatum L. Brutus instituit.
Lucius Brutus established political freedom and the consulship.
　Tacitus *Annales* 1.1

"The fifth century, by contrast [to the sixth century], is
something of a blank. Our knowledge of the material culture
of Rome in the fifth century is so poor that there is almost no
known artefact or monument that can be safely ascribed to it."
　Tim Cornell (2005, 55)

The history of early republican politics, especially in the fifth
century but also to some extent in the fourth, is surely the
most contested field in the half millennium after the end of
the monarchy, traditionally but rather hypothetically dated to
509. Scholarly disputes involve every kind of ancient evidence,
from the fragmentary literary tradition to the rare examples
of early epigraphic texts. Meanwhile, new archaeological finds
are stirring up increasingly heated debates rather than helping
to create any degree of consensus among the experts.[1] Interpretative models vary hugely, from the hypercritical, which
discards almost all of our literary evidence for the emergence
of a republican form of government, to a virtually fundamen-
talist reading of the texts, which simply accepts them as historically accurate and is willing to smooth over even major

[1]See esp. the new excavations of Andrea Carandini (1997, 2006). For an
overview of these finds and the debates, see *Archaeology* July/August 2007,
22–27, and Carandini 2008.

discrepancies between different types of ancient sources.[2] For
the nonspecialist, even the student of later republican politics,
these problems can appear virtually insoluble. This section will
attempt to address the history of Rome's emerging republican
culture from the specific point of view of chronology, with the
idea that some kind of time map is essential to an understanding of Roman history in general.

It would, of course, be possible to give up on this subject and
simply start a historical analysis of Roman republicanism at a
later date. A number of scholars and teachers effectively end
up doing just that. One may also note that not all Roman historians before Livy treated the whole history of the city from
its foundation.[3] In other words, one could start with the famous figure of Appius Claudius Caecus, censor in 312, the first
Roman whose political biography and legislative program we
can talk about in any meaningful detail.[4] Some would begin
even later, with the reforms of 287, which have been described
as the end of the so-called Conflict of the Orders and the beginning of a fully developed republican form of government.
Nevertheless, events become quite a bit better attested for us
in 264, with the outbreak of the First Punic War and Rome's
first overseas military engagement. Much is lost, however, by
taking no account at all of earlier times, even if one classi-
fies them all as proto-historical or proto-republican. Certainly,
for later Romans, images of their earlier history were an important part of the shared culture, both within the community and in its self-presentation to outsiders. In other words,
why not explore what can be said, at least in terms of a basic
outline?[5]

---

[2]For early Rome, see Millar 1989; Cornell 1995; Forsythe 2005; Raaflaub
2005; and Smith 2006, esp. his overview at 176–83.

[3]Most "annalists" wrote universal histories starting with the foundation of
the city. However, Polybius started with 264 and Q. Claudius Quadrigarius
with the Gallic sack (on the grounds that evidence about early Rome had
not survived the destruction caused by the Gauls). Coelius Antipater wrote a
monograph on the Second Punic War, while Sempronius Asellio and Cornelius Sisenna wrote contemporary histories.

[4]Humm 2005 is detailed and comprehensive.

[5]Raaflaub (2006) makes an eloquent argument in support of an attempt at
reading the evidence for early Rome, although for him the historically accurate period emerges in the late fourth century with the Great Samnite War.

One relatively easy way to deal with the issue of chronology is to use the dates of external wars as largely undisputed markers for various stages in the community's development.[6] Such a dating scheme, however, does not provide a periodization that is descriptive of political history. In fact, the problems posed by chronology beg the whole question of whether we are dealing with one single republic or several. How can the archaic community of the Romans be said to be the same republic as the one that conquered Carthage or the one described by Cicero?

The first issue that must inevitably be addressed in this inquiry is the nature of the sources for Rome's early political structures. This problem is multifaceted. In the first place, it is unclear exactly how much information about early times survived in Rome. The Gallic sack of the early fourth century (390 or 387) may or may not have caused a significant loss of archives, inscriptions, and other materials that could have been used by later Romans to understand their past.[7] The physical effects of this traumatic defeat by the Gauls have proved hard to establish with any degree of certainty. Similarly, the very sparse archaeological record for Roman life during the entire preceding century (the fifth) has been interpreted in very different ways. Some have posited a poor and struggling early republic, under attack from its neighbors and no longer able to maintain the lifestyle associated with the opulent regal city of the sixth century. By contrast, others see the new austerity as a deliberate lifestyle choice in a new political climate, where the lavish customs of earlier times had gone out of fashion in a young republic that was cultivating more austere tastes.[8] Material evidence in itself has not provided definitive answers to these types of questions.

Historiography at Rome was first written in the very late third century, by Q. Fabius Pictor, a Roman senator and a member of an ancient patrician family.[9] It is easy to appreciate the

---

[6]Oakley (2004, 23–24) gives a convenient synopsis of Rome's early wars.
[7]For the Gallic sack, see Cornell 1995, 313–18; von Ungern-Sternberg 2000; and Kolb 2002, 140–41. Oakley (1997, 105–6) discusses chronological confusion around the Gallic sack.
[8]E.g., Smith 2006, 316.
[9]See Beck 2003 and Kierdorf 2003 for an overview.

challenging task that Fabius faced in writing Rome's history over the roughly 450 years since the city's foundation. Naturally Rome's story had already attracted the attention of Greek historians of various kinds, but none we know of had dedicated a special work to the topic of the city's history before Pictor's time.[10] Few can now doubt that earlier times tended, both consciously and unconsciously, to be re-created by a succession of Roman writers in light of conditions in the third and second centuries. This was true even before the crisis of 133 gave rise to a new political climate in which historians had more urgent motives to project the political concerns and conflicts of their own times onto earlier Roman history. Although the fourth century is an obscure time to the modern reader, at least before its last decades, it is an even greater challenge to understand the fifth century in any meaningful detail. Our evidence improves steadily in the third century.

As many modern researchers have noted, the pattern of Roman historical writing is typical of the characteristics of oral traditions as these have been studied in a variety of societies, both traditional and more recent.[11] Information can be preserved reliably over a span of about three generations, but then becomes scarcer and less detailed once a society contemplates times that are beyond living memory. Fabius Pictor was probably born around the year 270 and would have had access to the memories of older Romans stretching back a few decades before the time of his birth. Naevius, who wrote about the First Punic War in the first historical epic poem in Latin, seems to have been a slightly younger contemporary of Fabius, but probably published first.[12] Historical writing in both prose and in verse, therefore, grew out of the context of the Second Punic War, in relation both to the perils and to the triumphs of those very exciting times. Consequently, it is possible to ascribe the pattern and focus of the Roman histo-

---

[10]Greek historians (now lost) who mentioned Rome before Fabius Pictor included Timaeus of Tauromenium, Heraclides Ponticus, and Diocles of Peparethos.

[11]The classic treatment of oral tradition remains Vansina 1985. For oral tradition and the Romans, see also von Ungern-Sternberg 1988 and 2006a.

[12]For Naevius, see Goldberg 1995. For Fabius Pictor, see Dillery 2002; Beck 2003; and Walter 2004, 229–55.

riographical tradition to the circumstances of its creation by Fabius, who made use of a certain body of information that was available to him in the historical times in which he was living and writing.

However, another way of interpreting Roman historical writing is also available, one that complements rather than discounts the pattern suggested by the dictates of oral tradition and community memory. The three generations of Fabii in the family of Pictor coincide with the emergence in the late fourth century of the characteristic political culture of the *nobiles*, the office-holding class composed of both patricians and plebeians. One might, therefore, connect the timing of Rome's first historical writing with the desire of Rome's political elite to record and to celebrate their particular political story in their own voice, even though Rome's histories were written in Greek until around the middle of the second century. There can be no doubt that educated Romans had been reading Greek historians for many years before the time of Pictor, apparently without feeling the need to write such works themselves. Moreover, these same *nobiles* had already developed an elaborate culture of memory in rituals, monuments, and inscriptions for the purpose of commemorating their political story and the role of leading individuals and families within this celebration of Roman values.[13] The identity and influence of the *nobiles*, with particular emphasis on their achievements, was regularly celebrated in the city before the eyes of all the citizens. Indeed the urban landscape in Rome had itself been constructed for at least a century to serve as a memorial and a stage set for this particular political elite.[14]

It is impossible for us to know whether Pictor and his generation had become aware of the limits of orally transmitted collective memory and community rituals. Nor can we know whether they ever explicitly discussed the relative advantages of more formal historical writing in the Greek manner with a view to preserving the story of Rome's characteristic political culture, a republic whose leaders had by now asserted themselves in Italy and against a variety of formidable foreign enemies.

[13]For various cultures of memory, see Flower 1996, 2004, and 2008.
[14]Hölkeskamp 2001 and Hölscher 2001.

Historiographical writing certainly did not displace the more popular and traditional ways of commemorating the past and its heroes. In fact, written histories may never have reached a very wide audience, but were probably circulated among an elite readership, both at home and in other cities throughout Rome's sphere of influence. However, historiography certainly did serve the purpose of preserving a story (eventually a variety of stories) of the *nobiles* and their values just at the time when their political system was reaching the natural limits of most oral traditions and was perhaps already seeming venerable in its own particular way.

It is notable that the pattern of Pictor's history, as far as we can grasp it, seems to have been precisely to focus on more recent times and to connect these with the story of Rome's first origins.[15] In other words, he did not apparently concern himself in any detail with the early republicanism of the fifth century. Rather he wrote about the founding of the city and then concentrated on a fuller narrative of the much more recent history of Rome's political community, in essence as it functioned in his own times. As far as we can tell, he was followed in this by other historians who wrote soon after him. It was not until later that Roman historians wrote more elaborate accounts of earlier republican times, accounts that seem to have been embroidered and expanded with a view to filling the gap in the earlier historiographical tradition.[16] Therefore, both the narrative shape and the publication time of Fabius Pictor's history make sense in terms of the notion of several Roman republics: Pictor wrote about the republican culture he knew and made connections between his political community and the famous origins of the city.

The tradition of Roman historiography before Sallust, which is often referred to as the annalistic tradition, has certain recognizable shortcomings, at least from the point of view of a modern reader. It is generally agreed to have been subject to a number of distortions, including omission, reduplication of episodes, family bias (especially on the part of aristocratic historians like Pictor), anachronism, rewriting of past episodes

[15]Dion. Hal. 1.6.2 provides our evidence for the shape of Pictor's history.
[16]Badian 1966 remains the classic discussion.

in the light of present concerns, simple ignorance of earlier conditions, and the imitation of patterns in Greek history and historiography.[17] Some of these narrative strategies were self-conscious on the part of individual authors, who had literary or political agendas, while others simply mirrored accepted ways of thinking about past events. It is not easy to see exactly how we can compensate for all these various tendencies, even if we argue that a genuine layer of historical information underlies later elaborations and storytelling.[18]

In addition, and perhaps even more importantly, we can only glimpse these republican historical writings at second hand or in very fragmentary direct quotations preserved in later authors. Most of the principal extant writers whose accounts of early Rome we can actually read lived much later. They are Polybius, Livy, Dionysius of Halicarnassus, and to a lesser extent Plutarch.[19] All except Livy are Greeks, and only Polybius, who has very little to say about early Roman history, experienced republican politics in person. Consequently, the accounts of early Rome that we have are written by outsiders to republican politics, who are offering their own versions of what the lost works of several generations of republican authors, with all their own limitations, had to say. The situation is far from ideal.

Two historical examples can serve to show some of the effects in our sources. We can see that an important feature of early republican and pre-republican politics was groups called

[17]For the fragments of the republican historians, see Beck and Walter 2001, 2004 (German edition); and Chassignet 2002, 2003a, 2003b, and 2004 (French edition). For discussion, see Oakley 1997, 21–108; Walter 2004; and Forsythe 2005, 59–77.

[18]Cornell 2005, 52: "We are in fact entitled to conclude that the surviving literary accounts are firmly based on a common body of tradition that outlined the main developments in the history of the city. This tradition was constantly being reinterpreted in the light of new historical circumstances and filled out with rhetorical elaboration as the art of historical writing became increasingly sophisticated. On the other hand there is no reason to think that the tradition was consciously deformed or systematically contaminated in the course of its transmission."

[19]Polybius wrote in the second century BC and Livy and Dionysius in the late first century BC. Plutarch wrote in the late first and early second century AD.

curiae, which seem to have been based on kinship associations.[20] These *curiae* had buildings throughout the city and met in an assembly of citizens that had various political, military, and legal functions. A highly modified form of this assembly survived to the end of republican times. Many scholars have reconstructed the early Roman community on the basis of hypothetical roles assigned to the *curiae*.[21] Yet no ancient source provides secure information about their composition and original functions. Livy himself, the author of our most important narrative of republican times, seems not to know about them in any real detail. They provide a fascinating example of a really important civic group whose history seems to have been lost once they were largely replaced by other assemblies, organized according to tribes or to army units.

Similarly, it is interesting to note the focus of Roman sources on the figure of King Servius Tullius, the great reformer who is associated with many institutions that would be important for republican politics and the Roman army.[22] Since he lived well before republican times, Servius is associated with republican values in spirit and sentiment but not in a traditional historical chronology. He manages to be both republican and pre-republican at the same time. This is especially striking since he is not matched by any equivalent founding figure, who implemented a series of reforms at the time when the monarchy was overthrown and the traditional narrative posits the establishment of a consular system of government. Again, the early history of republican politics has been obscured, this time in favor of traditions about the regal period. Yet no Roman writer was so bold as to move Servius into a republican context and to make the whole story fit in more neatly with the stridently antimonarchic tendencies of so much Roman thought.[23]

The consequences of our limited sources for any chronological scheme will now be briefly sketched. By the time historiography was first written in Rome, the Romans themselves did not know many details about their early political history,

---

[20]Smith (2006) presents a comprehensive and new discussion of the *curiae*.
[21]See Palmer 1970 and Carandini 1997.
[22]For Servius Tullius, see Forsythe 2005, 97–99, 101–6. See Wiseman 1998 for the foundation legends of the Republic.
[23]Martin 1994.

because it was about two hundred years since the monarchy had come to an end and well over four hundred years since the city was thought to have been founded. The survival of accurate data and traditions was limited. At the same time, the very nature of the historiographical project, especially as it was first envisioned by senatorial writers of the late third century, was most probably shaped by a desire to tell the story of their present political system, a republic dominated by *nobiles*, and to describe and celebrate the military and political values associated with this quintessentially Roman elite culture. Such an intellectual project made particular sense at a stage when Rome had become much more influential and ambitious than she had been at earlier times in her development. The *nobiles* now had a story to broadcast and an increasing audience of Mediterranean elites with whom to share this heroic narrative of civic virtue, leadership based on personal valor and merit, and superior republican institutions.

The resulting historiographical genre is the product of a society that had seen several republican systems, rather than the confused story of a single republic whose evolution had simply been obscured by the passage of time. It should come as no surprise that earlier republics had been forgotten once their institutions and way of life had been superseded by more recent political developments.[24] Their politics could be of only limited relevance to the *nobiles*, and hence they were simply not memorable. Meanwhile, archives in the city of Rome were not numerous and tended to be priestly rather than civic or political.[25] The content of earlier political experiments was not explicitly the subject of senatorial historiography, even in cases of writers whose families had played an ancient and venerable role in Rome's early history. In fact, it proved quite

[24]Geary 1994, 176–77, on the subject of historical writing after the year 1000: ". . . the raw material of the past was transformed in ways similar to those described by Frederic Bartlett: to the extent that the past could be made to conform to the present, it was retained. Persons, events, and traditions that eluded contemporary systems of understanding and perceiving were quickly lost or transformed. These transformations, whether of kings or princes, or of dragons and grandfathers, owed more to superimposed interpretative schemes than to the raw materials by which eleventh century people encountered them."

[25]See *La mémoire perdue* 1 for a wide-ranging discussion.

possible for Fabius Pictor to celebrate the early exploits of a range of patrician Fabii, whether exaggerated or not, without apparently providing detailed explanations of the political and social contexts of the very different times in which his ancestors had lived.[26] Rather, contemporary political patterns and concerns, which were generally well established by the late third century, and especially the very success of the *nobiles* themselves, shaped what was interesting and worth discussing about earlier times. Senatorial historiography served self-advertisement first and foremost, and only gradually developed more academic and antiquarian interests during the course of the second and first centuries. It is interesting that the first attested work of this kind is Junius Gracchanus' book *De potestatibus*, about the legal powers of Roman magistrates and therefore about how republicanism had developed at Rome.[27]

As a consequence of all these considerations, and for our present purposes as modern historians, a number of useful chronological frameworks can be envisioned for the study of early republican Rome. I will discuss two of them here. The first seems to me more partial and less useful, so I will essentially be making an argument in favor of the second. However, the situation of our various types of sources for Roman politics makes any time map of fifth and early fourth century Rome hypothetical.

Time Map 1: Patricians and Plebeians

The traditional annalistic accounts present a vivid picture of an early community that was dominated by the bitter clash between patricians and plebeians—represented as *the* two exclusive social groups—over political power and the control of material assets within the community. According to this story,

[26]Forsythe (2005, 195–200) argues that the whole episode of the Fabii at Cremera is a literary imitation of the three hundred Spartans at Thermopylae. Contrast with Smith 2006, 298: "Patricians must have made a significant contribution to the full military levy, but the Fabii at Cremera could operate independently."

[27]Sehlmeyer (2003) explores antiquarianism in Roman historical writing as a separate genre that emerged in the 120s. See also Rawson 1985, 234.

the patricians were descendants of the senators who had advised the kings and had assumed political and religious leadership as soon as the monarchy was overthrown. All consuls and other magistrates had been patricians before the reforms of 367/6. The plebeians, a diverse group of Romans who were not patricians, slowly gained political influence within the community over many generations of struggle, first succeeding in creating their own magistrates (the tribunes of the plebs and the plebeian aediles) and then, in the fourth century, in managing to gain access to the political offices of the patricians (consulship, praetorship, censorship, dictatorship) and eventually to most of the important priestly offices (*decemviri*, augurs, pontiffs). This narrative elaborates on the ancient inherited customs and privileges of the patricians, who were said only to have permitted intermarriage with plebeians by a law of 445 (the *lex Canuleia*). The republican culture of the *nobiles* was represented as the product of an elaborate compromise between patricians and plebeians. However, the patricians still retained many of their old, inherited rights under the new system. This story makes Roman society appear highly traditional and slow to change, even under intense pressure from external enemies and from internal social tensions.

A time map based on the traditional annalistic narrative about such a Conflict of the Orders can yield one or more patrician republics, which were firmly based on a hereditary system of eligibility to hold political office. This principle was completely different from the qualifications for magistracies recorded by Polybius, whose guidelines are based on property ownership and a record of military service. The earliest patrician republic might therefore be said to have come to an end with the decision to allow intermarriage with plebeians, in the years immediately after the creation of the written law code known as the Twelve Tables. The time between the *lex Canuleia* allowing intermarriage in 445 and the great reforms that permitted plebeians to be consuls in 367 could be termed a second patrician republic.[28] Even scholars most wedded to

---

[28]The *lex Canuleia* of 445 legalized marriages between patricians and plebeians (Livy 4.1–7; cf. Cicero *Rep.* 2.61–65). Forsythe (2005, 225–30) argues against the historicity of the original ban.

these Roman accounts would benefit from the greater precision and accuracy that results from distinguishing between hereditary patrician regimes and then differentiating these from the subsequent political compromise: the republican culture dominated by the *nobiles*, whose preeminence was based on repeated election to magisterial office rather than simply on birth. Early Roman republics could, therefore, have been characterized by a steady and logical pattern of power sharing.

To accept such a scheme, however, which centers around the inherited status of the patricians, and defines the plebeians purely in opposition to them, entails the acceptance of patrician claims at face value, despite evidence to the contrary in various ancient sources. There is no space to rehearse all the evidence and the history of various scholarly arguments here; one example will suffice for present purposes. The lists of consuls (*fasti*), which stretch back to 509 and which are preserved in more than one source, clearly seem to indicate that there were plebeian consuls, especially in the earliest period after the monarchy.[29] Similarly, doubts have been raised about the idea that the patricians were ever a closed caste, who married only members of other patrician families.[30] Yet, as soon as we recognize such elements of distortion and exaggeration in our ancient traditions, the framework of our chronology can become unstable and even be lost. A more nuanced approach is called for if we are to make sense of the surviving ancient evidence.

Time Map 2: An Alternative Chronology

It is not the aim of this section to solve the complex problems associated with the archaic republican community, but rather to suggest a chronological outline that might be useful for a range of possible interpretations of the extant evidence.

[29]Cornell 1995, 12–16.
[30]Cornell 1995, 242–71; and Forsythe 2005, 157–70. The latter has nineteen patrician family groups in the Middle Republic. For the continuing distinction between patrician and plebeian, see von Ungern-Sternberg 1990 and 2005; Forsythe 1994, 266–68. For the Roman family in general, see Hölkeskamp 2004c.

My alternative time map contains four chronological periods, some much more republican in nature than others. All are clearly distinct in tone and practice from the political systems of the *nobiles*, which are much more fully attested.

The initial phase of uncertainty and war that followed the expulsion of the kings is probably most conveniently described as a time of transition. It seems to have been essentially pre-republican in character. Conflicting traditions ascribe a leading role in the drama to King Lars Porsenna of Clusium.[31] No individual or political group seems to have emerged with a ready-made constitutional solution. It is possible that two consuls were already the executive magistrates elected each year, at least according to the *fasti*. An inscription quoted by Livy, however, refers to a magistrate called the *praetor maximus*.[32] He may have been one of the consuls (who were at first known as praetors), but he may equally well have been a chief magistrate of another kind (more like a dictator) or part of a board of magistrates, in which case the superlative in his title may suggest that there were at least two others in his group. Roman historical traditions preserve no memory of his role or of the time when he could be found in Rome.

Consequently, we are simply not in a position to classify the Roman government of the years between about 509 and at least 494, when the plebeians first emerged as a political community with their own magistrates.[33] The chronological markers for these early political events can be associated with the traditional foundation dates ascribed to the great temples in Rome: the Capitoline temple of Jupiter, Juno, and Minerva (traditionally dedicated in the first year of republican government), and the Aventine temple of Ceres, Liber, and Libera (traditionally dedicated in 494), which served as the headquarters

---

[31]For Lars Porsenna, see Cornell 1995, 215–39.

[32]See Livy 7.3.5–7 with Forsythe 2005, 151–53.

[33]Hölkeskamp 2007, 51: "Die 'Fremdheit' der Verhältnisse nach dem Ende der Königsherrschaft und in den folgenden Jahrzehnten, ihre archaische Andersartigkeit im Vergleich zu den politischen und institutionellen, sozialen und ökonomischen Strukturen der 'klassischen' Republik ist uns zwar immer deutlicher geworden" ("We have become ever more clearly aware of the 'foreign' nature of conditions after the end of the regal period and in the subsequent decades, their archaic otherness in comparison with the political, institutional, social and economic structures of the 'classic' Republic").

for the plebeian magistrates.[34] It is certainly possible, however, that the political aspirations of the patricians and plebeians have been synchronized in an artificial and perhaps anachronistic way with their principal religious centers.

The second identifiable period can be described as proto-republican and stretches from around 494 to the year 451/0, when the Romans decided to appoint a board of ten men (*decemviri*) to govern the city and to draw up a written law code, the famous Twelve Tables, which provided open access to the community's laws.[35] The end of this period is marked by a significant political and legal reform, which formed the basis for the later history of Roman law and for the use of public writing within the city. As in the Greek city-states, a written law code introduced within the Roman community the important concept of the equality of citizens before the law. This principle, often referred to in Latin as *libertas*, was a vital foundation of republican politics. Although this first law code survives only in fragments, its importance is well attested. Even in Cicero's day, educated Romans learned this archaic code by heart in school. Consequently, it makes sense to recognize the creation of the Twelve Tables as the actual beginning of the first republican period in Rome. The fact that many of the individual clauses probably reflected accepted practices or norms does not detract from the significance of the decision to systematize and publish all this material as a single legal and political document, which served in effect as the foundation of community life.

We are very poorly informed about the circumstances and debates that brought the Romans to this political revolution. The proto-republican period was one of unwritten laws and apparently of significant strife in society. Rome may or may not have been governed by annually elected consuls during these years. Plebeians may have held high political office but have come under increasing pressure from patricians who

[34]For the Capitoline temple, see Tagliamonte (*LTUR* 1996); for the Aventine temple, see Coarelli (*LTUR* 1993). Purcell (2003) argues that the date of the Republic has been fitted to that of the temple's foundation. The Aventine temple burned in a large fire in 31 BC and a new structure was not rededicated until AD 17.

[35]Watson 1975; Cornell 1995, 272–92; Forsythe 2005, 201–33.

aimed to control the executive magistracies. Alternatively, the plebeians may have demanded and enjoyed a more separate political community, especially since their political and religious centers on the Aventine were outside the ritual city boundary known as the *pomerium*. Since we know so little, caution seems preferable to elaborate hypothesis.

After the middle of the fifth century, there was a change in politics, and the first republican period was marked by political experimentation over many years. Particularly notable, as well as singularly obscure, is the variable pattern of tribunes who exercised the powers of consuls.[36] In some years, consuls served as the chief magistrates, while in others, authority rested with boards of magistrates (consular tribunes), consisting of up to six or even eight men of apparently equal rank. These boards of consular tribunes came to predominate by the end of the period (the late fifth and early fourth centuries). It is during this period that the patricians really do seem to have dominated political office for a generation or two. In other words, the new political situation created by the written law code led to less, rather than more, sharing of executive office between patricians and others in Rome. Still, it is essential to note that, however little we may know about this alternative republic, it was very different from what came next in the fourth century. Once heredity had emerged as a key qualification for political leadership, collegiality was differently constructed within a board of patrician magistrates.

At the same time, the consular tribunes did not enjoy the customary religious sanctions for power, in the form of the auspices, nor did they ever celebrate a triumph. These features set them apart from the later culture of the *nobiles* and also from the well-known claims made by later patricians to enjoy a special monopoly over auspical rites and knowledge. If the patricians dominated Rome during these years, they did not represent their power in the same ways as they later would, nor was individual achievement apparently celebrated in the

[36]Cornell 1995, 333–44. Table 8 on p. 336 covers seventy-seven years of this political experiment. P. 336: "In all humility we have to admit that we do not know why the new magistracy was instituted, nor what determined the decision to have tribunes rather than consuls in any given year or series of years." See also Oakley 1997, 41 and 367–76 (with table on 368).

same rituals or to the same political effect. Indeed, the nearly eighty years of regularly choosing consular tribunes instead of consuls must have decreased the number of Romans who could represent themselves as descendants of consuls.

It seems relevant to make explicit that the whole concept of boards of magistrates with equal powers was completely at variance with the later model of a hierarchy of offices culminating in two annually elected executive magistrates (consuls). The history of Rome's wars in this period does not suggest that boards of consular tribunes were chosen to meet special military needs. These boards of tribunes inevitably recall the ten tribunes of the plebs, who remained the most important plebeian magistrates throughout Rome's history. It is possible that the patricians, who did over many years hold a monopoly of the office of consular tribune, were imitating the republic of the plebeians in various ways. Similarly, after 366 the patricians elected their own pair of aediles, who were initially distinguished from their plebeian counterparts by their right to use the curule chair, otherwise reserved for the praetor and the two consuls. It is possible, however, that the dominant discourse in our ancient sources has obscured the political dialogue and mutual influence between patrician and plebeian concepts of a republic. It is not necessarily the case that early republics consisted exclusively of plebeians being excluded from or aiming at magistracies held by patricians. Patricians could also serve on their own board of tribunes, with different roles and rewards from those cultivated later by the *nobiles*.

It is interesting to note that this first republic, which may have been a patrician creation, was a political experiment that came to an abrupt end in 367/6, following what may have been a few years of anarchy.[37] The radical political reform of those years abolished the boards of consular tribunes and laid the foundation for a system of government led by two consuls, shared between patricians and plebeians.[38] The period between 367 and 300 appears, therefore, as a second republic, the one in which the *nobiles* emerged to power. Some scholars have argued that

---

[37]Forsythe (2005, 236) sees six tribunes with consular power replaced by five curule magistrates (two aediles, a praetor, and two consuls).

[38]Cornell 1995, 340: "The Licinio-Sextian Laws transformed the political structure of the Roman state."

the consuls were first created for this republic, which would make the break with earlier politics even more definitive.[39]

We are, in any case, much better informed about political life in the later fourth century. During these years, the other main political offices were either created or more clearly defined, notably the praetor (originally just one) and the censors. These offices do not appear to have been in a hierarchical relationship at that time, and patterns of competition for various offices were in flux. After 342 there was regularly one plebeian consul every year.[40] The censorship gained considerable ground toward the end of the century, partly as a result of the activities of Appius Claudius Caecus.[41]

The auspices, which comprised the religious authority to discern the will of the gods and to gain their favor for the community's actions, now appear to have been very important, and the final struggle between patricians and plebeians came over membership in the priesthoods, rather than over access to political office.[42] It seems likely that priestly office now became more overtly political, even as it was increasingly integrated into a competitive career structure. With the concession by the patricians of most of their claim to a monopoly on religious leadership, the stage was set for a new kind of political life, in which an increasing number of ambitious families and individuals had access to prestige and influence. Social concerns centering around land and debt are attested in legislation and in the policy of colonization, which provided real benefits to poor citizens and relieved need in the city.

The culture of the *nobiles* can also be closely associated with the continual warfare that marked the end of this period, as the Romans began to play a much more aggressive role than before both in Latium and in Italy. The values of the new elite were defined in terms of achievements in war and personal merit, rather than by inherited status or specialized religious

---

[39]Gellius 5.43 with Beck and Walter 2001, 118–20.

[40]Hölkeskamp 1987, 102–9.

[41]The introduction of official lists of senators and their scrutiny by the censors suggests that the role of the senate was evolving, as much as it contributed towards the senior status that the censors came to enjoy among elite Romans. For the censorship, see Suolahti 1963.

[42]Linderski 1986.

knowledge. All political leaders needed to demonstrate their ability to communicate effectively with the gods on behalf of the community. Indeed, the religious qualities of Roman life in general were fostered by the openness of the new political system and by the sense of manifest destiny that was emerging with Rome's imperial ambitions.

An argument can be made that the period of the new republic of the *nobiles*, the third in my scheme, did not start until 287, when a *lex Hortensia* is recorded, a measure that (once again?) made plebiscites binding on the whole Roman people.[43] However, I have opted for the year 300 as my time marker, on the grounds that the sharing of the major priesthoods represents the last significant barrier to plebeian emancipation and to the new kind of republic it created.[44] The sharing of all types and varieties of positions of leadership, even if the patricians still enjoyed a distinctly privileged position because of their small numbers, was the basis for a revolutionary type of republicanism that was to be strikingly more dynamic and successful than any previous regime. Yet the principle of heredity had not been completely discarded and the position of the patricians had not been destroyed. Rather the concept of compromise had emerged, which was to be a powerful political precedent in its own right. No major issue was left for which political compromise could not be a solution: political competition became fiercer, but it was also fully integrated as part of the way politics operated in Rome.

Conclusions

The argument I have presented in this section is that a scheme of four distinct political periods makes better sense of our infor-

[43]Hölkeskamp 1988a and Forsythe 2005, 345–48.

[44]For the system of magistrates, see Brennan 2004. For the emergence of the *nobiles*, see Hölkeskamp 1987 and 2004a, with Forsythe 2005, 276. Bleckmann 2002 discusses developments during the First Punic War. Goldmann 2002 elucidates the meaning of the term *nobilis*. For artistic developments, see Hölscher 1978, 1980, and 1990. For the importance of the year 300, see Hölkeskamp 1988b. Forsythe (2005, 369) considers the list of consuls secure after the year 300.

mation about the fifth and fourth centuries, however incomplete
and disputed that body of evidence may be. The framework outlined here consists of a pre-republican period, a proto-republic,
and two full-fledged republics. The first of these republics consisted of various experiments with larger boards of magistrates
in patterns that were not imitated in later republican politics.
The second was the republic that saw the emergence of the new
political class of the *nobiles*, who were to be very influential
well into the principate. Meanwhile, we must acknowledge and
take into account some consequences of this scheme.

This proposal must remain hypothetical and is designed to
be no more than a useful outline. It is not an argument for a
fixed system of interpretation. On the contrary, various read-
ings of our extant sources can be accommodated within this
same chronological pattern. As a result, this time map does not
presuppose a certain approach toward or level of criticism of
the historiographical traditions about early Rome. Our lack
of detailed information about these early republics and their
experimental predecessors reflects their distance in time and in
substance from the political system dominated by the *nobiles*,
which had certainly emerged by 287.

Meanwhile, an examination of Roman life and traditions
reveals that religious knowledge and customs could be preserved for generations, in the same society in which the details
of obsolete political practices and systems had been forgotten.
Not all evidence about the past was preserved in the same way
or for the same purposes. The value accorded ancient religious
rites was not matched by what would have amounted to a
purely academic interest in outdated political procedures.

As a result of these considerations, a scheme of multiple republics inevitably presents a picture of a much more dynamic
and fluid early Roman society, whose history was marked by
bold experiments in different republican models and by revolutionary moments of reform, when sweeping changes were
introduced in a short space of time. Our own understanding
of Roman political culture is enhanced by the realization that
many alternative histories have simply not been preserved for
us. Thus our picture of early Rome is distinctly partial and
represents certain specific points of view. Two examples can
help to elucidate this point.

The early history of the plebeian tribunate has been lost, with the result that our impression of this magistracy has been strongly affected by events and habits of later republican times.[45] We do not know exactly what powers the early tribunes enjoyed or how they used them. The question of whether or not they had their own form of auspices is particularly difficult to answer. Scholars have been divided about how soon the legislation the tribunes introduced had authoritative force for all Romans. This situation reflects the fact that Roman historians apparently did not have access to or make use of plebeian archives to write a systematic history of this magistracy and its development.

Similarly, it is hard to elucidate the general nature of the relationship between clients and patrons, and in particular the role of private militias in a city-state that from an early date apparently also had a regular citizen army based on a levy.[46] Should we imagine fifth-century Rome as dominated by warlords with private armies, or were these militias a more sporadic and isolated phenomenon? At the moment, our answers are heavily based on arguments from probability.

It seems important to make four general observations before concluding this section. To begin with, the rhetoric of patrician power and privilege needs to be read as an assertion, not necessarily a factual description.[47] Such claims represent a type of political platform expressed in idealized and generalizing language. While it should not be doubted that patrician families could and did preserve and transmit ancient traditions, these were often subject to distortion and exaggeration according to the political needs of the moment. The self-contradictory claims about patrician exclusivity make a simple reading of even their own story impractical.

---

[45]Badian 1996 provides a nuanced and bold treatment of the early tribunes. He stresses the idea that the plebeians could have established their own separate community. See also Bleicken 1968, 1981; Thommen 1989; two essays in Hölkeskamp 2004b; and Kondratieff 2003. For an overview, see Lintott 1999a, 121–33.

[46]Livy 2.49.5; Dionysius of Halicarnassus 9.15.3; Festus 451L; Servius ad *Aen.* 8.337. See Cornell 1995, 143–50, 174–75, 306, 311; and Forsythe 2005, 195–200.

[47]Smith 2006, 278–80.

Second (and similarly), the plebeian story is not a straightforward one, for its very complexity indicates a combination of material from a number of different historical situations and debates. Most notably, plebeian aims vary widely across time, from demands for their own separate political system with its own magistrates to their desire for full integration within the patrician hierarchy of offices. To classify these competing objectives as the pattern of a single republican system is unrefined and inaccurate.

Third, the sharply drawn dichotomy between patrician and plebeian in our sources must surely obscure the political roles and aspirations of other groups and subgroups of citizens. At the very least, some plebeians probably identified more closely with the patricians, while others agitated more or less stridently for political reform. If we had access to narratives from other groups, our picture would surely look very different. Yet the chances of recovering such narratives seem slim.

Finally, a central paradox presents a daunting challenge. Any reconstruction of early Roman society that is based on a highly critical reading of the unsatisfactory and self-contradictory ancient sources available to us runs the risk of simply producing its own independent modern narrative with no basis at all in the evidence.[48] This danger needs to taken seriously, since even for better-attested periods generations of earlier scholars have succeeded in recreating the Roman past in the image of their own times and political concerns.

In conclusion, early Rome remains a wild frontier land, where even experienced and well-equipped travelers will continue to face rugged terrain and harsh conditions. Meanwhile, bitter disputes among scholars have not helped to alleviate this

---

[48]Cornell (2005, 54) says the following about the critical reconstructions of early Roman history by Païs, Gjerstad, and Alföldi: "These radical theories are demonstrably erroneous and have always been unlikely to win acceptance, since they offer historical reconstructions that are far less convincing than the traditional account, which at least has the authority of the sources to back it up. The main positive argument in favour of the tradition is that it provides an account of Rome's historical development that is not only plausible and internally consistent, but also compatible with the continually increasing body of evidence that has come from more than a century of scientific archaeological research." Raaflaub (2006, 140) advises caution and the admission of our ignorance about early Roman history.

situation, especially for those of us who are only trying to pass through on a longer journey. The present discussion does not aim to produce a detailed new reading of the diverse source material. Indeed, change is in the air at the moment, since new excavations and a new edition of fragmentary historical texts promise to alter our picture of Rome's early history.[49]

By contrast, my argument has been that the framework of a single republican chronology is not supported by any reading of the ancient evidence. The concept of one long republic is especially unhelpful as a tool for understanding the complex debates and political experiments that characterized the first two centuries after the end of the monarchy. During these centuries there was no single political system at Rome, nor did politics operate in the same way as it would later in the third and second centuries. As a result, much can be gained from a scheme of multiple republics punctuated by periods of transition. A more nuanced framework brings out the conflicts, failures, and revolutionary moments of change that Romans experienced. It also suggests the elaborate compromises required to achieve a new republic in which political offices with well-defined tasks were shared between members of elite families from a variety of gentilicial backgrounds. The emergence of the *nobiles* and their particular political culture in the late fourth century is well attested by a variety of literary and material sources. This elected political elite then formed a radically new type of republican regime, which built Rome into a Mediterranean capital and invented literature in Latin.

The dynamic republican cultures of the third and second centuries, with their competitive values and aggressive foreign-policy objectives, produced a variety of narratives to describe their origins, to celebrate their success, and to shape their self-

[49]Several ongoing excavations in the center of Rome promise to reveal much new material. In addition, a major new edition of the fragments of Rome's historical writers now in press (T. J. Cornell, E. Bispham, J. W. Rich, and C. J. Smith, eds., *The Fragmentary Roman Historians* [Oxford]), a multivolume collaborative project, will offer the first modern critical edition of these authors since Hermann Peter's of 1870 (second edition 1914). Both these areas of research will surely change our picture of Rome's early history in many significant ways. See the announcement by Cornell (2005, 62–64). For updated information about current excavations, see http://www.fastionline.org.

image in the sophisticated Hellenistic world that had emerged at about the same time. As often happens, the past was appropriated and recalled in terms of present conditions and hopes for the future. Historiography, although a relative latecomer, proved a powerful medium for expressing identity and political meaning. Its serious tone and international audience reflect the political ambitions of the senators who wrote these early texts. They were directly involved in politics and were themselves *nobiles*; they were not scholars who aimed to produce a detailed archaeology of lost political systems or archaic customs and modes of thought. Consequently, the way in which they wrote about the early republic is fundamentally at variance with the purposes of a modern historical inquiry. A carefully constructed chronological framework is therefore all the more vital as we strive to make sense of the types of traditions that have survived about early Rome. These traditions are often episodic and were not necessarily recalled in their full historical or political contexts, nor did the general outline of the several earlier republican and almost-republican regimes have the same significance for the Romans as it has for us.

Part Two

CHANGE

IV

POLITICAL INNOVATIONS

A Community in Transition (Second Century)

eo anno rogatio primum lata est ab L. Villio tribuno plebis, quot annos nati quemque magistratum peterent caperentque. inde cognomen familiae inditum ut Annales appellarentur.
In that year for the first time a law was passed on the initiative of the tribune of the plebs Lucius Villius [that specified] at what ages men could stand for and hold each magistracy. Consequently, members of that branch of the family [of the Villii] were called by the *cognomen* "Annales."

Livy 40.44.1

meministine te saepe legisse quantas contentiones excitarit lex tabellaria quantumque ipsi latori vel gloriae vel reprehensionis attulerit?
Do you remember that you often read about what great contentions arose as a result of the law about the secret ballot and how much glory or blame that legislation brought to the man who had proposed it?

Pliny *Epistulae* 3.20.1, a letter written in the time of the emperor Trajan

Any discussion of the flourishing or disintegration of republican political culture needs to find a context in which to understand decisive change and how we want to define it. Often the "beginning of the end" is situated in 133 and is marked by the introduction of violence between citizens into Rome's civic space. Even in antiquity, the death of the tribune of the plebs Tiberius Sempronius Gracchus, which was the occasion for the first such violence, was already seen as a watershed.[1] Before turning to the topic of violence in the next section, however, this discussion will first attempt to find a broader background for a more general understanding of the nature of change in Roman political culture. The natural focus on the types of innovation in political practices and in rhetoric brought by the age of the Gracchi can easily distract our attention from the longer-term developments of the second century (and indeed the hundred years after Hannibal's invasion of Italy in 218), a time that had seen vast transformations of many kinds in Roman life. For it would be a mistake to imagine that the time before the Gracchi was characterized by a static political system that was not subject to reform or to substantive political debates. Similarly, even after violence first came upon the political scene in the late 130s, initiatives for change using regular political means, notably legislation, did not disappear. This section will explore the issue of non-violent political changes and how these took place in the decades before Sulla's first march on Rome in 88.

Most discussions of "Late Republican" politics have tended to focus on three areas: (1) the violence already alluded to, which intensified into repeated episodes of civil war, (2) party politics construed as the opposition between political groupings, especially those designated as *optimates* and *populares*, and (3) the repeated failures to pass various reform programs to address pressing issues, notably legislative attempts introduced by tribunes of the plebs before assemblies of the people.[2] While there is no reason to deny that these three features had a vital role to play, too narrow or exclusive a focus on

[1]Cicero *Rep.* 1.19.31: *mors Tiberii Gracchi, et iam ante tota illius ratio tribunatus, divisit populum unum in duas partes* ("The death of Tiberius Gracchus, and already before the whole political tenor of his tribunate, divided a single populace into two factions"). Cf. Velleius Paterculus 2.3.3; Plutarch *TGracch.* 20; Appian *BC* 1.17. Badian (1966) notes that partisan contemporary history emerged after the death of Tiberius Gracchus. See also Meier 1980, 129; von Ungern-Sternberg 1998, 614–18. Mackay 2004, 106: "Tiberius Gracchus' tribunate marks the beginning of the spiral of violence in the Late Republic that would eventually kill thousands and bring down the Republic."

[2]Taylor 1949; Meier 1980 (orig. 1966); Gruen 1974; Lintott 1999a; Bleicken 2004; Bringmann 2007.

them can tend to create its own repetitive pattern of political inaction characterized as a stalemate between political parties, a stalemate that resulted in obstruction to all change in a world that was facing ever-new challenges at home and abroad.[3] In the resulting story we encounter a series of tragic flaws that were somehow inherent in republican politics, in a manner reminiscent of Greek tragedy. A (usually unexplored) presupposition of these apparently systemic patterns of inaction and political partisanship is the model of a fundamental Republic, the republic of the preceding two centuries since the end of the Conflict of the Orders, which was weakened and eventually destroyed by these same new and revolutionary behaviors. This section will argue that a different, organic, view of ongoing change in Roman politics can provide the essential background for a more nuanced interpretation of politics and its violent phases in the years before Sulla's preeminence.

It has often been noted that our sources for the years between 133 and 70 are patchy and incomplete. In fact, our sources for the decades immediately before, notably the 150s and 140s, are hardly much better. After Livy's surviving narrative breaks off with the year 167, the course of republican history is inevitably much harder to chart. All the arguments of this section are affected by the lack of clarity both about what actually happened and, more notably, about why things were changing. Our ancient sources are especially poor on the nature of political debate and how such internal discussions were shaped in the generation after the death of Cato the Censor in 149. This situation does not, however, warrant the assumption that political debate came to an end and that there was a golden age of harmony and agreement before Tiberius Gracchus. We should assume, rather, that Romans continued to argue about politics as they had in the years covered by Livy's third, fourth, and fifth decades. Innovation marked the

---

[3]Meier 1980, 3: "Ansätze zu Reformen blieben vereinzelt, wirkten nur an der Oberfläche und haben die Lage oft verschlimmert" ("Initiatives for reform remained isolated, had only superficial effects, and often made the situation worse"). Lintott 1994, 53: "Although the Romans tended to equate 'new things' with revolution, their constitution was continually altering through statutes and precedents creating new traditions, which were acceptable, if they could be reconciled with the basic ethos of society."

turn of the second century, as the Romans boldly decided to engage, both diplomatically and militarily, in the Hellenistic world of the eastern Mediterranean rather than to retrench at home after the long war with Hannibal. This choice, which was to bring them vast wealth and prestige, only encouraged subsequent generations to innovate further and to think beyond traditional roles and societal boundaries.

The second century was a time of enormous and fundamental changes in most areas of Roman life.[4] While the present discussion will focus on political changes, other transformations in society at large also need to be kept in mind. Three areas seem especially worth mentioning: the huge increase in the number of slaves, who worked in all types of skilled and unskilled jobs; the vast influx of wealth in the form of precious metals and material goods, which was very unevenly distributed in Rome and Italy; and the growth of the city of Rome itself into a Mediterranean capital. Since the turn of the second century Roman material culture had been transformed by the huge increase of resources brought by military victories, followed by trade and tax revenues, especially in the eastern Mediterranean. One result of these victories was the huge influx of slaves, which went on to produce new citizens through regular manumission and family building, and the attendant widening gap between richer and poorer freeborn Romans, both in the city and in the countryside.[5] The size of Rome itself also resulted in various social pressures, including the question of the government's role in guaranteeing the price and availability of food in the city.[6] In many ways Rome in 100 (when Marius was consul for the sixth time) was a very different city, with a very different kind of population, from the one that had celebrated the victory over Hannibal at the triumph of Scipio

---

[4]Classic discussions are by Gruen (1984, 1990, 1992). Morstein-Marx and Rosenstein 2006, 634: "It is surely to the early and middle second century that we need to look more closely for the factors that heightened the potential for elite division to the inflammable level reached in 133."
[5]Bradley 1994 offers a general introduction; Dumont 1987 is a detailed treatment. For the period before 200, see Welwei 2000.
[6]Kolb 2002, 175–249; Scheidel 2001 and 2004. For the food supply, see also von Ungern-Sternberg 1991; Virlouvet 1985 and 1995.

Africanus in 201. Some degree of political evolution was the natural and inevitable consequence of changed circumstances.

A closer look at the character of the "Middle Republic" of the second century, therefore, reveals a mature political system but one that was dynamic, not static or fixed. There were real changes taking place in political practices, but these were mostly not violent or subversive. The republican culture of the *nobiles* was continuing to develop in an organic way, in response to perceived needs at home and abroad in circumstances that were obviously changing rapidly. The rest of this section will review some of the most striking and effective of these changes, to provide a more multifaceted and lifelike picture of republican politics in action in the generations immediately before and after the birth of Sulla around 138.

As discussed before, the concept of a *res publica* was based on political debate and commonly undertaken initiatives designed to further the public interest, rather than on close attention to a fixed paradigm such as a written constitution or a system of practices enshrined in religious law. In other words, the concept was itself dynamic. It is possible to get some idea of the patterns of political evolution, even in the absence of detailed sources that elucidated individual debates and issues as they were viewed at the time when the new directions discussed below were undertaken.

The Political Career

Our discussion may usefully start with a brief glance at the *lex Villia annalis* of 180. This legislation fixed the minimum ages for men to stand for and to hold political office and, therefore, established a hierarchy of offices and a standard career pattern. We know about this law only from a short notice in Livy, and its details are hard to recover.[7] Yet, it reminds us that the shape of the political career (*cursus honorum*), which was so central to aristocratic self-definition and influence, was still being developed during the second century. There is every

---

[7]Livy 40.44.1, quoted in the epigraph to this section, with Cicero *Phil.* 5.47. See Beck 2005a, esp. 51–60.

reason for us to pay close attention both to the fact that such legislation was still being passed at this date and to the lack of fanfare that apparently accompanied this important law. In another society such a law would have been seen as a milestone in the constitutional history of the community; for the Romans at the end of the 180s it seems to have been part of business as usual, so much so that it would have been easy for it to have escaped the historical record completely. Moreover, even if we imagine that this law merely codified practices that had essentially been in use for some time before, that does not explain why the law was thought to be necessary. In fact, such an interpretation begs the whole question. Either the law represented new content or it indicated a more formalized use of legislation to enshrine accepted political custom. Consequently, I have chosen to designate it as a decisive chronological marker, a point of legal and political reform that distinguished two types of republic dominated by *nobiles*.

Colonization

We are even less well informed about how and why the Romans stopped founding citizen colonies in Italy after the year 177 and reorganized their whole strategy of establishing new settlements.[8] The foundation of new cities, with the status of either full Roman citizenship or of Latin (allied) rights, had been integral to Roman practice since the later fourth century. Colonization had been, therefore, a typical policy of the *nobiles*. Colonial expansion had served many functions, including defense and security, the gathering of information on the ground in recently conquered areas, and the regular offering of new opportunities to the poor or newly demoted in the city, or to anyone else in Rome who felt the need for a new start.[9] Colonies also helped to spread Roman culture and values, whether according to plan or not. As has often been

---

[8]Patterson 2006b is an accessible and insightful introduction to this large subject.

[9]See Keaveney 2005a; Mouritsen 1998; Lomas 2004, 207–13; and Patterson 2006c, for an outline and bibliographical guide.

noted, many tensions over land ownership, rising debts, and the social condition of potential recruits to the Roman army by the time of the Gracchi can be traced to the decision to stop founding colonies after 177. It cannot be pure chance that no more colonies were founded, nor was it the case that land was completely unavailable in Italy by the mid-second century. A connection with foreign policy, especially in the eastern Mediterranean, may be posited but must remain hypothetical. Clearly, however, this was a deliberate policy decision and one that departed in striking ways from a successful Roman custom that had been in place for over 150 years. It was this policy choice that shaped the lives of ordinary citizens in Rome over the coming generations, and especially before Marius' army reforms at the very end of the century gave the landless a regular opportunity to better their economic situation through a military career. This new climate also emphasizes the break around 180.

The Political Calendar

Another striking change occurred starting in 153, when the Romans decided to move the beginning of their political year, with regard to the offices of their chief magistrates and for many other purposes, to January 1.[10] Previously, March 1 had been the first day of the political year, whereas in earlier times the new consuls had taken office when convenient rather than according to a fixed calendar date. Whether or not the reform of the mid-second century reflected a return to an older, Etruscan-style calendar in use in Rome in the regal period, it is notable to see such a change after a much more flexible approach to the start of the political year in earlier times. Little evidence survives about the reason for this calendar reform, which much later ancient authors simply connect with troublesome wars in Spain.[11]

---

[10]Mommsen 1859 is still a classic discussion. See Livy *Per.* 47; *Fasti Praenestini*, Cassiodorus; with Michels 1967, 97–100; Rüpke 1995, 193–95; and Feeney 2007, 171–72.

[11]Richardson 1986, 128–32.

It is hard to imagine, however, that such a permanent calendar change was no more than a reaction to the wars in Spain, which were hardly Rome's first overseas commitments. Moreover, it seems no coincidence that the new political prominence given to January 1 marked the first year of Rome's seventh century, immediately after the six hundredth anniversary of the city's foundation, according to the chronological scheme that would later be favored by Varro.[12] Our sources do not preserve for us any account of the larger rationale for this reform that would permanently change patterns of Roman office holding through the synchronism of the political with the calendar year. Whatever other celebrations may have marked this epochal time, innovation and a new beginning were apparently the order of the day. The senior consul of 153 was the son of the M. Fulvius Nobilior who put up a famous inscribed calendar in his temple of Hercules of the Muses.

The new calendar gave consuls who did not need to leave immediately for distant wars much more time in office in Rome before the traditional start of the campaigning season for the armies on March 15 (the Ides of March). In this sense, whatever the original rationale of a (re)instatement of January 1 as New Year's Day, its long-term effects were heavily political.[13] Some consuls were now faced with the need to work together in the city for two and a half months before setting out for the field and their separate army commands. The flavor of city life and politics must have been markedly affected by the celebration of a new political year in midwinter, soon after the shortest day and the great festival of the Saturnalia, rather than in the spring, shortly before the troops set out for war again. Early January was also a time that often saw the observance of the movable feast of Compitalia, a celebration of life and politics in the local neighborhoods of Rome.[14] Certainly by the late first century Augustus connected the New Year in a special way with festivities and gift giving involving ordinary

[12]See Brind'amour 1983, 131, and esp. the discussion in Brennan 1995, 53–54 n. 22.
[13]At one time the old year had ended with the festival of the *Regifugium* on February 24 and the new consuls took office on March 15, so that each year had celebrated the end of a king, a hiatus, and then two new consuls.
[14]Fraschetti 1994, 213–61; Lott 2004, 33, 35–40, 49–50, 114–15.

citizens in the neighborhoods, whom he cultivated in a special way as their *princeps*.[15] It is difficult to say how far these later Augustan practices reflect the way the beginning of January was conceived of in the new political year of 153.

The Court System

Shortly afterward, the year 149 saw the creation of Rome's first permanent jury court (*quaestio perpetua*), with a jury composed of senators.[16] While the shape of the new court drew on special courts that had been set up occasionally before to deal with exceptional challenges, such as the tribunals of 186 connected with the suppression of the Bacchanalian cult, the new permanent court was a milestone in the history of Roman law. Later many more such courts would be permanently established, and they would become the cornerstone and most visible forum for the administration of justice in Rome. The new court's importance is marked by the fact that it was staffed by senators as jurors. Its area of inquiry was defined as *res repetundae* or extortion by Roman elites, especially magistrates, in Rome's overseas provinces.

Juries composed of senators (and eventually also of elite non-senators) often failed to police the behavior of their own peers. Indeed, the general level of extortion in the provinces was evidently high, on the part of both republican senators and the tax collectors and publicans of the equestrian class who administered the collection of revenues for Rome.[17] However, the intention of dealing with the problem of imperial finances and their particular temptations was publicly articulated by the Romans in 149 and represented a new vision in terms of political and judicial reform. The fact that the court did not prove as effective as had been hoped should not obscure the innovative vision represented by its original establishment.

---

[15]Fraschetti (1994, 13–49) gives a general introduction. Lott (2004) discusses the Augustan urban reform in detail.

[16]Kunkel 1962 provides the classic treatment.

[17]Badian 1983, esp. 67–81. See Griffin 2008 for an important discussion of Roman self-criticism for their treatment of provincials.

Clearly Romans felt that existing systems of justice did not address the behavior of senators abroad. This situation is also a commentary on the ineffectiveness of the political families in policing their own members once they had left Rome, especially in situations in which those same family groups might be significantly enriched as a result of the new money acquired overseas.[18] Again we see a good example of a striking departure from ancestral tradition that involved careful thought and a challenge to the senators to act as a group to preserve their own reputation and that of the community in its new hegemonic role. This innovation seems also to represent a reaction to empire and to the resulting need for more centralized control. The principle that provincials should have the right to redress and compensation in a permanent Roman court was publicly articulated by this reform, although first steps had been taken already in 171.[19] It is not enough, however, simply to classify the new permanent court as a reaction to outside pressure: it must also have represented the political will and ideals of the leadership at home. The whole question of the role of permanent jury courts would now become a topic of ongoing discussion in Roman politics. Issues would include which crimes such courts should adjudicate and who should sit on the juries. These jury courts became one of the most important issues in political debate, and their eventual failures to administer justice fairly over the next one hundred years were symptomatic of the more general failures of a series of very different republican regimes.

Foreign Policy

Rome's changing attitude to her relations with outsiders is perhaps best exemplified by the sharp contrast between the new extortion court and a strikingly harsh and imperialistic new foreign policy, revealed in the decision to destroy the ancient cities of Carthage and Corinth in 146.[20] While pro-

---

[18]For the case of D. Junius Silanus in 140, see Flower 2006, 64–66.
[19]Brennan 2000, 1: 235–36.
[20]See Astin 1967, 272–76; Kallet-Marx 1995, 84–94; and esp. Purcell 1995. For the concept of Roman hegemony, see Kallet-Marx 1995 and von Ungern-Sternberg 1998, 610.

vincials were to have the right to prosecute corrupt Roman governors in court, those who resisted Roman hegemony were to be mercilessly destroyed. Both cities were completely razed to the ground, an operation that must have cost considerable effort, and both strategic sites were left empty, as erasures in the landscape that marked the power of the Romans. The balance in treatment between East and West in the same year can hardly have been a coincidence. Moreover, neither city at the time posed a credible threat to Rome: rather, these destructions were largely symbolic of a new rhetoric of Roman power. Both cities were by tradition older than Rome, and now lost their own calendars and the continuity of their traditions. By contrast, Gaius Gracchus can be interpreted as making a more traditionalist argument when he suggested the resettlement of the site of Carthage a generation later. Ultimately, it was Julius Caesar, as dictator, who colonized both sites with Roman veterans exactly a century after their destruction.

There is no compelling argument, therefore, to read these changes in Roman legal procedure or in the treatment of defeated rival communities as mere reactions to outside pressures. Political change at Rome appears instead to have been driven by internal concerns and debates whose details are lost to us. We do know that Cato had consistently called for the destruction of Carthage for many years, but we do not know why his wish was honored after he died. If anything, Rome faced fewer and smaller external military threats in the 140s than earlier in the second century. It is interesting, however, to see that the new aggressive stance abroad, which deliberately represented the Romans as sackers of major cultural centers, was soon followed by increasing military difficulties in the second half of the second century, notably in areas of previous success.

Agrarian Reform

In 140, Scipio Aemilianus' friend Laelius, who had proposed agrarian reform to address economic and social issues, earned the *cognomen* Sapiens ("the wise man," or perhaps alternatively "the shrewd one") for his decision to withdraw his

bill and avoid engaging with the vested interests of Rome's
wealthy landowners.[21] During the following decade of the
130s the signs of political change were even greater than in
the previous years, and many significant innovations predate
the momentous tribunate of Tiberius Gracchus in 133. At the
same time, it is important to remember that despite his violent death, the agrarian reform passed by Tiberius did go into
effect shortly after it was passed.[22] Before a quarrel with dispossessed Italian landowners came to the forefront of Roman
politics in 129, the Gracchan land commissioners seem to have
been very active in redistributing public land in small plots to
needy farmers and in (re)establishing the boundaries between
public and private property. It is important not to let the ultimate failure of the much more extensive reform program
of Gaius Gracchus overshadow the real political achievement
of his older brother, which produced significant changes on
the ground in a short time and which led to a whole series of
further agrarian laws being passed later in the second century,
apparently culminating in 111.[23] More is gained by looking
at the Gracchi brothers separately and in their own particular political contexts, rather than treating them as a unit in
the way that has become increasingly common and that dates
back to the paired biographies written by Plutarch.

The Secret Ballot

The 130s was the decade that saw the gradual introduction,
through separate pieces of legislation, of the secret ballot for
voting in the various Roman voting assemblies, for legislation, for election to magisterial office, and for trials of various
kinds.[24] Modern scholars have been somewhat unsure how to
categorize this change in voting procedure, since we do not

---

[21]Plutarch *TGracch.* 8, with the perceptive remarks of Astin 1967, 307–10.
[22]Lintott 1994, 73–77; Gargola 1995, 147–74, esp. 159–62.
[23]Lintott 1994, 86–87; Gargola 1995. For the background, see de Ligt 2006.
For the texts of the laws, see Lintott 1992 and Crawford 1996.
[24]The year 139: *lex Gabinia* (elections); 137: *Lex Cassia* (noncapital trials);
131: *lex Papiria* (legislation); 107: *lex Coelia* (capital trials of *perduellio*). See
Yakobson 1999 and Salerno 1999 for interpretation.

have much ancient evidence to indicate that it was seen as revolutionary at the time, nor does it seem to have subsequently produced many very different kinds of candidates for high office.[25] Yet, once again, lack of detailed evidence really proves nothing. The independence already shown by the voting assemblies in 133 is probably one result of these ballot initiatives.[26] The secret ballot should be seen as the political revolution that it surely was, a revolution that was phased in thoughtfully, as each assembly in turn was given the chance to try the secret ballot. The very concept of a secret ballot recalibrated the balance of power in Roman politics as envisioned by Polybius.

Before the secret-ballot initiative, Roman voters had to approach a voting official in charge of recording votes and announce their choice (yes or no to pass a bill, or the name of the candidates for office).[27] The official would then record the vote as a mark in the appropriate column on his list of possible choices. This open system of voting by public affirmation was traditional in Roman republican culture but carried some obvious consequences. Anyone standing nearby could hear the vote being declared. No effort was apparently made to stop someone from standing next to the official and finding out how individual citizens voted.[28] Similarly, it is unclear what checks, if any, there could be to prevent simple error or deliberate manipulation in the recording of the voting tallies by the electoral officials. Under the new system, voters were offered ballots made of clay. These were marked with yes or

[25]For the debate about the effects of the secret ballot, see Jehne 1993; Yakobson 1995; and Lintott 1999a, 47–48, 205. Badian (1990) gives an account of the consuls elected between the years 179 and 49. Note, however, Cicero *Amic.* 12.41 (written in 44), which does identify the secret ballot as a political watershed.

[26]Lintott (1994, 97–98) posits a radical sovereignty of the assembly over the details of government at the end of the second century. Cf. Mackay 2004, 107. It is not clear how far the increases in violence starting in the late 130s should be linked to the secret ballot and its effects. Extant ancient authors do not seem to draw any connections.

[27]For Roman voting practices, see Taylor 1960 and 1966; Nicolet 1976, 280–424; and Lintott 1999a, 46–49, 51–61.

[28]Livy 45.37–39: M. Servilius Pulex Geminus in 168 at the triumph of Paullus after Pydna.

no for legislation or with the name of candidates for office. The voter then placed the ballot of his choice in a basket designed to collect the votes. As tribune of the plebs in 119, C. Marius introduced further legislation that narrowed the gangways (*pontes*) leading to the baskets, thus assuring that no one could stand on them and look at the ballots as they were cast.[29] In 104 the use of the secret ballot was extended to elections to some major priesthoods.[30]

The introduction of the secret ballot was a political revolution at the very heart of the republic dominated by the *nobiles*, whose elite status depended on election success and on public acceptance by ordinary citizens in civic contexts. It is implausible to imagine that such an extensive change was introduced casually, without any debate, or without a reasoned political objective. Two of the tribunes who introduced these bills, L. Cassius Longinus Ravilla (cos. 127, cens. 125) and C. Papirius Carbo (cos. 120), came from prominent political families and went on to distinguished careers. It is not possible for us to say exactly why the senate and Roman people supported this change throughout the 130s and beyond, but they must have had a political reason that included dissatisfaction with the existing mechanics of voting. The original intention of the secret ballot has been interpreted as an anticorruption measure.[31]

Regardless of the terms in which that reason was articulated at the time, the reform suggests a concern with the integrity of each citizen's vote and of the final result of the voting process, which must have been conceived of as an accurate reflection of the will of those present in the assembly. Now it would be verifiable in a more permanent record on clay. In a basic way, therefore, this reform changed republican political culture on the initiative of successful tribunician legislation and gave the voters more independence. The secret ballot made it much more difficult to intimidate or bribe individual voters. It also afforded privacy to each citizen and to the neighborhood group he might belong to, and might vote with or

[29]For the *lex Maria* of 119, see Wiseman 1971, 5; Lintott 1999a, 46. Note esp. *RRC* 292.1, of 113 or 112.
[30]The *lex Domitia* of 104: Hantos 1988, 120–21; Lintott 1994, 94.
[31]Lintott 1994.

against. Further, the reform shows a real concern on the part of the community with the voting process itself: voting was not a civic exercise that was merely taken for granted. Despite criticism of the secret ballot in some later Roman authors, it is notable that it was maintained in the constitutional settlement of Sulla. These ballot laws marked a political watershed. I would argue that they provide the most distinctive and useful chronological marker of the unstable, final republic of the *nobiles*, a time of political turmoil that looked different from what had come before.

Silver Coinage

A very visible change that has been associated with the introduction of the secret ballot is the marked shift in the Roman silver *denarius* coinage production, starting in the 130s and continuing until the eventual introduction of different minting patterns once there was a system of one-man rule.[32] Traditionally, the Roman mint had favored repetitive coin types in patterns similar to the coins of Greek cities, especially of those in southern Italy. Now coin types started to change annually and to reflect designs chosen by the individual officials in charge of the mint each year. The new coins displayed a varied array of types that could refer to religious symbols, political ideas, anniversaries of historical events, monuments or buildings in Rome, or to the achievements and status of the moneyer's ancestors. The effort put into coin designs suggests that an audience for these images was envisioned, presumably beyond the circle of the moneyer's immediate family and friends. At the same time, the shift gave the moneyers themselves and their traditionally relatively humble job at the mint much more publicity and symbolic political capital than ever before.[33] It has been argued that these new coin designs were aimed at the voters, who were now less open to more direct forms of pressure and influence.[34] However that may be, the

---

[32]For republican coins, see *RRC*. See also Flower 1996, 79–86.
[33]Hamilton 1969; Crawford 1974, 616–19; Burnett 1977.
[34]Wiseman 1971, 4; Crawford 1974, 728.

change in minting habits demonstrates that political shifts of various kinds were underway and that the 130s were a decade of significant evolution in both the content and the form of political expression. It would certainly have been a huge change to envision the images on coins as aimed mainly and more explicitly at ordinary citizens, rather than at foreigners who might use Roman currency as a standard for trade, or as a symbol of Rome's hegemony, as was often the case with the coins of Greek city-states and earlier Roman issues.

Army Recruitment

A reform with significant political consequences for the republic was the change in recruitment of soldiers for the Roman army, first introduced by Marius as consul in 107 and further implemented by him in 104.[35] This, too, was a peaceful reform that was put in place in a regular manner by a consul in office. It can be seen as the logical culmination of a long trend of enlisting men with ever-smaller amounts of wealth. Moreover, it did not mean that all Roman soldiers were suddenly landless overnight. Rather, new volunteers from the landless classes served for the first time alongside drafted peasants in the war against Jugurtha in Numidia. Voters were no longer necessarily identical with soldiers now, since the landless had little chance to vote in the *comitia centuriata*, although in practice men with little wealth had been serving in the army for some time. Veterans began to look to their commander for benefits at the time of their discharge. It is important to take note that Marius did not disappoint his veterans of the war with Jugurtha. His close relationship with his soldiers was well known and had its own effects during his lifetime, especially in 88, and it set an example for later commanders.

---

[35]For Marius' army reforms, see Rich 1983; Keppie 1984, 61–63, 69–70; and de Blois 2000. Lintott (1994, 92) sees criticism of landless soldiers in later authors as reflections of Roman armies after the death of Caesar. Nicolet (1976, 122–99) reviews the life of the soldier and the army during the Republic. Keaveney (2007) presents a different picture of Sulla as the creator of the new revolutionary army.

Concluding Thoughts

Marius' rise to extraordinary power, and the political initiatives that he took, were fundamental to the destruction of the traditional republican culture of the *nobiles*, which was far less resilient in the face of the changes his career and policies brought than has usually been appreciated.[36] This outcome is all the more startling since Marius had been born sometime in the early 150s and had, therefore, seen republican politics and army life in action before the age of the Gracchi. Moreover, political changes introduced in peaceful ways, especially in the last thirty years of the second century, emerge nonetheless as significant steps toward the violence and collapse of Roman politics at home and in Italy that started in 91. In other words, it was peaceful political reform, just as much as—and sometimes even more than—violence and the breaking of accepted norms, that initiated the momentum for changes of diverse sorts in republican political and military culture.

One of the principal challenges facing any discussion of the political chaos of the 80s is the almost complete lack of reliable evidence about what was going on in Roman politics in the 90s. Hence the immediate context of Livius Drusus' great reform program has been lost, probably irretrievably. There must have been ongoing political debates that followed from the violent events of the year 100 and the political eclipse of Marius, who had been preeminent for several years.[37] Whatever was happening during the 90s, it is notable that by the end of the decade Drusus proposed a full-scale program of reforms that would have rivaled and perhaps even surpassed the ambitious reform program of Gaius Gracchus a generation before. If they had succeeded, Drusus' reforms would have rewritten Roman history in a truly radical way, as is revealed by the collapse that followed his murder in the *atrium* of his own house by an unidentified (political) assassin.[38] Consequently,

---

[36]For Marius, see Evans 1994 and Lintott 1994, 86–103.
[37]Badian (1984) gives an excellent overview of the year 100.
[38]Meier (1980, 208–16, 262) puts Livius' tribunate in context, seeing four big reform suggestions between 95 and 80. Lintott (1994, 101) reviews the 90s. Gabba (1994) puts Livius and his death in an Italian context.

it seems worthwhile to note that Rome once again had the opportunity to pass fundamental political reforms based on a platform proposed by a member of the existing political elite, who had been duly elected to magisterial office and was amongst the wealthiest *nobiles* in Rome.

This section has sketched a broad second-century context that can serve as background for a more nuanced understanding of the types and the frequency of violence in republican politics after 133, which forms the subject of the next section. Exactly fifty years separated the death of Tiberius Gracchus from Sulla's invasion of Italy after he had signed the Peace of Dardanus with king Mithridates VI of Pontus. That half century has often been characterized as one of increasing violence and outside pressure on an old-fashioned republic that was incapable of meaningful internal change and of adapting to new external challenges.[39] A willingness to consider patterns of peaceful political reform and successful initiatives that departed in radical ways from inherited political practices can serve to modify this received model. Meanwhile, the recognition of a political break in the 130s, which is found in many ancient sources and modern discussions, makes sense.

In fact, traditional republican practices of the *nobiles* had already changed in several fundamental ways in the forty years before Marius was elected to the consulship of 107. As this section has outlined, radical and permanent changes had come in the areas of foreign policy, the law courts, voting, agrarian legislation, and the conditions and demands of army service. If we consider the sixty years before the unsuccessful reform proposal of Livius Drusus in 91, patterns of internal reform are even more striking. The rules of the game were far from the same as they had traditionally been. Calls for reform like those of Gaius Gracchus or Livius Drusus acknowledged a need for change and were based on the idea that reform was

[39]Meier 1980, ix: "Eine virulente Krise spielt sich ab, in der sich hundert Jahre lang keine Alternative zum Herkommen bildet" ("A virulent crisis took its course, during which no alternative to the status quo emerged for a hundred years"). According to Meier (xviii), Augustus offered the first alternative; Gotter (1996, 246–47) criticizes this view on the grounds that Cicero's political writings of the late 50s were suggestions for practical reform.

indeed integral to republican politics and to the ethos of its traditional leaders, the *nobiles*. A more dynamic understanding of the moments of republican reform, when combined with a nuanced picture of the interactions of internal and external pressures and demands, creates a subtler understanding of an adaptive, vital, but brittle republic, subject to a wide array of different influences that would lead to political collapse and military revolution in the decade of the 80s.

═══ V ═══

VIOLENCE AND THE BREAK-DOWN OF THE POLITICAL PROCESS (133–81)

ad summam perniciem rem publicam perventurum esse…
Conditions had reached the final destruction of the state/
republic…
> Fragment of Sulla's memoirs, Book 21 (quoted by Priscian 9.476H)[1]

si Latinis civitatem dederitis, credo, existimatis vos ita, ut nunc constitistis, in contione habituros locum aut ludis et festis diebus interfuturos? nonne illos omnia occupaturos putatis?
If you were to give Roman citizenship to the Latins, do you think that there would still be room for you at public meetings to hear political speeches or at the games and on public holidays, as you enjoy it now? Do you not think that *they* would take up all the spaces?
> Gaius Fannius, in a speech attacking Gaius Gracchus in 122 (quoted by Julius Victor 6.4)

In any interpretative scheme that has been or could be proposed, political violence is a characteristic—and perhaps the best-known—feature of the urban landscape in Rome after the time of the Gracchi. Such violence merits and has already received separate and detailed treatment as a subject in its

---

[1]The rather unusual impersonal construction of this phrase further obscures its original meaning and frame of reference.

own right.[2] There are many perspectives from which it can be viewed and as many analytical tools for its analysis. It was more than a political phenomenon, as it carried within it causes and results that were social, religious, economic, and cultural. The following brief look at violence in Rome, however, will concentrate on its political effects and implications. In a specifically political context, the nature of each episode has its own meaning, as is reflected in its precise aftereffects on republican practices. It has become easy to blur the different episodes and, as a result, to create a generalized pattern of violence in seemingly repetitive cycles across several generations of a slowly dying "Late Republic." Such a treatment can seem to trivialize the impact even of open civil war and of times of complete political collapse. As I will argue here, it is only by appreciating the particular political effects of violence that its full implications for traditional republican political culture can be gauged.

This section will sketch the developing violence between the year 133 and Sulla's dictatorship of 81, a time span of just over fifty years. The basic line of argument can readily be summarized: violence was devastating for Rome, especially between the death of Gaius Gracchus and his followers in 121 and the end of the proscriptions of Sulla in the summer of 81. It was violence, in its various typically Roman forms, that led to the complete collapse of the last traditional republic of the *nobiles* by the early 80s. That republic, already weakened and compromised by violence over more than a generation, was finally destroyed when Sulla marched on Rome in 88, in the immediate aftermath of the Social War.

---

[2]Appian *BC* 1.1–16 gives an overview of the period from 133 to 31, with a stress on violence. Other sources can be found in *MRR* and Greenidge and Clay 1960. For modern discussions, see Nippel 1988 and 1995, Lintott 1999b. For bibliography, see Bleicken 2004, 305–6. Mackay 2004, 129: "The oligarchy had introduced violence into the political system with the murder of Tiberius Gracchus and over the years the use of violence became increasingly acceptable as various political disputes in Rome led to more and more bloody discord. The refusal of the oligarchy to grant citizenship to the allies had eventually resulted in an armed revolt and then in civil war that saw a senatorial commander use the loyalty of his landless troops to seize control of Italy and to wreak on his enemies—and others—a form of vengeance that brought domestic violence to unheard of levels."

The received interpretation of Sulla's coup and reforms as no more than a brutal interlude in republican government misrepresents both the nature of the violence he unleashed and the character of politics at the time.[3] In fact, it must be stressed that this violence was much more corrosive of republican political values and practices than has usually been admitted. In political terms any violence was in itself a basic breach of republican principles. The use of force constituted an admission, or perhaps often an assertion, of the failure of the accepted political system to resolve conflict or even to manage some of the regular functions of government. As soon as such a failure occurred or was claimed to have occurred, it inevitably weakened republican norms, and at the same time a further precedent for violent behavior was being set. Moreover, these political effects came on top of the inevitable cycle of revenge that was unleashed by any killings. All this was much more serious in a city state that claimed to have solved the problem of societal strife and class warfare long ago by developing a community based on the equal access of all citizens to a law code regulated by a jury court system.[4] Roman republican law did not impose the death penalty on citizens, except in a few rare cases.[5] Rather, the standard punishment for the worst crimes was exile and loss of civil standing, thereby simply removing the offender from the community.[6] Hence there was virtually no societal or legal precedent to support any argument that a citizen should forfeit his life in an internal political conflict.

Both ancient and modern sources have tended to agree that political violence was unleashed in Rome when Tiberius Grachus, as a tribune of the plebs, and a significant number of his supporters were killed by a group of senators and magistrates (and their followers), led by the *pontifex maximus*

[3] On armed militias, see Dahlheim 1993, 103. For proscriptions, see Hinard 1985 and Flower 2006, 86–98. Strabo (5.11.249) notes the effects three generations later of the ethnic cleansing of Samnites.
[4] See Jolowicz and Nicholas 1972; Johnston 1999; and Alexander 2006.
[5] Mommsen 1899, 911–44, esp. 939; Levy 1963, 331–32.
[6] Kelly 2006 offers a detailed discussion and a prosopography of individual cases.

Scipio Nasica.[7] The ostensible cause was a serious breach of Roman political norms, namely, Tiberius' attempt to be re-elected to a second (successive) annual term as tribune of the plebs Tiberius Gracchus' desire to continue in office, which suggested an unrepublican attempt to seize power, came on the heels of other actions that represented clear contraventions of accepted rules.[8] Yet it was especially shocking to Romans that a sacrosanct tribune of the plebs had been killed in front of the temple of Jupiter Optimus Maximus on the Capitol during an inaugurated electoral assembly by the most senior of Rome's priests. The fact that Nasica was Gracchus' first cousin added the further sacrilege of the shedding of kindred blood. Nasica seems to have enacted an ancient religious ritual killing (*consecratio*) of Gracchus, presumably on the grounds that he was trying to seize power and overthrow the existing republic. The impact of this violence, especially when understood in terms of religious transgression and pollution, can scarcely be overestimated. Meanwhile, Nasica's claim that the republican government was in mortal danger became a self-fulfilling prophecy.[9]

Yet the first nonlethal violence had been introduced earlier that same year, when Tiberius' fellow tribune M. Octavius had persisted in his veto of Tiberius' agrarian bill in the voting assembly, despite the fact that ordinary people vociferously supported Tiberius' initiative. Tiberius proceeded to have the assembled people vote to depose Octavius, and then physically removed his fellow tribune from the assembly.[10] The initial political breach, therefore, came between two fellow tribunes of the plebs, elected together to represent the interests and views of the plebeians. Octavius insisted on enforcing his veto, even in complete defiance of the openly expressed will of

[7]See Flower 2006, 69–76, for a more detailed treatment.

[8]See Badian 1972, 722: Tiberius had destroyed collegiality and then threatened annuity and the very principle of annual political office.

[9]Valerius Maximus 3.2.17: *qui rem publicam salvam esse volunt, me sequantur* ("Let those who want the state/republic to be safe follow me"); cf. Plutarch *TGracch*. 19.

[10]Badian 1972, 701; Stockton 1979, 78: Octavius' veto broke constitutional conventions in force since the *lex Hortensia* of 287. Linderski 2002, 339: the revolution did not start in 60, as Asinius Pollio thought, but in 133 with the clash between two fellow tribunes.

his constituents in his own presence. In this sense, he used his office and its traditional rights as a political tool to support elite vested interests. Gracchus, in turn, first nullified the veto and then deposed and manhandled an elected tribune of the plebs, in a similarly unprecedented breach of political behavior. Their clash exemplifies a pattern of decay typical of the republic of the *nobiles*: neither Octavius nor Gracchus acted according to the existing rules of the political game. Rather, the breach of one (Octavius) led to the unconstitutional behavior of the other (Gracchus). Nevertheless, at the end of the day both men were in the wrong and republican habits had been broken.

In other words, it was the republic that stood to lose. Subsequently, the implications of Gracchus' political choices can seem all the more dire, for his actions suggested (whether rightly or wrongly) that traditional republican norms could not produce the types of economic reform needed by the people and the army. At the same time, the further Gracchan position was that a given political issue, in this case the redistribution of public land in order to boost army recruitment, could outweigh virtually every other political consideration, even the very structures of the republic itself. It is evident, therefore, that Gracchus paid too high a price, even before his death, for insisting on his view of reform, particularly within the brief span of his one year in office as tribune of the plebs. Moreover, political change at any cost must have seemed an especially strident demand in a decade such as the 130s, which had already seen so many reforms introduced in a peaceful and orderly fashion, at least as far as we can see from the existing evidence.

Nasica also, in effect, chose a course of political action essentially similar to that his cousin just had, for he refused to accept the considered opinion of the consul and jurist Mucius Scaevola that the existing laws were adequate to deal with any unconstitutional acts that might result from Gracchus' assembly.[11] Instead of abiding by this advice, which would have avoided violence and kept to republican norms, Nasica took matters into his own hands, even though he was not a magistrate in office but only a private citizen at the time. Not unlike

---

[11]Ungern Sternberg von Pürkel 1970, 4; Badian 1972, 711.

Octavius, he misused his office, in this case a religious one, to obstruct a voting assembly and to try to enforce a minority view. His religious justification for violence was archaic and had nothing to do with contemporary political norms.

As a result, the year 133 was momentous because it witnessed a wide range of unprecedented violations of political rules of behavior, which proved decisive in dividing the community in its reactions to what had occurred. The final introduction of deadly violence, both in 133 and then again in 132 in the senate's further pursuit of Gracchus' supporters, confirmed the divide between citizens with different political views. It also confirmed the distinctly un-Roman notion that senators (whether in office at the time or not) could or should use violence to enforce or to suppress a political solution—thereby silencing a group, perhaps even a majority, of their fellow citizens.

By the same token, the religious and ritual nature of the violence used against Tiberius sets it apart from any later violent episode in the period under discussion.[12] In that sense, it serves as something of a prelude to rather than a direct precedent for more formalized uses of armed force by elected magistrates in office. Of much greater significance are the events of 121, when Gaius Sempronius Gracchus, Marcus Fulvius Flaccus, and their followers were killed in an attack by soldiers under the command of the consul L. Opimius. Opinions have differed as to the exact legal implications of the so-called *senatus consultum ultimum* (or "final decree"), a special emergency decree passed by the senate for the first time on this occasion.[13] This vaguely worded senatorial decree declared a new type of "state of emergency," but without making clear exactly what difference that made to republican legal or constitutional norms or to the civil rights of citizens. This decree might appear to be a formalized suspension of the constitution. It is not clear, however, that Romans would have shared this notion, nor do later events justify the idea that a consul armed with such a decree could undertake with impunity any action that

[12]See Spaeth 1990 and esp. Linderski 2002.
[13]Ungern Sternberg von Pürkel 1970, 55–67; Stockton 1979, 176–205; Burckhardt 1988, 135–41; Nippel 1988, 71–79, 84; Lintott 1994, 77–86, and 1999a, 89–93.

he saw fit. It is also notable that such decrees never seem to have named a specific threat or group of enemies as a target. Rather, the decree was a more abstract expression of senatorial concern and of a generalized support for those already in executive offices to "defend Rome's republic." It is ironic, in this context, that the decree itself, in tone and in effect, seems to subvert the effectiveness of the existing norms of the very republican government that it purported to uphold.[14]

Whatever view one takes of the exact nature of the *senatus consultum ultimum,* the violence of 121 was a shocking escalation from anything seen in Rome in living memory. Civil war and street battles broke out in the city and the Gracchan supporters occupied the Aventine Hill. They were defeated in open combat by the consul Opimius, whose forces included specially trained Cretan archers who had clearly been summoned and deployed for this particular purpose. Although no Roman citizen was formally deemed an "enemy" (*hostis*), Opimius' opponents were certainly treated as such and the consul placed a price on the heads of his most prominent political opponents.[15] Subsequently, Flaccus' house was confiscated and razed in a rhetorical gesture that labeled him an aspirant to tyranny. Although Gracchus and Flaccus were not magistrates in office at the time, the overwhelming force used against them did have a number of political implications. Certainly the issue of civil rights for citizens in situations of emergency was raised in a highly public manner. Similarly, the split in the political community was now assimilated to an invasion and occupation by a foreign enemy. The use by the consul of select special-forces units, composed of foreign soldiers, to kill Roman citizens in and around Rome will not have made the solution more palatable and less like an outbreak of a civil war. Again the outcome was both violent and completely outside republican rules of conduct. A dangerous

---

[14]Cicero *Cat.* 1.2.4: *decrevit quondam senatus, ut L. Opimius consul videret ne quid res publica detrimenti caperet* ("The senate once decreed that the consul Lucius Opimius should see to it that the state/republic not suffer any loss"); cf. *Phil.* 8.4.14.

[15]Opimius is the first attested example of a Roman magistrate putting a price on a citizen's head, which he then paid to those who brought him the head of Gaius Gracchus. For sources, see Greenidge and Clay 1960, ad loc.

precedent was set here that suggested violence as the logical and more effective alternative to political engagement, negotiation, and compromise within the parameters set by existing political norms.

At the same time, there is every indication that Opimius recognized at least some of the unsettling implications of his actions. He performed a ritual purification of the city (*lustrum*) that acknowledged the pollution caused by the shedding of blood inside the community's sacred boundary. He then built an imposing new temple of the goddess Concord (Concordia) at the northwest end of the Forum adjacent to the senate house.[16] The honoring of this deity clearly represented a pious hope for a return to a renewed sense of political harmony within the civic community, which had been organized according to republican precepts. Care, thought, and expense were not spared in Opimius' efforts to bring acceptable closure to political strife and civil conflict. It is interesting and suggestive of things to come that many in Rome did not accept either his political apology or its religious dimensions. Traditional republican culture could not be restored by an executive order. At the same time, violent and illegal actions, regardless of who committed them, set unrepublican precedents of their own, precedents that proved destabilizing even after centuries of orderly civic life. In other words, Opimius' political experiment foreshadowed the later experience of Sulla, the dictator who tried and failed to impose a functional republic by force and through terror.

The next attested violence of the type and scale of that experienced in 121 is attributed to the year 100. What is perhaps most noticeable after the passage of twenty years is the variety of different types of violence now seen in Rome, such that even a seasoned general like Marius, consul for the sixth time in that year and known as an expert in guerilla warfare, was unable to control most of its manifestations. This is the first year in which we have firm evidence for organized and armed groups,

---

[16]Temple of Concord: Ferroni in *LTUR* 1993; Kolb 2002, 169, 241, 245. Purcell (*LTUR* 1995, 325) puts the temple just outside the Forum area but adjacent to the *comitium* and *rostra*. Opimius, who had destroyed the town of Fregellae in 125, can be seen as an anti-Italian consular candidate.

which have been termed "gangs" in modern discussions.[17] It is important to keep in mind the traditional ban on the carrying of weapons within the city limits, another rule of republican life that was now apparently no longer observed. In any case, the scale of unrest surely suggests that these militia-style political groupings may have been developing over a number of years. Similarly, political assassination now appeared as a means of eliminating a rival candidate (C. Memmius) for election to high office, even as exile was used as a political weapon against Metellus.

Both armed gangs and political assassination were closely associated with the plans of L. Appuleius Saturninus and C. Servilius Glaucia to try to place in office for the following year as many men as possible from their own political association, precisely by using a range of illegal and violent methods.[18] In other words, at the heart of the use of violence was the desire to appropriate political power for a small faction by circumventing republican practices, especially the free election of magistrates. Purportedly such pacts, if successful, would have allowed the passage of more extensive programs of reform, although at the price of a significant increase in the personal power of the politicians involved. Once again, other patterns of reform in these years, including legislation passed by some of these very same individuals, raises the whole question of the motives and methods espoused by a man like Saturninus. The kinds of compacts envisioned would have fulfilled all the worst fears voiced by traditionalists in 133, when some felt that Tiberius Gracchus' election to a second consecutive term as tribune of the plebs would undermine republican government and values. Eventually such a political compact would be realized, first under Cinna in the mid-80s and then in the 50s, with the alliance between Caesar, Pompey, and Crassus. Such an arrangement, whether directly bought with the price

---

[17]Lintott (1994, 96, 103) describes Saturninus' violence as calculated and political. See also his discussion at 1999b, 67–88, esp. 74–88, with a stress on the local neighborhood culture. Mackay (2004, 119–20) gives an overview in outline.

[18]Burckhardt (1988, 141–49) sees Saturninus and Glaucia as a serious threat to the state.

of citizen blood or not, was simply not compatible with republican culture.

Voting in various situations was now also affected by direct pressure, including violence, exercised by soldiers. It is vital to note that in less than ten years after Marius' army reforms were implemented, his new landless recruits were fighting in the streets of Rome and intimidating voters in the voting assemblies. With rapid and dire consequences for community politics, the essential and characteristic republican link between voting and military service had been broken, since the landless recruits had little chance to vote in the assembly.[19] Moreover, these consequences manifested themselves even though Marius had apparently succeeded in gaining land and benefits for his first set of veterans, many of whom had fought Jugurtha in Numidia.[20] It has been argued that most veterans were poor men from the countryside, but detailed information about recruitment is not available.[21] It is not easy for us to trace the exact relationship between the armed urban gangs (or militias) and the disaffected soldiers who now entered the city to disrupt voting and the regular political process. However, the combination of both of these violent phenomena changed the urban political landscape forever. In other words, whereas Opimius had used foreign troops inside the city in an exceptional and short-lived crisis situation, Rome now faced on a regular basis the violent disaffection and political alienation of her armies and veterans.

Despite his prestige and military skills, including a distinguished record fighting insurgents in Spain and in North Africa, Marius was unable to control the violence in the city. In this sense also, therefore, the violence of 100 was very different and much more destabilizing than the relatively much more contained police action of 121. The consul, although he had been hailed as Rome's savior the year before, was not

---

[19]Potter (2004) gives a clear statement of the connection between military service and political activity, especially voting.

[20]Mackay 2004, 119.

[21]Morstein-Marx and Rosenstein (2006, 630–33) give a succinct statement of the issues. We do not know the details of recruitment in the late republican armies, nor how many recruits were poor or landless. See also Keaveney 2007.

ultimately in control. His decision to use force pitted a consul against other elected officials for the first time. Saturninus and his followers seized the Capitol after their unsuccessful attempts to control the elections for the following year, and although Marius easily managed to capture them, he was not able to guarantee their safety. The consul's prisoners, who had been locked inside the senate house with a promise of due process, were lynched by a mob, despite the sacred nature of that space.

Marius' subsequent retirement from politics in the 90s is a reflection of his failure as a leader in Rome. The outcome is all the more surprising when we consider that this same Marius had apparently received widespread and spontaneous divine honors the previous year, in the aftermath of his victory at Vercellae.[22] However, the man who had saved Rome from her foreign enemies was unable to rescue his city from the effects of political violence and virtual anarchy. His failure has sometimes been seen as an inability to adapt to political life in Rome after many years as a commander in the field. In fact, however, what he experienced was essentially a type of military defeat in a landscape of extreme urban violence, in which veterans and city dwellers from a variety of social groups turned to arms and to political assassination in defiance of their elected consul and his attempts to restore at least a semblance of order. In this situation violent means were used by many Romans of very different backgrounds, and the results showed widespread erosion of confidence in republican institutions and practices.[23]

As noted in the previous section, our lack of information about politics in Rome in the 90s is a serious impediment to the reconstruction of political issues and debate in the crucial decade before the Social War. The events of the years 91 to 88 represent the final unhinging of the existing republic, as Rome faced first the revolt of a large number of her allies in Italy and then open civil war in the city, culminating in Sulla's march on Rome at the head of a Roman army. Depending on how we

[22]Honors for Marius in 101: Valerius Maximus 8.15.7; Plutarch *Mar.* 27.9 with Classen 1963, 327–29, and Simón and Pina Polo 2000.
[23]In addition, the use of religious obstruction is first attested in the year 100. See Lintott 1994, 99 and 101 (the *lex Caecilia Didia* of 98 enforced the precedence of negative auspices by law).

read the Social War, that conflict can also be seen as a type of civil war, particularly in light of Rome's military dependence on Italian manpower for her position in the Mediterranean.[24] Although it may be classified as an external war, by virtue of the cultural independence and autonomous political identity of the Italians, its intensity of violence and closeness to home nevertheless created the level of instability in Italy that very soon led to the dissolution of traditional republican politics. The military conditions of that war also gave rise to the armies and generals who played the key roles in the violence of the 80s. In a number of senses, therefore, Rome's "victory" in the Social War should be considered a Pyrrhic one at best. In the end it was the persistent Italian question, which republican politics had been unable to solve, that led both to the Social War itself and to the issue at the heart of the confrontation after the war, which culminated in Sulla's march on Rome in 88.

In 88 the reform program of the tribune P. Sulpicius Rufus was centered around the issue of how Rome's new Italian citizens should be integrated into her political system, particularly in the voting assemblies.[25] In other words, this issue was a replay in different terms of the same basic question: should the Italians be given full citizenship or not? The subsequent decision to transfer to Marius the command against Mithridates, a choice that reflected Sulpicius' own need to gain Marius as a political ally, was actually a secondary issue in the political landscape. By agreeing to promote the career of Marius, Sulpicius effectively decided to throw republican norms aside in his bid to control the political scene in Rome and get his reforms established. Yet, Sulla's decision to march

---

[24]On the Social War, see Brunt 1988, 257–65; David 1996, 140–56; and Patterson 2006c. Lintott 1994, 92: "In fact, Roman armies were only to be used for civil war after their scruples had been drowned in a blood-bath of fighting with their own Italian allies, and the Roman soldiers who served were raised by wholesale conscription. It may as well be argued that the civil war created the self-seeking unprincipled soldier as the converse." Florus (2.6.18) calls the Social War a civil war.

[25]For the transfer of the command, see Livy *Per.* 77; Velleius Paterculus 2.18; Plutarch *Mar.* 33–34, *Sulla* 7–8; Appian *BC* 1.56, with Meier 1980, 221. For the Italian issue in 88, see Meier 1980, 217; Dahlheim 1993, 104–10.

on Rome with the army, which was encamped at Nola in preparation for the expedition against Mithridates in the East, was a devastating choice that led to the complete collapse of the traditional republican culture of the *nobiles*.[26]

No doubt Sulla would have argued (and perhaps did in his memoirs) that the republic was not functioning and that he had to save himself from his political enemies or face annihilation. Nevertheless, in the event it was Sulpicius who lost his life. One might wonder to what extent republican politics was still functional in the confusing aftermath of the murder of Livius Drusus and during the Social War. Our evidence simply does not provide details of political life in the city between 91 and 88.[27] However, at the end of the day, it was Sulla's march at the head of his client army in 88 that overthrew republican government. It was also Sulla who on this occasion introduced the new custom of openly designating a Roman citizen as a *hostis*, or "foreign enemy."[28] As we have seen, such a label had been implied already in 121 but had never been enunciated in principle. This new custom was also a clear signal that the era of republican politics that gave all citizens a share in the political arena had come to an end. In 81 Sulla himself established a very different kind of republic, described in more detail below in section VII.

Many if not most narratives of the Roman republic would classify the time of Cinna's domination in the city (87–82) as a part of republican history.[29] Direct evidence to support this view, however, is very thin. In fact, we do not really know what Cinna's political program consisted of, or even if he had one

[26]Mackay 2004, 125: "At this point, Sulla took a step that would seal the fate of the Republic, even though it would continue to function (more or less) for another four decades." For discussion, see Volkmann 1958; Meier 1980, 222–28, 298; Levick 1982; Keaveney 1983; Dahlheim 1993; and von Ungern-Sternberg 1998.

[27]The meager sources for the 90s can be found at Greenidge and Clay 1960, 111–50. See Lintott 1994, 101.

[28] Velleius Paterculus 2.19.1 and Appian *BC* 1.271, with Ungern Sternberg von Pürkel 1970, 74–75; Nippel 1988, 91; and Christ 2002, 81.

[29]L. Cornelius Cinna (*RE* 106 Münzer): Meier 1980, 229–46; Christ 2002, 99–103; and esp. Lovano 2002. But see Cicero (*Brut.* 227) who calls Cinna's time *sine iure et dignitate* ("without the rule of law and a code of precedence").

beyond his own personal ambitions for absolute power. All reconstructions of his program must remain purely hypothetical. What is clear is that Cinna and his associates controlled the elections, and surely many other aspects of political life, with the result that Cinna was elected consul every year.[30] Cinna's regime was also marked at its beginning and end by the political assassination of leading Romans. These years saw the first display of Roman heads on the *rostra* in the Forum. Meanwhile, Sulla was declared a *hostis*, his house was razed, and his family had to flee for their lives. Another Roman army was sent out to fight Mithridates, as if Sulla were no more than a warlord in charge of his own personal client army. In this sense, Cinna and his associates set up the inevitable future conflict that was looming over Rome during the 80s, a conflict with Sulla, who had originally been assigned his command as a regularly elected consul with an army of regular Roman soldiers. After Cinna was killed by his own troops in 84, Carbo served as sole consul for the rest of that year.

It seems safe to say, then, that Rome in the mid-80s was ruled by a political faction, a situation that hardly conforms to republican principles. Moreover, that faction had come to power in a coup of their own staged in 87, although Cinna was in fact the lawfully elected consul for that year. However we choose to describe the vestigial (or renewed) republic left behind by Sulla when he departed for the East in 88, it crumbled rapidly in the face of Cinna. These circumstances justify and support the argument that conventional republican government did indeed collapse in 88, and that afterward no group on either side of the new political conflict was operating according to the previous republican rules. The civil war of 83–82 was fought between a rogue regime in the city and a rogue general Sulla, who intended to set up a new republic along very different lines.

Sulla himself was obviously no stranger to violence either on the battlefield or in political life. His was a novel and momentous decision, in 88, to turn his army on Rome rather than to seek a solution within existing political structures or rules of conduct. This strategy also reflects his own political

[30]*MRR* for the years 87, 86, 85, 84, and 83.

experiences since 107, when he first went on campaign to Numidia in the new army of Marius, as an officer with political ambitions. In this sense, Sulla came of age at the same time as the client armies he commanded. It had been Sulla who was credited with the delicate diplomatic negotiations that led Bocchus, king of Mauretania, to hand over his kinsman Jugurtha to the Romans and end the war with a huge victory for Marius late in 105.[31] However, in the chaos of Roman politics after the end of the Social War, Sulla apparently did not hesitate to choose civil war over diplomacy. Sulla was both an individual making a choice—one not anticipated by many of his contemporaries—and a man shaped by Roman politics since the revolutionary decade of the 130s that had seen his birth.[32]

As has often been noted, Sulla's new regime was marked by a significant escalation of violence. On the battlefield, among the prisoners of war, in the streets of Rome after his victory at the Colline Gate on November 1, 82, and most notoriously in the proscription and hunting down of thousands of Romans whose names appeared on lists put up at the command of Rome's new dictator, Sulla's answer to Rome's political troubles was a bloody one.[33] Whether or not we interpret this exceptional level of violence as a logical development of Roman political behavior, especially since the events of the year 100, its effects were devastating. Any vestige of a republic was gone and in its place there were rivers of blood and a dictator who imposed his own political vision by force in the form of a new constitution.

Some of the violence, especially the episodes of ethnic cleansing against the Samnites, reflected unfinished business from the Social War. In Rome, Sulla set out to eliminate his political opponents completely, by killing them and by banning any of their descendants from political careers. It is important to remember that the political and civic rights of these relatives of the proscribed were not restored until Julius Caesar became

---

[31]The most detailed source is Sallust *BJ* 102–13.
[32]Christ 2002 is the most recent biography of Sulla. Keaveney 2005b is an updated version of the standard treatment in English. See also Hölkeskamp 2000a and, for an extensive bibliography, Santangelo 2007.
[33]Hinard 1985 gives a full prosopography.

dictator. Moreover, the violence was deliberately open and advertised, just as the heads of the proscribed who were from prominent families were left to rot slowly at the *rostra* in the Forum. In this sense, terror and intimidation were also important weapons used by Sulla. Sulla aimed to establish a New Republic, but that system was to be marked by and built upon the most brutal political violence Rome had ever seen. The caesura in the political landscape at Rome was stark and long remembered. The multitude of the dispossessed and the corresponding army of beneficiaries of the new order enshrined the violent transfer of private property and of civic spaces throughout Italy. Any analysis of Roman society needs to take the effects of this civil war into account. Factors included not only loss of life, experience, and talent, but also psychological trauma and a sense of discontinuity with ancestral republican traditions. The result was fear for an uncertain future.

It is significant to note that no political leader in the fifty years before Sulla captured Rome had achieved long-term success or political security by using force. After the death of Tiberius Gracchus, Scipio Nasica was soon forced to leave Rome because of the odium he had incurred, and he died abroad while serving on an embassy to Pergamum.[34] Opimius initially seemed successful in his firm measures against Gaius Gracchus, but he was eventually tried and exiled some ten years later, once the political climate had changed at the time of the war against Jugurtha.[35] Even the great Marius found himself eclipsed after his loss of control in 100.[36] Similarly, Cinna did not achieve any lasting political legacy and was killed by his own soldiers, who resisted leaving Italy to face the armies of Sulla.[37] Some consideration of these previous incidents must

[34]Nasica at Pergamum: Valerius Maximus 5.3.2e, Plutarch *TGracch.* 21, *ILS* 8886 = *ILLRP* 333.

[35]Livy *Per.* 61, with Lintott 1994, 84–85, 89; and Kelly 2006, 76–81, 170.

[36]Cicero *Brut.* 1.5.3c; Plutarch *Mar.* 31; *ILLRP* 343 (Delos). For Sulla in the 90s, see Brennan 1992.

[37]Livy *Per.* 83: *Cinna ab exercitu suo, quem invitum cogebat naves conscendere et adversus Syllam proficisci, interfectus est. consulatum Carbo solus gessit* ("Cinna was killed by his army, which he was forcing to embark on ships and to set out against Sulla. Carbo held the consulship without a colleague"). Cf. *Vir ill.* 69 (Cinna stoned by his troops for his cruelty); Velleius Paterculus 2.24; Plutarch *Pomp.* 5; Appian *BC* 1.76–78.

have been in Sulla's mind: he seems to have thought that only the most extreme violence would achieve his political goals. Meanwhile, everyday violence had infiltrated Roman life and affected political debate and procedures in legislation and in the courts. Civil rights were increasingly eroded by political conflict and the senate had lost the moral authority it had enjoyed during the later third century, and especially immediately after the victory against Hannibal. There is also reason to think that issues of everyday lawlessness and lack of order contributed to the degradation of the quality of ordinary life in the city, as well as in the Italian countryside.

It may seem a truism of history that violence offers few political solutions and that dictators are rarely successful in their attempts to kill all their political opponents. Yet it seems that most interpretations of republican Rome have seriously underestimated the devastating effects of violence on Rome's traditional political culture. It did not take generations to wear the Republic down slowly; rather, the violence associated with the age of the Gracchi ushered in a new era that produced virtual anarchy and serious challenges to the political system by the watershed year of 100. The attempt by the consul Opimius to restore concord by force in 121 had failed, despite appeals to traditional political values and to divine help. No republican consul after Opimius was even as successful as he had been. Marius' stunning career was eclipsed by the uncontrolled violence and political chaos of 100. Soon after, Rome faced dangerous revolt in Italy and had to modify her hegemony over her Italian allies by extending citizenship to any who would accept it rather than turning against the Romans. Consequently, it was hegemony in Italy and the related issue of citizenship at Rome that caused republican government to falter. The gravity of this forced political concession to the Italians led to a collapse of civic discourse at home and the violent emergence, after a decade of fighting, of a completely New Republic designed and imposed by a dictator who had taken the city by storm. In other words, the last republic of the *nobiles* did not survive political dissension over the question of extending Roman citizenship and full voting rights to the Italian allies after the Social War.

⟵ VI ⟶

EXTERNAL PRESSURES ON
INTERNAL POLITICS (140–83)

bellum scripturus sum, quod populus Romanus cum Iugurtha
rege Numidarum gessit, primum quia magnum et atrox vari-
aque victoria fuit, dein quia tunc primum superbiae nobilita-
tis obviam itum est; quae contentio divina et humana cuncta
permiscuit eoque vecordiae processit, ut studiis civilibus
bellum atque vastitas Italiae finem faceret.

I am about to write about the war that the Roman people
waged with Jugurtha king of the Numidians, first because
it was big and terrible and victories alternated with defeats,
second because it was then that the first attempt was made to
oppose the arrogance of the political elite. This struggle threw
all human and divine affairs into confusion and reached such
a point of madness that it ended in full-scale civil war and in
the devastation of Italy.

　　Sallust *De bello Jugurthino* 5, written around 40 BC

C. Mari, ecquando te nostrum et reipublicae miserebitur?
Gaius Marius, when will you take pity on us and on the *res*
publica?

　　Claudius Quadrigarius, writing in the mid-first century (quoted
　　by Aulus Gellius 20.6.11 = F84)

In 1734 Montesquieu argued that it was the size of Rome's
empire that had overwhelmed republican politics, a republic
designed to govern a city-state, not a Mediterranean empire.[1]

---

[1]Montesquieu (1734) was following a line of argument already sketched out

His analysis has been highly influential since that time.[2] It is not the aim of this section to question Montesquieu's basic explanation for why Roman politics evolved, over a long time, into a system of one-man rule that provided a much more stable and equitable administration of the provinces. According to the model for republican change outlined in this essay, however, the collapse of republican government came long before one-man rule was established, and can be linked directly to external pressures felt in the late second century and subsequently. The collapse of republican government culminated in the terrible combination of revolt in Italy with the threat of Mithridates VI of Pontus, which Rome experienced in the early 80s, just as her political system slid into a spiral of civil war. This picture is, therefore, very different from the standard one that would place the fall of a single republic somewhere in the 40s, at a time when Rome did not face anything like such direct or dangerous threats from abroad. In this sense, to put the decisive moment in 88 is to give more credence and weight to the fundamentals of Montesquieu's argument, but in a rather different historical context.

It is no secret that war was a way of life for the Romans and that they were constantly in combat, often on several fronts,

---

by Machiavelli. For modern bibliography, see von Ungern-Sternberg 1998, 611; and Morstein-Marx and Rosenstein 2006, 629–30.

[2]For reactions to Montesquieu, see Meier 1980, 151–61, 203; von Ungern-Sternberg 1982 and 1998, 624: "Die Wirkung der Weltherrschaft war eine andere: sie enthob die herrschende Elite, die Nobilität, des Zwangs zum Kompromiß aus außenpolitischen Rücksichten. Die sich aufstauenden sozialen Probleme führten zu einem Legitimitätsverlust, der sich besonders sinnfällig im ersten Marsch römischer Soldaten auf Rom im Jahre 88 v. Chr. zeigte, allgemeiner, in der Eskalierung der Gewalt vom Blutvergießen in der Stadt Rom im Jahre 133 bis zu den reichsweiten Bürgerkriegen" ("The effect of world domination was quite different: it relieved the ruling elite, the nobility, of the necessity to compromise from considerations of foreign policy. The buildup of pressure caused by social problems led to a loss of legitimacy, which manifested itself especially in the first march of Roman soldiers on Rome in the year 88 BC, and more generally in the escalation of bloody violence within the city of Rome from the year 133 to the civil wars that were fought all over the empire"). Mackay 2004, 176: "Basically, some way had to be found to curb the elaborate military setup necessary to maintain control over the vast territory held in the name of the Roman People."

before the Augustan settlement. This was especially the case after 241, after the first war with Carthage, which drew the Romans into Sicily and led to the acquisition there of their first overseas province. The relationship of Roman republican culture to war continues to be a subject of considerable debate, as it has been for over a generation.[3] Romans at all levels of society expected wars to be frequent and were obviously much more tolerant of casualties than citizens of modern democracies are. It is not my aim to engage with the arguments about whether the Romans were especially warlike and expansionist, even by ancient standards, or whether it is more helpful, for example, to see their conflicts as natural reactions to the aggressive international atmosphere they found themselves in, particularly once they entered the competitive world of Hellenistic politics that had been shaped by the successors to Alexander the Great.[4]

From the perspective of political culture in the city, it is interesting to see that similar external pressures did not always have the same effects on Roman society at home in different historical periods. During the third century, Rome was subject to direct attack by a Hellenistic king who invaded Italy (Pyrrhus of Epirus), and then by her principal rival city-state (Carthage), who also invaded. There can be no doubt that both the first and second wars with Carthage put tremendous strains on Rome over many years of harsh warfare, which cost huge losses of material and men. Yet it was precisely these challenges that have been seen as forging the characteristic political culture of the so-called Middle Republic (which I have termed the first and second republic of the *nobiles*), a culture based on debate and the image of consensus, on confidence in Rome's political and military leaders even in moments of terrible defeat and danger, and on a shared ethic of sacrifice for the community. A sense of imperial destiny emerged as the city overcame what surely seemed at some moments to be insurmountable challenges. In fact, one might posit that Rome's wars helped her society to cohere and to move beyond the

---

[3]Raaflaub 1996 discusses the development of Roman attitudes in the fifth century. For bibliography, see Bleicken 2004, 307–8.
[4]For the Roman attitude to war, see Harris 1979 and Eckstein 2006.

situations of internal dissension (*stasis*) that were so typical of many Greek city-states.

With this political and military history in mind, it is all the more striking to see the Romans apparently falter after the 140s, when they faced increasing pressures abroad and were less successful in many areas in which they had been victorious before, notably in Spain, in North Africa, and in keeping invaders from the north out of Italy. Subsequently the combination of widespread revolt in Italy with the aggressive military ambitions of Mithridates VI of Pontus created what would have been a nightmare scenario for any imperial power. Despite her huge reserves of manpower and her strong republican traditions, Rome was struggling. Morale and discipline in her armies were not consistent with expectations, and issues surrounding the draft of new recruits had started to emerge as early as the 150s.[5] In the absence of detailed ancient sources, the accepted model of a slow republican decline and a teleological view of Rome as inevitably destined for world dominance have tended to prevent a more realistic and sober assessment of the difficulties the Romans experienced abroad in the fifty years before Sulla's dictatorship and of the strong effects these setbacks had on the political climate in the city. A full military history of these years is obviously beyond the scope of the present study.[6] This section will proceed to sketch out the major wars Rome was involved in from the 130s to the 80s, with particular emphasis on their political impact at home.

In many ways the long and bitter struggle in Spain in the 130s, culminating in the brutal siege of Numantia, remains the essential unwritten chapter in the history of Rome's republican decline.[7] It will be noted, however, that I have chosen 139 as the turning point of an era, with the introduction of

---

[5] Draft issues became more frequent after 151, but are sometimes attested before that date. See Polybius 35.4 with Taylor 1962, 19; and Astin 1967, 161–65, 167–72, 337, who notes that from 156 onwards Rome was continuously at war, often on several fronts.

[6] See *CAH*[2] 9 (1994), with Bleicken 2004; Mackay 2004; and Bringmann 2007.

[7] Burckhardt (1988, 118) traces unrest back to the Spanish wars. See Richardson 1986, 126–55, and 1996, 59–69.

the secret ballot, rather than the wars in Spain in the mid-130s or the tribunate of Tiberius Gracchus in 133, which appears in my scheme as an effect of the decay of consensus rather than as its cause. The Numantine war saw military service by many of the principal players who were to have key roles in the politics of the later second century. One may especially note Scipio Aemilianus, Marius, Jugurtha, Calpurnius Piso (historian and consul in 133), and Tiberius Gracchus, the reformer of 133 who would become the first prominent victim of political violence in the city.

The long war and the strains it put on recruitment were apparently themes that Gracchus raised in his speeches.[8] He claimed that his consciousness had been raised by his journey to Spain, through a countryside worked only by slaves in chain gangs, and by his experiences in the demoralized army at Numantia. His agrarian reform, whatever one may think of its design or its chances of success, was explicitly aimed at rebuilding an army of small peasant farmers who would be more willing to fight for a community in which they had a tangible and perhaps even inalienable stake.[9] Tiberius is generally recognized as a reformer who wanted to turn the clock back to an earlier age. Gracchus had been a distinguished soldier in his own right and had received singular recognition as the first man over the wall when Carthage was captured in 146. It may well be that he was a believer in the aggressive military policies of his cousin and brother-in-law, Scipio Aemilianus.

It has also been argued that a rebuff that Tiberius had suffered—when the treaty that he had negotiated as quaestor in Spain under the command of C. Hostilius Mancinus was refused by the senate—was a key factor in the way he behaved during his tribunate in 133.[10] According to this theory, Tiberius had suffered a loss of face and could preserve his own ambitions and standing only by successfully proposing a political intiative.[11] Consequently, it was also this earlier rebuff that led to his distrust of the senate as a body and his subsequent

---

[8]Tiberius' speeches: Plutarch *TGracch*. 9 and 15; Appian *BC* 1.11.
[9]See Gargola 1995; Rosenstein 2004.
[10]Rosenstein 1986; Brennan 2004, 50–55.
[11]Von Ungern-Sternberg 2004.

refusal to compromise in the traditional way over the details of his legislative proposals. In fact, we will never really know what Tiberius' personal motives or ambitions were.

If the interpretation offered above is accurate, then there would be an even more direct connection between the stalemate in Spain, together with the ways in which the senate had reacted to it, and the political debates over land issues and military recruitment at home. Tiberius' intentions have been a notorious problem for historians, since his distinguished family and fine military service should have assured him a stellar career without the need to take bold political risks for revolutionary causes. Nor is it even evident that he really cared for the plight of the poor in ways that some later tribunes seem to have. Meanwhile, his unwillingness to play by the traditional political rules of the game was much more of a factor in unleashing deadly violence than was the substance of his agrarian law, which was put into effect even after he had been murdered and his body had been thrown in the Tiber.

In 134 Scipio Aemilianus successfully restored the morale of the Roman army in Numantia, and in the following year he brought the long Spanish war to a decisive end by capturing the town.[12] It may be an irony of history that his success came just too late to defuse the tense political standoff in Rome, which centered partly on the issue of army recruitment and Rome's ability to meet her military obligations abroad. In another age, Scipio would have returned to a hero's welcome and a huge triumph that everyone was happy to share. Under the new circumstances, he soon came into political difficulties himself when he was unable to give what the crowd saw as a credible answer to a tribune's question about his opinion of the deaths of Tiberius and his followers.[13] He suffered serious political consequences because he appeared to endorse the violence in the city and the fate of his cousin. It was he who went on to defend the interests of the Italian landowners

---

[12]Astin 1967, 137–60, esp. 147–60. Badian (1972, 685) argues that the Republic would have ended sooner if Aemilianus had not captured Numantia in 133.

[13]For Aemilianus at the *contio*, see Astin 1967, 226, 233–34; and Nippel 1988, 83.

whom Tiberius' agrarian commission provoked, as they traveled around Italy surveying and dividing up land that Rome had claimed to own on the basis of earlier conquests.[14] He may have seen himself as the champion of the Italians because of their role in the army and in making Rome's overseas hegemony possible. He was unable, however, to negotiate the tensions in the political debate and seems to have succumbed to a stress-related illness as he saw his own position in Rome challenged and as Rome's relations with her allies began to deteriorate.[15] Scipio Aemilianus' experiences in the 130s, ending with his sad death in 129, were symptomatic of how Roman politics had already changed as citizens split into factions bitterly opposed to each other and leaders from political families were forced to justify themselves. The political framework of the republic seemed to be at risk.

It is important to note that the first slave war in Sicily took place at the same time in the 130s. It was a war that presented another set of consequences of the large-scale slaveholding that Rome's imperial policies had made possible, and another external issue that Tiberius had apparently referred to in his political speeches in the city.[16] Here, again, it took several Roman initiatives and a full-scale military engagement to bring the situation under control. Because of Rome's close connections with Sicily, an important source of food for the metropolis, this external war threatened to destabilize conditions at home. In addition, if the Sicilian slaves had succeeded and gained independence, unrest would very likely have spread to slaves in Italy, especially in the south, which had large concentrations of unfree labor. The first slave war was not ended until the year after Tiberius' tribunate, and it must have loomed over events in Rome. Eventually the senate decided, on the advice of the Sibylline books, to send an embassy to make atonement to Ceres at Henna in Sicily, the ancient shrine at the location where the slaves had made their headquarters, in expiation of the death of Tiberius Gracchus and of subsequent

---

[14]Astin 1967, 238–41, for Aemilianus and the Italians. Gabba (1994) sees Tiberius Gracchus' land bill as setting off the whole Italian issue in Roman politics.

[15]On Scipio's death, see Astin 1967, 241.

[16]Appian *BC* 1.9, with Shaw 2001, esp. 79–106.

events in Rome.[17] In the psychology of the Roman senate, apparently, events in Sicily were closely and fatefully connected with the violent death of Gracchus and the political strife in Rome.

Subsequently, external affairs seem to have been relatively calm in the 120s, and serious pressures did not emerge again until the year 113, when the first Roman general suffered a defeat at the hands of the Cimbri, a wandering tribe that was beginning to move into the sphere of Rome's influence in search of a place to establish a new home.[18] It is unclear exactly why the Cimbri, originally from Jutland in modern Denmark, decided to leave their home and migrate south, collecting other tribal peoples as fellow travelers. One theory attributes the impetus to flooding and natural disaster in their native territory.[19] Whatever the reason for the migration, the movement was a direct threat to Rome—even though it was almost certainly not caused by any actions the Romans had taken, or perhaps even by any knowledge of Rome or of the geography of the Italian peninsula. The threat posed by the Cimbri and Teutoni (a tribe who had joined the Cimbri on their journey), a military challenge that was to become ever more serious over the next dozen years, can be directly linked to further political strife in Rome and to the rise of Marius, the first great general of the period, who led the new volunteer army he had raised to save Italy from the northern invaders.

Consequently, it should be recognized at the outset that the Cimbri and Teutoni had devastating effects on Rome's internal politics, culminating in the brutal violence of the year 100. Their arrival may well have been largely a matter of chance, but it laid bare for all to see the existing weaknesses in the Roman army and in the political equilibrium at home. In the face of this danger, Rome's republican culture experienced tremendous strains from which it never really recovered. As a consequence, the Italians who revolted a decade after the defeat of the Cimbri, along with Mithridates, who took the opportunity the Italians provided him to make a bid to end

[17]Flower 2006, 72–75, provides discussion and bibliography.
[18]Trzaska-Richter 1991; Timpe 1994; and Goetz and Welwei 1995.
[19]Posidonius in Strabo 2.3.6, 7.2.

Roman domination in the eastern Mediterranean, easily overturned the seriously impaired republic and caused civil war
and dictatorship in Rome.

In other words, the years before and immediately after
113/112 set in motion the terrible drama that would unfold
both at home and abroad. Rome faced a problem of over-
extension and of being unable to evaluate or step back from
her role abroad, as that role had been developing over the
previous century. For it was the coincidence of the conflict
in Numidia following the death of king Micipsa with the
much more pressing threat from the Cimbri and Teutoni in
the north that created a situation of military challenge abroad
and political disintegration at home. The looming threat of
the migrating peoples was not easy to deal with, and yet the
Romans allowed themselves to be drawn into a long and difficult guerilla war in Numidia, fighting over the succession
among the descendants of Masinissa, who had been a loyal
ally of the Romans in their struggle against Carthage. In this
situation, the Numidian royal bastard Jugurtha emerged as
a typically threatening figure in a colonial setting; the loyal
ally who has been trained by the conquerors and knows their
military and political system, but who goes on to become one
of their most effective enemies. It is also relevant to note that
the final clash with the Cimbri coincided with the second slave
war in Sicily and with the special command held by M. Antonius against the pirates in the eastern Mediterranean.[20] It
was the combination of these several military threats that produced both the unparalleled career of Marius and the decision
to accept landless volunteers in the Roman army. As we have
seen, the existing political system was overthrown by Sulla, in
response to the unprecedented ambitions of Marius in 88, and
by means of a client army that emerged from the violence of
the Social War with no qualms about marching on Rome in
order to achieve its own economic advantage and its general's
political power.

While there is little reason to imagine that Sallust's analysis of
Jugurtha's motives in the monograph he wrote around 40 was
based on any reliable source of evidence, his basic argument

[20]Shaw 2001, 107–29.

in the *De Bello Jugurthino* does seem to be credible.[21] Sallust
says that he undertook to write about the war against Jugurtha
partly because that was the time when there was the first real
political movement by ordinary Romans to question their traditional leadership and the basis on which their foreign policy
was being administered. One might rephrase this to mean that
they questioned the condition of their republic.[22] An argument
could be made that this Sallustian reconstruction fails to take
into account the fact that a political watershed had already
happened in the age of the Gracchi, when (as Sallust himself
admits) deep divisions apparently emerged in Roman political
life.[23] Sallust, however, makes a different and more effective
argument.

The events of these years, and especially episodes such as
the *rogatio Mamilia* of 110 (a tribunal that held Roman commanders responsible for their actions and their defeats), the
resulting exile of various *nobiles*, the replacement of Metellus
by Marius as commander in Numidia, and especially the devastating Roman defeat at Arausio (modern Orange in the
south of France) in 105, created a situation of utter panic and
despair in Rome. The population turned to Marius and his
armies to save the city. The *nobiles*, both individually and as
a group, were seen to have failed the republic that they were
supposed to be leading. Meanwhile, old resentments created
during the time of the Gracchi emerged, and Opimius, the
man responsible for the death of Gaius Gracchus, was sent
into exile. Without these new external pressures, events would
presumably have unfolded quite differently.

Indeed, it is not unlikely that continued Roman successes
abroad would have helped the following generation of Romans to weather the bitterness of Gracchan political strife,
especially if a negotiated settlement had been reached early on
in Numidia, and if the Cimbri had stayed in Jutland. Similarly,
a Roman victory over the Cimbri in 106 or 105 would have

[21]Conte (1994, 234, 239–40) gives an overview. Syme 1964 remains the classic treatment. Paul 1984 is a commentary in English.
[22]See the epigraph of this section. Sallust's view is also endorsed by Meier
(1980, 138).
[23]Sallust (*BJ* 41–42) stresses the lack of an external threat for Rome after
146.

made events in Numidia seem much less important. In this sense it may seem surprising that Sallust chose the struggle against Jugurtha, rather than the war with the Cimbri and Teutoni, as his subject.

We have no surviving detailed account by an ancient author of the fateful clash with the Cimbri and Teutoni, a war that made the new army of fully trained professional soldiers (both volunteers and more traditional recruits) seem essential to Rome's survival. The massive defeat of the Romans at Arausio in 105 was by far the largest since Cannae, the biggest loss of the Second Punic War, and portended an imminent invasion of Italy.[24] It was this event that led to the extraordinary political and military power that was handed to Marius, but without the revival of the temporary republican office of dictator that had been used to such good effect during the war with Hannibal. Instead, Marius' career became a pattern of irregularity that suggested that Rome could not survive without a strong man who operated outside the rules. Metellus had already been deprived of his command in Numidia by popular vote, in contravention of the senate's assignment of the war.[25] Metellus did not resist—but when Marius tried the same tactic again twenty years later, Sulla marched on Rome. Marius was also elected consul in succession for the years 104–100 (amounting to five years of continual executive power), on several occasions *in absentia*, that is to say, without appearing as a regular candidate in person in Rome. The logical culmination of this popular adulation came with the spontaneous divine honors he received from ordinary Romans after his final victory over the Cimbri at Vercellae in 101.[26]

It should come as no surprise, therefore, that Marius' precipitous fall from political favor in 100 left him embittered and hoping to return to power and to a new command one day. The republican culture of the *nobiles* could not, and did not, properly accommodate a Marius, either at the height of his powers or in his reluctant retirement during the 90s. The

[24]For Arausio, see Greenidge and Clay 1960, ad loc.; for the sources, and Mackay 2004, 118.

[25]Sallust *BJ* 73.7, 82.2, 84.1; with *ILS* 59.

[26]Valerius Maximus 8.15.7 and Plutarch *Mar.* 27.9, with Classen 1963, 327–29; and Simón and Pina Polo 2000.

seeds of the very personal conflict that erupted in 88 were already sown in the reactions of Marius' colleague Q. Lutatius Catulus and his close ally L. Cornelius Sulla to Marius' extraordinary power and to his claim to be the sole savior of Rome. He had, after all, reaped glory at the expense of colleagues from old political families, whether those men were of equal or more junior standing.[27] In this way, Marius' career, consisting of six consulships by the end of 100, broke the republican pattern of collegiality, annuity, and the sharing of political and military duties and rewards among a group of men calling themselves the *nobiles*. Rome had been saved from the Cimbri and Teutoni but the political price was enormous, encompassing both the failure of traditional republican structures to rescue the city and the specter of a single strong man.

If we are to look for a turning point in terms of historical processes, rather than in the personal ambitions and self-glorification of a Marius, a Catulus, or a Sulla, then the defeat at Arausio in 105 looms large. The senate simply did not have the political will or talent to pull the Romans together after this crushing defeat. The explanation for the situation must be sought in a combination of factors. For many reasons Rome was a much less coherent or unified society by this time, and tensions between classes had surfaced over the previous five years, ever since the tribune Mamilius set out to make Rome's leaders more responsible for their failures abroad.[28] One does not need to look back to the Gracchi to find sources and subjects of friction between citizens and politicians.

Sallust also claims that criticism of the *nobiles* had been a principal theme of Marius in his election campaign of 108 for the consulship of 107, and in his speeches before leaving for Africa with his new recruits.[29] Many modern historians have seen the speeches in Sallust's monograph as essentially free compositions by the historian himself. The main ideas, however, may still reflect the rhetoric of the times and of the "new man" Marius, who had no ancestors with political office in

[27]Flower 2006, 87–90.

[28]Lintott (1994, 89–90) stresses the political views of the rich equestrians. See Doblhofer 1990 for the *populares* between 111 and 99.

[29]Sallust (*BJ* 85) provides the most famous example. No fragments are listed for Marius in *ORF*.

Rome. His line of argument was related to the rhetoric of earlier self-made Romans, notably Cato the Censor, a rhetoric that was based on the argument that by hard work and integrity the new man could embody the values and habits of the ancestors just as well as, if not better than, their biological descendants. But Marius' words seem to have had a much more corrosive tone, especially his sweeping criticisms of the established political families as incompetent and dishonest. His version of the new man's self-presentation comes at the expense of denigrating much that was republican in Roman political culture.

Typical of the earlier republican culture of societal harmony had been the practice of excusing generals for defeats, which were most often blamed on the gods or the soldiers.[30] This is not to say that no earlier general had ever been questioned or prosecuted after a defeat, but earlier criticisms of generals tended to focus on religious faults and omissions, not on issues of personal integrity or military competence. These societal practices of cohesion and consensus had allowed Romans to survive military setbacks and to preserve the continuity provided by an experienced group of leaders, even if they had been defeated on occasion. Some commanders emerged as beacons of hope in moments of great crisis, after or perhaps even because of huge defeats. This republican habit was something that the Romans themselves saw as setting them apart from cities like Carthage, which habitually crucified unsuccessful generals.

Now the political climate had changed, and the result was not necessarily what anyone, even the most radical tribune, could have foreseen or would have wished. Romans were already disillusioned with their leadership, and especially with those from the political families, as a result of events during the war in Africa and the earlier setbacks against the Cimbri and Teutoni. One may also recall the treatment of C. Hostilius Mancinus, consul in 137, who was surrendered to the enemy in Spain in order to invalidate the treaty he had made. It is revealing of the political climate that the defeat at Arausio was publicly connected with class animosity between the

---

[30]Rosenstein 1990 gives a valuable and detailed treatment.

two commanders. It was alleged that the patrician Q. Servilius
Caepio (consul of 106) refused to cooperate with Cn. Mallius
Maximus, a new man who had been elected consul for 105,
and that the Roman armies suffered enormous casualties after
Caepio would not combine his forces with those of Mallius,
despite appeals from a senatorial commission.[31]

We will never know whether this clash of personalities was
the most essential feature of what actually happened on that
field in southern France. However, the fact that people be-
lieved and repeated such an explanation later is suggestive of
attitudes and reactions. The leaders produced by republican
elections, even under the new secret-ballot system, simply did
not command the confidence and credibility that their ancestors had. It is all the more notable that Sallust, in his typically
elusive manner, chose to record the defeat very briefly but in
strong words (*male pugnatum*), thus relying on his readers to
know the story and to draw their own conclusions from it.[32]

Defeat had not drawn the Romans together in 105, and it
seems that victory in the years that immediately followed was
not able to do so either. The Romans gained decisive victories
over their enemies at Aquae Sextiae in 102 and at Vercellae in
101, as a result of which the Cimbri and Teutoni were eliminated as a threat and were not heard from again. Given the
circumstances, the whole story should have had a rousing and
patriotic tone, as well as a happy end. Yet the political discord
and open violence in Rome in 100, already discussed in the
previous section, is well known. By now republican politics
was far from business as usual.

Only ten years after Marius' historic victory at Vercellae,
the great Social War with the Italian allies erupted, and in the

[31]Caepio and Mallius: Gruen 1968, 161–65; Meier 1980, 137; and Gotter
1996, 244.

[32]Sallust *BJ* 114: *per idem tempus advorsum Gallos ab ducibus nostris Q.
Caepione et Cn. Mallio male pugnatum, quo metu Italia omnis contremuerat.
utique et inde usque ad nostram memoriam Romani sic habuere, alia omnia
virtuti suae prona esse, cum Gallis pro salute, non pro gloria certare* ("At the
same time our generals Q. Caepio and Cn. Mallius suffered a defeat at the
hands of the Gauls, with the result that all of Italy was shaken by fear. Moreover in those days and even up to our own time the Romans held this belief,
that every other contest is winnable through their military prowess, but that
a war against Gauls is fought for survival, not for glory").

face of this challenge republican government finally disintegrated. In truth, "Rome" itself was redefined at the very start of the conflict because the only way for the city to survive was to offer full Roman citizenship to any Italian community that would accept it, in return for siding with Rome against the separatists.[33] The first republic of the *nobiles* had emerged as Rome gained her position of preeminence in Italy, especially toward the end of the fourth century. Now a reversal had set in, and the loss of her hegemonic power over the Italians (and simultaneously over the very definition of Roman citizenship) led to constitutional change. This characteristically Roman pattern of a hegemonic republic in Italy has been eclipsed in many modern studies by a closer focus on Rome's overseas possessions. Yet it was really Rome's position in Italy, and her ability to divide and conquer the Italian peoples, that had created the power of the *nobiles* and the simultaneous rise of their particular political culture. In turn, it was Italian manpower that went on to extend Roman hegemony first to Sicily, then to southern Spain, and next to North Africa and the eastern Mediterranean.[34] Losing control of Italy was, in this sense, the ultimate failure of Rome's political system. Although Romans and Italians had long fought and worked so closely together abroad, the outcome of the Social War was a political revolution.

Moreover, it is evident that the admission of all free adult males in Italy to full citizenship, with the voting rights that this concession implied, completely changed the nature of politics in the city. Whereas the voting assemblies had rarely accommodated a truly significant percentage of eligible voters, their

[33]Gabba 1994, 127: "The Roman state in fact ceased to be a city state and became a state made up of numerous *municipia*, at any rate as far as the organization of its territory was concerned: political institutions remained for all practical purposes unchanged." There is a lack of logical connection between the two parts of this sentence. Gabba 1994, 105–6: "It was not simply a manifestation of proud and stubborn exclusiveness, though that of course existed and displayed itself in the unprecedented harshness of some Roman magistrates towards the allies; rather it will have been the result of a not unreasonable fear that the whole political and institutional structure of the Roman state would collapse." According to my argument, that collapse did indeed ensue in the 80s.

[34]See Brunt 1971; Scheidel 2001 and 2004; and Rosenstein 2004.

traditional function was now undermined by the huge numbers of possible voters, most of whom would never make the
journey to Rome even once in their lifetimes. The question of
how electoral politics should now function remained a subject
for discussion and bitter division until well into the Augustan
principate and even beyond, to the time when the emperor
Tiberius transferred voting for the highest magisterial offices
to the senate. The common ground of politics had to be rein-
vented in an Italy united into a type of proto-nation-state, but
deeply divided by different languages, customs, and heritages,
as well as by recent violence.

At the same time, the decisive conflict in Italy provided
Mithridates VI of Pontus with the opportunity he had been
looking for to challenge Roman power in Asia and Greece
and to establish a new empire of his own.[35] Here again, to
an even greater extent than at the end of the second century,
Rome faced a combination of military threats that constituted
a "perfect storm." The stress produced in 88 by the need to
field an army against Mithridates while there was still resistance in Italy was a vital aspect of the political collapse of the
80s. It is important to note that the Romans did not manage
to defeat Mithridates until 63, some twenty-five years after he
first invaded the Roman province of Asia. He was an enemy
who posed a serious threat, but Sulla and other Romans could
not deal with him because of the political unrest in Rome. The
fact that he was a new type of Hellenistic king from the Black
Sea region also presented an unpleasant reversal of the victories of the 190s and 180s in the eastern Mediterranean.

It has been argued that Rome became much more aggressively imperialist in the decades immediately after Sulla.[36]
Certainly the image of "empire" loomed large, and the shrill
insistence on Rome as a world capital, which may have been
developed in a special way by Sulla, is a reflection of the loss

[35]See McGing 1986 and Kallet-Marx 1995. Dahlheim (1993, 98) completely
underestimates Mithridates.
[36]Kallet-Marx (1995, 335–342) makes a strong argument for a new epoch
with the first war against Mithridates, noting (335): "That the age of Sulla
was a turning point in the history of Rome's relations with the foreign people
of its *imperium* did not escape contemporaries." For Sulla's organization of
the East, see Santangelo 2007.

of control and identity at home and in Italy.[37] In any case, the first war with Mithridates must be viewed as a watershed. According to the argument presented here, it coincided with the fall of the last republic of the *nobiles*, the fifth republic in Rome since the late sixth century.

The interpretation proposed in this study stresses the immediate and direct effects of external pressures and military demands on the delicate balance of traditional politics in Rome. In 133 military conditions abroad, particularly in Spain and in Sicily, formed the essential background to the reform proposals of Tiberius Gracchus, who was concerned about recruitment for the army and about the dangers posed by slave revolts. In this sense, empire provided the context for political discourse in Rome and for the increasingly divisive politics of the later second century. The citizen army was challenged by the military demands of a growing empire. Conditions on the land and in food production had been transformed by the large numbers of slaves, who were either prisoners of war or captives sold by pirates. The slave trade had become so huge that free populations in places like Sicily were unequal to the task of controlling their chattel. At the same time, the lawlessness of the pirates, who had grown rich in an eastern Mediterranean dominated by Rome, was in itself a threat, and the Romans felt the need to respond to it repeatedly between the late second century and Pompey's special command against the pirates in 67.[38]

Sallust asserts that it was the largely unnecessary and long, drawn-out war against Jugurtha in Numidia between 112 and 105 that caused the decisive rift in domestic politics and in the ability of the community to work together to meet the steep challenges posed by its ambitious foreign policy, for at the very same time Rome was facing the real threat to her home territory posed by the Cimbri and Teutoni. By the end of the century, despite great success abroad and in Italy, political irregularities and violence by soldiers and civilians were rampant in the city. In the final analysis, however, it was Rome's

---

[37]See Thein forthcoming.
[38]For pirates, see Ormerod 1924; Pohl 1993; Kallet-Marx 1995, 227–39; and de Souza 2000.

inability to reward the Italian allies for their part in building Rome's vast hegemony abroad—even though the difference between Roman and Italian had become increasingly blurred in many situations outside Italy—that caused the final collapse of the existing republic, even as it struggled to retain its imperial role in the East in the face of chaos at home. The riches and demands of empire had not only divided society in the city and in Italy: it had changed Roman life and identity beyond recognition.

Part Three

AFTERMATH

VII

AN ALTERNATIVE TO A CRISIS

Sulla's New Republic

L. Sullam... solus rem publicam regeret orbemque terrarum
gubernaret imperique maiestatem quam armis receperat iam
legibus confirmaret...
Lucius Sulla... alone ruled the state and governed the whole
earth and now confirmed through legislation the majesty of
the empire that he had won with arms...
   Cicero *Pro Roscio* 131, a forensic speech delivered in 80

cuius illi pietati plenam populus Romanus gratiam rettulit
ipsum viritim civitate donando, duos filios eius creando prae-
tores, cum seni adhuc crearentur.
The Roman people expressed their full gratitude to him for
his loyalty by giving him an individual gift of the Roman
citizenship and by electing his two sons to the praetorship, at
the time when only six were elected annually.

Velleius Paterculus 2.16, ca. AD 30, speaking of his ancestors
who had attained the praetorship before Sulla's political reforms over a century before

The period from 133 to 78 (and beyond) was far from being a long crisis to which no alternative was ever proposed
or implemented.[1] Rather, it was a dynamic time that saw

[1]Meier 1980, chap. 5 (201–5), with further arguments at xiv–lvii, endorsed in
general by Hölkeskamp 2004a. Morstein-Marx and Rosenstein 2006, 633:
"The power of [this] tradition, continually reinforced for the citizenry in mass

numerous successful reforms of various kinds, unsuccessful attempts at new legislation, and three major proposals to create a new type of republic to modify or to replace the existing system. The first thoroughgoing reform program was drawn up and partially implemented by Gaius Gracchus in 123–122. However, after his death in 121 his legislation, as well as his brother's earlier agrarian reform of 133, was modified in fundamental ways. The Gracchan reforms did not achieve their authors' original objectives. The second attempt at reform was put forward in 91, some thirty years later, by M. Livius Drusus, a leading aristocrat who was the son of a political opponent of Gaius Gracchus. This initiative seems already to have come to nothing by the time Drusus was assassinated late in that same year. Both Gracchus and Drusus proposed their reforms as tribunes of the plebs. Sulla was the third of these republican reformers and he implemented by far the most wide-ranging and drastic reforms; he was in a position to enforce his political ideas because he had captured the city with his army and subsequently chose to assume the office of dictator. Sulla's revolutionary program, which shaped the political agenda for the next generation, is the topic of this section.[2]

---

oratory and civic rituals such as elections, was such that no alternative model of state organization seen in recent history seems to have been realistically conceivable."

[2]See Hantos 1988; Hölkeskamp 2000a; Mackay 2004, 131 (a one-page outline); and Keaveney 2005b. Meier (1980, 235, 246–60, 140) speaks of Sulla's "umfassenden Versuches, das Senatsregime wiederherzustellen" ("comprehensive attempt to restore the regime of the senate"). Walter 2004, 328-9: "Für Cicero war die Diktatur Sullas eine isolierte Katastrophe der römischen Geschichte, ein negatives *exemplum*, dessen an sich mögliche Wiederholung zu verhindern die Pflicht aller *boni* war. Für Sallust bildete sie den kausalen Anfang eines Verfallsprozesses aller politischen Normen und Sitten, aus dem allenfalls noch die Erinnerung an bessere Zeiten und einzelne Erwiese von *virtus* herausragten" ("For Cicero, Sulla's dictatorship was an isolated catastrophe in Roman history and a negative example; it was the duty of all good men [*boni*] to avoid its possible repetition. For Sallust, [Sulla's dictatorship] was the beginning in a chain of events that led to the decay of all political norms and customs, although memories of better times and individual examples of *virtus* could still be found").

It is regrettable that we do not have access to Sulla's own ideas about his new constitutional program, a set of reforms that he put in place rapidly and efficiently in 81 during the year of his dictatorship.[3] These reforms represented his commentary on the unrest and divisive politics that he had witnessed during his lifetime in Rome. After his retirement from public life, at the end of his consulship of 80, he devoted himself to writing his memoirs. Although these were published in twenty-two papyrus rolls (books) after his death, they apparently did not contain, at least as far as we can judge from the limited surviving fragments, a detailed rationale or account of his reform program.[4] Surely this was only because Sulla ran out of time. Had he lived longer, he would have had the opportunity to publish his thoughts about the *res publica*, whether these reflections would have taken a more or less theoretical form. It would be far easier to discuss his achievements and aims today if we had access to more of his own arguments and ideas, whether in speeches, pamphlets, or in the books of his memoirs.

Although his constitution was certainly the product of his own political imagination, it must also have been influenced by political debates that he had witnessed and taken part in. It was not conceived in a vacuum. Some reconstructions have him as a close imitator of Livius Drusus, the tribune of 91, but it is difficult to be sure about all these details.[5] It is equally possible that some (or many) of Sulla's ideas have been retrojected by our sources onto the earlier reformer. If he was closer to Drusus, this eventuality would suggest that the need for a whole new republic was already perceived *before* the Social War and the rapid collapse of a traditional republican system in 88. In other words, the argument over a new

[3] I follow Badian's argument (1970) that Sulla resigned his dictatorship at the end of 81. This chronology also fits in with Hurlet (1993), who describes the republican qualities of Sulla's dictatorship. In other words, Sulla held the dictatorship for twice the usual six-month term and then the consulship of 80 to mark the new era of his constitutional settlement. Keaveney (2005c) also supports this line of argument.

[4] See now Chassignet 2004 for a new edition of the fragments, most of which are from Plutarch. For discussion, see Ramage 1991, 95–102; Lewis 1991; Behr 1993, 9–21; and Scholz 2003.

[5] Sources for Livius Drusus: Greenidge and Clay 1960, 128–36. See also Gabba 1976, 131–41; Linke 2005, 95–100, 132.

republic could be seen as one of the causes of the ensuing conflict. On balance, however, it seems more likely that a completely new republic was called for in the early 80s simply because the old one had collapsed.

It may be that Sulla had already attempted some reforms before he left for the East early in 87.[6] If he did, it is clear that these initiatives were almost immediately overturned. Skepticism is in order here also, especially given time constraints and the relative weakness of Sulla's political position in Rome that year. It is more probable that there was a single Sullan reform moment in 81, a political revolution that was brought about by and informed by the extreme violence and partisan politics of the 80s. Much had happened in Roman politics since the tribunate of Drusus ten years earlier.

Both in form and in content, Sulla's New Republic represented a radical departure from what had come before.[7] The use of the same names for magistrates and for other political functions should not obscure the degree of innovation (as it has not for the political settlement of Augustus). There is also every reason to imagine that the reforms were presented in Rome as a coherent and new system, with Sulla as its primary author. Recent studies of Sulla's self-presentation, of his celebration of victory, and of his inauguration of a new age fully support the interpretation of his reform program as a new republic rather than a restoration.[8] The rest of this section will be devoted to a closer look at how different Sulla's republic really was and at some of the results of the changes he made. At the same time, the violence of the times forms the essential background to political reform. The Social and Civil Wars of the 80s had created a huge discontinuity in Roman politics. Many died or were driven into exile or lost their social status, from the most exalted to the humblest. In this sense alone, things could not be the same after the violence stopped. Hence it is important to keep in mind that although the focus of

---

[6]Reforms of 87: Livy *Per.* 87; Appian *BC* 1.59 (seems confused); and Festus 464L.

[7]Sources: Greenidge and Clay 1960, 211–22. *Contra* Gabba 1976, 137: "Sulla showed no great originality and he was a long way from being an extremist.... His hope was to re-establish the government of the oligarchy."

[8]Frier 1971; Ramage 1991; Mackay 2000; and esp. Thein 2002.

the present discussion is on politics, its structures and practices, there was an equally dramatic and immediate change in personnel. There were new actors in the political landscape after 81. For example, one might wonder how Cicero's career would have developed without the constitutional reforms that Sulla instituted, just at the time when Cicero was making his debut in Rome.[9]

Sulla's reforms will now be sketched out and evaluated, with a special emphasis on their novelty. It seems fitting to start with the senate, which was the group that Sulla is usually thought to have put in charge of political life.[10] Sulla greatly increased the size of the traditional republican senate from three hundred to perhaps as many as six hundred senators, although the actual number of senators alive in 81 must have been far fewer than three hundred.[11] In other words, in practice, the senate was increased by more than 100 percent, and most of these new men had no previous experience of political office in Rome, since the majority of them had not been chosen by the voters in the city for any public duty at all. In practice, this new senate was filled with novices, mostly from the ranks of the equestrians and many from Italian towns. Since the number of quaestors was increased, it was even more the case now that the vast majority of senators would never reach high office. In fact, many might not go on to be elected to anything. Rather their function was to serve as jurors in the extensive new system of permanent jury courts (*quaestiones*) created by Sulla. Senatorial debate was inevitably very different, even when not everyone was present, and one wonders how many of the newcomers ever spoke at all during their political careers.[12] Sulla seems to have done away with the powerful position of *princeps senatus*, the leading senator who had shaped debate and mediated conflicts in earlier times.

[9]Cicero was born in the year 106, so he was only twenty-five at the time of Sulla's reform program.

[10]For the senate of Sulla, see Wiseman 1971, 6; Hantos 1988, 45–61.

[11]Santangelo (2007, 100–102) argues for a new senate of about 450, rather than 600. If we had more evidence about the size of Sulla's new enlarged senate house, we would have a clearer idea about how many senators he envisaged.

[12]Ryan 1998 provides an analysis of senatorial debate.

It goes without saying that this reform was a startling and complete departure from any republican precedent. Most senators had always been former magistrates, chosen by the censors in the republic of the *nobiles*, but according to Sulla's arrangements, future recruits were now to be drawn automatically every year from ex-quaestors. When the senate's numbers had dropped as a result of casualties in the Hannibalic war, new senators had been chosen from among Roman citizens who had distinguished themselves in single combats and who, therefore, had enemy armor displayed as spoils in their homes in the city of Rome. Sulla, by contrast, recruited a large number of new senators from the Italian towns.[13]

Sulla, then, had changed the shape and functions of the senate in numerous ways. Inevitably the result was more of a two-tiered (or rather multitiered) system in which the inner circle of the powerful opinion makers, men who had repeatedly and consistently been elected to high office by the voters, were separated from those who spent their lives as jurors. Under the Sullan republic, magistrates in high office, specifically consuls and praetors who were invested with *imperium* (the power to command an army), spent their year of office in Rome and only went to commands abroad afterward. This new pattern meant that consuls were nearly always in Rome to convene the senate, as opposed to being out of the city after the Ides of March. It also meant that consuls and praetors were in the senate all year long and were present for most debates, which would have given these a more formal structure according to participation and rank. The relationship between colleagues in office changed, perhaps most noticeably between the consuls who now had to work with each other in the city during their year of office. Clashes between consuls had certainly happened before, but had often been defused simply because the two men did not see much of each other as they undertook tasks in different spheres of operation outside the city. The praetors found their jobs changed also, as they were

---

[13]Livy 23.23.6. Cicero *Verr.* 1.2 says that before Sulla the censors chose senators according to character and service. See Hantos 1988, 19–33, on Sulla's system of political recruitment.

now mostly busy with the courts during their year of office and with governing a province immediately afterward.[14]

The abolition of the censorship was another striking innovation, which interrupted a time-honored political rhythm, repeated every five years, and which highlighted the demise of the army of small landowners, who no longer needed to be counted for the draft.[15] The office of censor had existed since the late fifth century. It was the censors who had made and edited the list of senators. They had kept a similar record of who was an equestrian and what military service each horseman could be called upon to render. The censors had put each Roman citizen in his place and had set a moral tone, for which the elder Cato had been the most famous. They had auctioned the contracts for public buildings in the city and had allotted the similar contracts for the collection of taxes in the provinces. The growth of their various spheres of responsibility since the later fourth century had thus been another characteristic feature of the republic of the *nobiles*.

The last censorship had been in 86/85 and the next census was not conducted until 70, in the consulship of Pompey and Crassus that saw the decisive revision of many central aspects of Sulla's political plan.[16] After that, the next completed census would be under Augustus in 28. Sulla's decision to abolish the censorship also affected the career patterns of office holders, for attaining the censorship had long been regarded as the pinnacle of the political career of an ex-consul. During the second century, elections for the censorship had often been hotly contested and the activities of the censors had served as a type of barometer for Roman society. During these Sullan years, the only censors to be seen were those represented by wax masks of ancestors worn by actors at the funerals of office holders, who must now have seemed even more like figures from a lost past.

Sulla redefined the careers of all magistrates, even as he changed the numbers of quaestors and praetors, as well as

---

[14]Brennan 2000, vol. 2.
[15]Hantos 1988, 24–33. Kolb (2002, 162–63) stresses the effect on the city of Rome where censors had supervised public contracts for building projects.
[16]See Wiseman 1994b, 327–29, for the census of 70. See *MRR* for a failure of the census in 65–64, dubious evidence for 61, another failure in 55–54, and the interrupted census of 50–49.

aspects of their tasks.[17] The result was a much more rigid and hierarchical pyramid of office holding that started with the post of *quaestor*, which a man could not hold before he was thirty years old. It was also this office that allowed a man a seat in the senate. In this age pyramid Sulla was probably drawing on earlier ideas and concepts: nevertheless, now everything was to be a matter of law rather than of custom. Each year the voters were to elect twenty quaestors, four aediles, eight praetors, and two consuls. The compulsory waiting period of ten years before holding the same office again was reinforced and spoke to the feelings Sulla and others had about Marius and his seven consulships. The overall picture was certainly of magistracies and career patterns that had been given a definitive new shape by Sulla. No contemporary, especially a senator, would have mistaken this new system for the old one.

Most striking of all, when it came to political office, was the drastic reduction of the powers of the ten tribunes of the plebs.[18] Tribunes were no longer to introduce legislation to the assembly of the plebs, and their power to block other magistrates was reduced. In other words, the tribunes were now limited to helping individual citizens who were threatened by the arbitrary power of a magistrate. Moreover, any man who had been tribune could not now hold any further political office afterward. In this way Sulla reversed some of the most basic agreements that had been made with the plebeians during the Conflict of the Orders, while making the tribunate a dead-end job. What ambitious young Roman would want to be tribune under these circumstances? Sulla in effect reduced the tribunate to a very primitive form of the original office and removed it completely from any relationship with the structure of other offices. It was now little more than an isolated plebeian vestige. In this sense the weakening of the tribunate must have seemed like a reversal of one of the essential elements of the political alliance between patricians and plebeians that underlay the Roman sense of a unified community in a republican system of government led by *nobiles*. The patrician Sulla aimed to eliminate the political influence of the tribunes of the

[17]Brennan (2004, 61–65) gives a convenient and concise overview.
[18]Bleicken 1981; Hantos 1988, 74–89; Thommen 1989.

plebs. It remains unclear how Sulla thought that most everyday laws would be passed without tribunician legislation.

Political life changed radically in Rome as a result of Sulla's
actions, and not only for the office holders on whom many
modern studies tend to concentrate. Ordinary people no longer heard political speeches (*contiones*) being made from the
rostra in the Forum, speeches that had been frequent and popular, not least those by Sulla himself.[19] Nor could they vote in
their own assemblies on legislation drafted by the tribunes of
the plebs. In future they were simply called upon to ratify laws
that had already been approved by the senate and that were
proposed by the highest magistrates. They had lost much of
their political presence and their occasions for civic expression: the silence must have been deafening.

It would be interesting to know whether one result of the
drastic reduction in political rhetoric in the Forum was a
higher level of political debate in the local neighborhoods of
the city (*vici*), the home turf of the men who had joined the
armed militias in the time of Saturninus twenty years before
and would serve again under Clodius and Milo in the next
generation.[20] There were certainly issues to discuss, not least
of which was the fact that Sulla had completely abolished
the grain dole, and indeed the now-accustomed government
role in controlling the price of food in the city.[21] His policies,
then, had both practical and symbolic results. Sulla effectively
changed the relationship between the ordinary citizens—especially the plebeians in the city—and the government, represented by the magistrates and the senate. Meanwhile, it is
interesting and suggestive that he did not do away with the
secret ballot, or apparently introduce any reform into the actual mechanics of voting.

Sulla's actions also affected the role of freedmen, the humblest citizens, notably in the city of Rome. For Sulla apparently took for himself a large number of the able-bodied male
slaves of the proscribed. He freed ten thousand of them in
his own name and settled them in the city as his agents and

---

[19]Cicero *Pro Cluent.* 40.110, with Morstein-Marx 2004. Public meetings had
been very active since 133, and probably before. See also Pina Polo 1996.
[20]Lott 2004, 28–60.
[21]Sallust *Hist.* 1.55.11 (speech of Lepidus); Licinianus 34F.

supporters throughout Rome.[22] Because they owed their
freedom to him, each of them had his name of L. Cornelius,
together with their slave name as their *cognomen*. The impact of this unprecedented action must have been enormous.
Moreover, the price of ten thousand strong young slaves represented a significant economic investment, since Sulla could
have sold these slaves, just as much of the other property
of the proscribed was sold at large public auctions. In addition, one must assume that he did not simply turn these men
loose to be homeless in the city: they must have received some
money or other support in kind, perhaps from the resources
and real estate of their former masters, to help them start a
new life and to encourage them to stay in Rome.

Sulla's ten thousand Cornelii, therefore, represented an ex-
pensive urban initiative. Surely many would then have married and have gone on to have children, all of them Cornelii.
This action of Sulla's suggests the importance of the local
neighborhoods of the city, especially in political terms. Based
on epigraphic evidence, there is reason to believe that Sulla
received special honors, including statues, in these *vici*, probably at the focal point of the *compita*, or crossroads, where
local shrines were usually to be found.[23] Sulla's actions can
be taken to indicate that, just as we know was the case later
under Augustus, the local officials who tended the neighborhood shrines and had a leading role in local life were mostly
freedmen. Furthermore, Sulla himself seems to have taken the
political role of these freedmen seriously.

Sulla also passed various reforms with regard to the state
cults that were run by the elite priests. A law of 104, proposed
by the tribune Cn. Domitius Ahenobarbus, had introduced
a form of election for the major priesthoods. Sulla now apparently abolished these elections and went back to the older
system of cooptation by existing priests.[24] In other words,
new priests would be chosen by the group remaining on each
board. This system was now also applied to the office of *pon-*

---

[22]Appian *BC* 1.100, 104; *ILLRP* 353 = *ILS* 871.
[23]*CIL* 6.1297 = *ILS* 872 = *ILLRP* 352 (*vicus Laci Fundani*), with Ramage
1991, 110. These honors need not reflect the specific influence of the ten
thousand Cornelii alone.
[24]Hantos 1988, 120–29.

tifex maximus, the most influential and prestigious priesthood in Rome. Sulla increased the number of priests in the colleges, including an augmentation in the number for consulting the Sibylline Books, despite the fact that these had been lost in the Capitoline fire of 83. His interest in the state religion can be seen in a number of measures.

Sulla himself was a deeply religious person, both in a traditional and in a less conventional, more mystical, sense.[25] Upon his return from the East, he had dedicated a tenth of his huge booty to Hercules.[26] As is very clear from the fragments of Sulla's autobiography, most of which are to be found in the biography written by Plutarch, he felt that he had a special relationship with a number of deities, most obviously Venus. In the East he took the extra name Epaphroditos, or "favorite of Venus," which was not equivalent to his triumphal name of Felix that he assumed after he had captured Rome.[27]

However, it would be a mistake to interpret his reforms of the state priesthoods simply in light of his personal spirituality. Rather, these reforms demonstrate how closely state cults and their boards of priests were connected to the political system. A thorough reform of republican politics needed to consider the number of priests, who were all leading senators anyway, and their role in society. Sulla and his contemporaries would simply not have seen a divide between religion and politics, just as they did not see these priesthoods as special vocations or as the main occupations of their incumbents.

Note should be taken of Sulla's new system of permanent courts staffed by large senatorial juries.[28] There seem to have been at least seven of these courts, each under its own praetorian magistrate. The large size of the juries was partly designed, at least in theory, to prevent bribery. Since the time of the Gracchi the juries had been staffed by equestrians; now

---

[25]Santangelo (2007, 197–223) and Giardina (2008) give nuanced assessments and full bibliography. Sulla did not become *pontifex maximus*, despite the vacancy in the office in 82 with the death of Q. Mucius Scaevola.

[26]Plutarch *Sulla* 35 paints a vivid scene.

[27]Behr 1993, 144–70; Thein 2002, 20–32.

[28]Hantos (1988, 63–68, 154–61) gives an overview of the court system. Brunt (1988, 194–239) offers a different point of view. See Alexander (1990, 149–50) for trials.

they were to be exclusively run by senators again, as had been the situation when the first such court was established in 149. However, these new "senators," and especially those who spent most time on jury duty, were equestrians who had been promoted directly by Sulla. In other words, Sulla cut a huge swath through the ranks of the equestrian order, first by killing thousands, and next by promoting hundreds of the survivors—many of them from wealthy families in the Italian towns—to become his new senators, replacing the large number of prominent men in Rome who had died. However, their sudden cooption as senators did not make them the equals of Roman senators of earlier generations. These jurors were now given the task of policing Roman society, and especially the behavior of its most powerful senatorial elites, in a much more organized way than had ever been envisioned before.

Special attention must be paid to Sulla's new *maiestas* (treason) law, which enforced a code of conduct for Romans abroad, notably the governors of Rome's ten overseas provinces, who were also the commanders of Rome's armies in the field.[29] Sulla changed the previous system, which had been much more informal, as regards both the precise relationship of each general to his peers at home in the senate and particularly what actions he could undertake on his own initiative while he was on campaign. It had increasingly become the case that a Roman general might go abroad for years and would only be able to communicate sporadically with anyone at home. As a result, many commanders had effectively become independent operatives with big armies and wide discretion, as they marched around the Mediterranean and made decisions according to the situations they met.[30] The instructions they had received prior to leaving Rome would probably have been general and unspecific in most cases. Under Sulla's new laws, little room was left for negotiating the fine points of a commander's task. At the same time, the whole concept of a province had become defined as a specific geographical area with fixed borders, rather than as a specific military objective. The Roman governor was to go to that area (his province)

---

[29]Cicero *Pis.* 21.50, *Ad Fam.* 3.11.2, *Cluent.* 35.97, with Bauman 1967.
[30]Eckstein (1987) provides a wealth of insights.

and to stay in it until the next governor arrived from Rome. He was not to leave the province without permission or to start a war without instruction, especially one that took him beyond the borders of his province. His task had now been clearly enunciated for him, and the penalties for infringement of the new guidelines were severe.

Sulla's republic was a political constitution based on laws and their regular enforcement by a system of courts.[31] This system did not correspond to the Roman experience of a traditional republic, namely a republic that had been based on deliberation in the senate, debate in front of the people, and on elaborate rituals of compromise and consensus building in both settings. The republics of the *nobiles* had been founded on a shared political experience in the city and on the words and leadership of the elected politicians, who were specifically identified as being the best and brightest in the community. These *nobiles* were promoted by the electorate at each stage of their careers, and so they were seen to be answerable to the voters. By definition, such a republic had more fluidity and a less formal shape because the possibility for debate and change at any time was one of its most defining features. While the appeal to ancestral custom (*mos maiorum*) was always strong, dynamic changes had been continual and political debate was expected to be lively, both between rival politicians and in the interactions of leaders with crowds in various urban settings. The elections had often been fierce competitions between elite candidates.[32]

The new system relied almost entirely on the rule of law and on norms and guidelines that had been clearly encoded in Sulla's legislation. In other words, *lex* was to replace *mos maiorum*. The basic foundation of Sulla's republic was new, therefore, even to the extent of being a revolutionary change in political life at Rome. At about the age of 60, Sulla the dictator effectively declared that a traditional republican system led by *nobiles* had failed within his own lifetime. We may suspect that he was not alone in holding this opinion, even if others might have proposed a solution different from the one he

---

[31]Hantos (1988) sees it all in terms of control. See Crawford 1996 for republican statutes and Riggsby 1999 for the court system as seen by Cicero. Williamson (2005) offers a new interpretation of law in a republican context.
[32]Yakobson (1999) discusses a later period. See Flower 1996, 60–90.

implemented. It is vital to understand that his New Republic was not a restoration of any kind, although it certainly used many components and ideas that had been employed or suggested at various earlier times. Sulla was definitely not trying to "turn back the clock," let alone to any particular period of Roman history. Sulla was a pragmatist, not an antiquarian. In the end, it took a patrician like Sulla, whose status in Roman society was not wholly dependent on elected office, to refuse to restore the *nobiles* to power. In other words, the outcome of Sulla's dictatorship could have been very different. He deliberately chose to install a new political system rather than to resurrect the one that had been in place immediately before.

The innovative nature of Sulla's program can be gauged by the fact that it proved to be essentially unworkable, despite the logic and care that had gone into its complex design.[33] Even among its beneficiaries it had only partial support, depending on the personal interests of each individual or group. The land allocations were difficult to undo, despite the fact that many Sullan veterans did not prove to be successful farmers.[34] Unrest and lawlessness resulted in many places in Italy over the next generation. It took another patrician dictator, this time Julius Caesar, to remove the civic disabilities imposed upon the families of those who had been proscribed.[35] Sulla's political plans were dismantled piecemeal, both before and after the watershed year of 70, the consulship of Pompey and Crassus.[36] The "restoration" of the tribunate at that time went on to shape the increasingly chaotic and divisive politics of the 60s and 50s, which will be discussed in the next section. Many of Sulla's new senators simply did not have the background or the training for their new jobs.

Similarly, many Romans, like Cicero himself, chose to follow Sulla's example in turning down provinces in order to stay in Rome, with the result that expertise and prestige became more

[33]*Contra* Gruen (1974), who sees no fundamental changes to the Sullan system.
[34]For Sulla's colonies in Italy, see Santangelo 2007, 147–57.
[35]Vedaldi Iasbez (1981) documents the individual descendants.
[36]Sources in Greenidge and Clay 1960. Reforms were passed in 75 (*leges Aureliae*) and 70 (reforms of tribunate, censorship, and courts). Failed attempts at reform are attested for 78, 76, 74, 73, and 71. Continuous agitation can surely be assumed during the 70s.

concentrated in the hands of a smaller circle. Meanwhile, generals in the provinces were often unwilling to abide by the new guidelines. The most obvious example is provided by Caesar in Gaul in the 50s, where he broke every new rule and a few older ones as well. Caesar's *De bello Gallico* is an extensive example of the special pleading he thought might help him to avoid prosecution and political ruin. But above all, it was the lack of tradition, of the societal restraints produced by inherited behavior patterns, and of true conservative principles that doomed Sulla's republic, virtually from the start. It was difficult to be a conservative politician after Sulla's revolution because there was so little of a former way of life left to conserve.

The new social and political framework of Sulla's republic gave rise to a new physical setting, which acted as the stage for political drama after Sulla. Just as he had finally put an old republic to rest, Sulla tore down the old speaker's platform (*rostra*), repaved the whole area around it (*comitium*), and demolished the old senate house (*curia Hostilia*).[37] Apparently there was no delay in implementing these changes, and work started immediately during his dictatorship of 81. The new senate house was in a slightly different location and much bigger than the old one, in order to accommodate the larger senate. The *rostra* were also higher and angled differently. Next to the new *rostra* stood the monumental equestrian statue of Sulla, the first such gilded statue in the city.[38] There is every reason to believe that the new senate house was called *curia Cornelia* after its founder.[39] It is difficult to recover the exact design of the Forum under Sulla, but enough has been revealed by excavations and finds to show how original and striking the new design was.

The principal political structures of senate house and speaker's platform were also given a new backdrop with the construction of the huge structure we now refer to as the "Tabularium,"

[37]See Coarelli on the *comitium* and *curia* (*LTUR* 1993) and Purcell (*LTUR* 1995, 331) on the Forum. Cf. Ramage 1991, 113–15; Behr 1993, 124–35.
[38]Sehlmeyer 1999, 204–9; Coarelli and Papi (*LTUR* 1999). Cf. *RRC* 381, of 80.
[39]Faustus, Sulla's son, was chosen to restore the senate house after the fire of 52, despite his relatively low status as a politician (Cicero *Fin.* 5.2; Dio 44.5). *LTUR* has entries only for *Curia Hostilia* and *Curia Iulia*.

a building that has been connected with the more systematic keeping of records and government documents, especially laws.[40] In this way even the view behind the political area was reshaped, as the eye took in the Capitoline Hill behind. Meanwhile, the temple of Jupiter Optimus Maximus on the Capitol, which had been destroyed in the fire of 83, was also being rebuilt. Its new incarnation recalled Sulla's times, but it was labeled with the name of his close political associate Q. Lutatius Catulus (cos. 78).[41] That particular rebuilding was occasioned by an (apparently) accidental destruction, but the rest of the urban renewal showed elaborate planning and a desire for a completely novel design, even at the expense of working around some older features that were hard to move. The Temple of Veiovis, for example, was now surrounded by the new Tabularium.[42] Sulla was the first leader since the regal period to extend the sacred boundary of the city (*pomerium*).[43] The New Republic of Sulla had a face, and that image was carefully designed to suggest a new beginning for a world capital (re)founded by a unique and charismatic leader.

Finally, the matter of Sulla's retirement, which has been a perennial topic for debate, also relates to the image of his New Republic. The best ancient evidence supports the argument that Sulla laid down his dictatorship at the end of 81, before becoming consul for 80. There is no reliable evidence for his holding both titles at once. Scholars have cited a wide variety of causes for Sulla's retirement from politics to his country estate at Puteoli on the bay of Naples: political eclipse at the hands of rivals, a religious sense of impending doom, poor health due to chronic illness, a feeling of political failure, a conviction of political success, a purely personal reason of some kind, or some combination of these factors.[44] It has

[40]See Mura Sommella in *LTUR* 1999; for a different view, Tucci 2005. Kolb (2002, 254) sees the Tabularium as the most important extant republican building in Rome today.

[41]See De Angeli in *LTUR* 1996: the new temple was dedicated in 69 although it was not quite finished then.

[42]Albertoni in *LTUR* 1999.

[43]Andreussi in *LTUR* 1999; Baraz in *TLL*. Kolb (2002, 101, 145, 255, 400) identifies Sulla as the new founder of Rome.

[44]For Sulla's retirement, see the succinct discussion in Hölkeskamp 2000a.

been argued that even people alive at the time found his decision hard to understand, although there is no real evidence for what most people thought. I would suggest, however, that the retirement appears to have been part of a carefully laid plan.

As has been persuasively argued, Sulla conceived of his dictatorship in quasi-republican terms, as a special office undertaken to perform a specific task, namely, the establishment of a constitutional (republican) form of government.[45] He was preeminent in this sphere in holding the office of dictator for a year (or perhaps slightly more), which amounted to two times the normal term of six months held in succession. He then became ordinary consul in the first year of the New Republic. This was a clear sign of the restoration of constitutional government and the rule of law, as well as being a recognition of his preeminent position in Roman society. After his consulship he retired to Puteoli, and seems not to have come back to the city again before his death in 78, although his funeral was celebrated in Rome.[46]

What did Sulla think he was doing and why? The simplest answer is that he saw himself as fulfilling the role of the lawgiver, a figure unprecedented in Rome but well known in Greece and the Near East. Like Solon, the famous Athenian, Sulla aimed to give Rome a new constitution that would put an end to political and social strife. Like Solon, who had left Athens for ten years to let the Athenians make the system work for themselves, Sulla left Rome. The paradigm of Athens' most famous lawgiver makes perfect sense of Sulla's decision and of how he would most probably have presented it to his fellow citizens.[47] Sulla's proximity and the power of his veterans all over Italy, however, made him a figure who must have seemed

---

[45]Hurlet 1993 is detailed and convincing. Similarly, the *lex Titia* of 43 assigned such a task to the triumvirate of Antony, Octavian, and Lepidus.

[46]Appian *BC* 1. 104; *Vir ill.* 75, with Meier 1980, 260–62.

[47]Cicero *Rep*. 2.30 and 2.1: *nostra autem res publica non unius esset ingenio sed multorum, nec una hominis vita sed aliquot constituta saeculis et aetatibus* ("But our form of government was not the product of one person's intelligence, but of many, nor was it created in the lifetime of one man, but over several centuries and ages"). This conception of republican development may go back to Cato; see Walter 2004, 291, for discussion. See also Gotter 1996, 247–49, 254; *contra*, Giardina 2008. Hölkeskamp (1999) treats Greek lawgivers in context. See Santangelo 2007, 214–23, for Sulla as a new founder of Rome.

much more threatening than any Greek lawgiver had been. Moreover, he was still active in politics, and was writing his extensive memoirs, which were to be decisive in shaping the picture of his times handed on to future historians.

He was also a lawgiver in a local setting, and had given a new law code to Dicaearchia shortly before his death.[48] Many codes may have been implemented and many eras inaugurated under Sulla throughout Italy, as seems to have been the case with the *Fasti Ostienses*, the famous local chronicle of Ostia that apparently started in Sullan times.[49] Needless to say, the interpretation of Sulla as a lawgiver for the Romans does not preclude some of the more traditional explanations of his withdrawal, for example, his chronic illness or his desire to write an extensive account of his life in his own words before he died.

Meanwhile, the Romans did not accept Sulla, partly because the figure of the lawgiver was simply not a part of their political tradition. Sulla's New Republic failed not just because of its untraditional form, but also because of the way in which it had been imposed on Rome, without political debate, by a strong man, whether he wanted to appear as a "republican dictator" or not. A top-down solution did not fit with a republican system of government in the Roman sense. In that way, Rome was very different from Athens, or Sparta (which claimed Lycurgus as its lawgiver), or many other Greek city-states. At the same time, the Romans did not want to accept the sovereignty of law envisioned by the self-appointed lawgiver Sulla and reminiscent of the role of law in fourth-century Athens.[50] The content, style, and origins of Sulla's New Republic were too revolutionary and too foreign to last in Rome, especially after they were imposed by a man who was not present to enforce them himself for any length of time.

[48]Plutarch *Sulla* 37. See Santangelo 2007, 168–69, for Sulla on the Bay of Naples.

[49]Bargagli and Grosso 1997 (originally proposed by Degrassi in *II* 13.1 [1947], 173–241). Note also the striking break in Roman wall painting at both Rome and Pompeii with the advent of the revolutionary new "Second Style," characterized by the use of perspective and illusions of space (Pappalardo 2004).

[50]Ostwald (1986) explains the development of Athenian law from the fifth to the fourth centuries.

VIII

AFTER THE SHIPWRECK (78–49)

amissa re publica…
The republic/state has been lost…
    Cicero, writing to Atticus in January 60 (*Att.* 1.18.6)

de re publica quid ego tibi subtiliter? tota periit.
What can I say to you in detail about the republic? It is completely in ruins.
    Cicero, writing to Atticus in midsummer 59 (*Att.* 2.21)

The menace of despotic power hung over Rome like a heavy cloud for thirty years from the Dictatorship of Sulla to the Dictatorship of Caesar.
    Sir Ronald Syme (1939, 8)

W e now move from the 80s to a brief consideration of the period of some thirty years between the death of Sulla in 78 and Caesar's invasion of Italy in January 49. These years are traditionally associated with the "Fall of the Republic," but in the periodization that I propose here, they come after the fall of a fifth republic, one dominated by the *nobiles*. According to this new interpretation, Sulla's republic should be considered a separate constitutional system in its own right, a sixth republic, albeit one that lasted in its original form for barely a decade: in the year 70, the consuls Pompey and Crassus introduced major changes to Sulla's carefully conceived system. A realistic assessment of politics in the decades immediately after Sulla reveals many features that are distinctly unrepublican, not least the corrosive violence that soon reasserted itself in so many spheres and contexts of Roman life. The essentially stable and dynamic republican culture of the third and second centuries had been replaced by a government that was volatile and that soon collapsed into a repeating pattern, one that alternated between narrow oligarchies of two or three leading men (Pompey, with Caesar and Crassus, then Antony, with Octavian and Lepidus) and systems of one-man rule (Caesar the dictator, then Octavian/Augustus the *princeps*). Most importantly, between 80 and the outbreak of civil war in 49 Romans failed to reach a basic agreement on the rules of their political game.

Despite the many Romans who had a clear stake in Sulla's New Republic, from senators to veterans throughout Italy to freedmen in the city, the divisive politics of the 80s and the way in which revolutionary political change had been imposed by one man had disrupted the very basis of the traditional social contract. Violence had broken down relationships both within the city of Rome and between Romans and many Italians. The sense of disconnect with the past was tangible. Increasingly insistent rhetoric and iconography featuring traditional values and practices was a symptom of this sense of estrangement and loss, a malaise that only worsened as time went on. The same could be said of the appearance of "ancestors" in many more contexts in Roman life; such an assertive use of appeals to earlier figures and to the central importance of the political families was innovative and reflected deep-seated fears about the state of a republic that no longer belonged to the *nobiles*.[1]

The question of leadership in Sulla's republic was a pressing one that was at the heart of most political debates during the 70s and 60s. As discussed above, the decade of the 80s had already been dominated by factionalism, extreme violence, and the emergence of warlords such as Cinna and Sulla. Sulla's solution has often been described as putting the senate in charge, although insofar as he did so, he did it in an untraditional setting and by creating a new, huge senate that looked nothing like the republican senate of his youth. As is generally acknowledged, Sulla's senate did not fulfill the role he had assigned to it,

---

[1] Sulla's successors appealed to republican pasts in much more overt terms than he seems to have. See Flower 1996 for a discussion of ancestor images on coins, seals, statues, and in other media in the city, in addition to a steady increase in the number and splendor of aristocratic funerals.

and this contributed in many ways to the rise of the powerful generals Pompey, Crassus, and Caesar. The senators failed to lead, but that may be because many neither wanted nor were able to exercise power in the way that Sulla had envisioned. In the republics of the *nobiles*, the senate, which met and debated the questions posed by senior magistrates, had always been conceived of and represented as an advisory body, albeit one with great authority.[2] Consequently, the senate was never an elective body that represented any particular constituency. Sulla hoped that his comprehensive legal system, backed up by the senatorial juries, would control behavior and restore orderly and constitutional government. The Romans, however, had never had a political system principally or formally based on law rather than on custom, and they were not ready or willing to make that fundamental and revolutionary change.

Meanwhile, Sulla's own example clearly set an important precedent for all Roman leaders who came after him, even for Augustus. His exemplarity has often been expressed in simple terms: he was a powerful general who marched on Rome and seized power with a client army.[3] Afterward others did likewise, because he had proved that such actions could be performed with impunity. There are, however, other ways of reading the story. According to the interpretation offered here, Sulla set himself up as a lawgiver for the Romans, as symbolized by his gilded statue at the *rostra*. He wanted Romans to recall him as the man who had given them a law code and a republic that worked better than their previous one. He hoped to be remembered fondly, not only as a general and politician in all the usual spheres, but as the man who had established a new standard of law and order.[4]

---

[2]Lintott 1999a, 65–88.

[3]Cicero *Att.* 9.10.2 cites Pompey's words in 49: *Sulla potuit, ego non potero?* ("Sulla could, so why can't I?"); see also Meier 1980, 145, 265, 290.

[4]Cf. Augustus' wish in an edict quoted by Suetonius (*Aug.* 28): *ita mihi salvam ac sospitem rem publicam sistere in sua sede liceat atque eius rei fructum percipere, quem peto, ut optimi status auctor dicar et moriens ut feram mecum spem mansura in vestigio suo fundamenta rei publicae quae iecero* ("My aim is that the *res publica* be so safe and sound, so firm in its foundations and evidently prosperous that I be called the author of the best constitution and that when I die I should take with me the hope that the basis of the political system should endure according to the foundations that I laid").

In this sense, his project was an evident failure, because Romans were simply not willing to accept such a figure, let alone Sulla himself in that role. His negative example was in fact just as powerful as his positive one. None of his followers, especially Pompey, even attempted to propose a systematic alternative to his program. Piecemeal reforms, which aimed to make the new system look a bit more like earlier ones, undermined the logic of Sulla's constitution without offering a coherent political system to replace it. If Sulla's system was seen to be flawed and unworkable, then the Romans needed either a new lawgiver or the political will to debate the issues and come up with solutions through compromise and consensus. In the event, they did neither, until Octavian seized power by force and designed his own constitution.

Political failures in the 70s and 60s should not be attributed to a lack of talent or of ideas. Rather, the rejection by the surviving *nobiles* of Sulla's methods and the whole tone he had set discouraged the emergence of another single lawgiver. At the same time, the culture of compromise and open debate now lay in the distant past and proved effectively impossible to re-create in the prevailing political climate. There was simply no one left who was playing the old republican game, among either the old or the new senators, least of all an obstructionist like Cato. At the same time, the use of violence by all sides undermined the very concept of a political game with rules, in which losers accepted defeat and winners did not insist on making sure that their rivals had no future in politics. For all these reasons we must acknowledge the importance of the break in 88, which was a decisive watershed in republican life. The remainder of this section will look in a bit more detail at various episodes during the years after Sulla's retirement, according to their usual division into decades, as well as at the overall pattern of republican politics after Sulla.

The Seventies

The 70s are much harder to study than the two decades that follow, because we have much less material provided by Cicero, who was just starting his career and who spent some years away from Rome.[5] As a result, the 70s have also received relatively less attention from modern scholars. Yet several very important themes emerge. This is the decade that saw the essential failure of Sulla's republic. We know much more about the resulting reforms at the end of the decade in 70 than about the exact way in which events led up to that change. For present purposes the most important observation would seem to be that unrest, political opposition, and episodes of open civil war were common. In other words, there was no time when Sulla's republic was both fully functional and unchallenged as the established status quo. If we read resistance simply in terms of the personal ambitions of individual leaders like Sertorius or Lepidus, we miss the underlying political ideas and issues that were at stake. The intensity, variety, and immediacy of opposition to the new system is a powerful indication of its perceived revolutionary character.

Civil war on several fronts marked the year of Sulla's death in 78. Thus it is not accurate to say that Sulla had won the civil war before he established his new constitution. Rather, fighting continued in Spain until the late 70s, mainly against Q. Sertorius, who had been an ally of Cinna.[6] Given the charisma and the military gifts of Sertorius, and the resources that were required to defeat him, it would be a mistake to dismiss the conflict in Spain as a mere mopping-up operation. In fact, it was the immediate and pressing military need in Spain that created an opportunity for Pompey, the man who would go on to be consul in the year 70 at the early age of thirty-six, without having held any previous political office. While it is true that Pompey had already received military commands and a triumph from Sulla, things might have gone very differently for him if Sulla had managed to establish a stable republic. Without pressing military needs, Pompey's career would have returned to a more normal pattern or might even have petered out. Pompey's victory in Spain makes all the more striking his decision to amend the Sullan constitution,

[5]The fragmentary sources can be found in *MRR* and Greenidge and Clay 1960, 228–76.
[6]See Spann 1987 and Konrad 1994 on Plutarch's biography. It is notable that Sertorius controlled Spain through legates in a way that prefigured Pompey, both in Spain and in the East.

which is presumably just what a victorious Sertorius would have done under different circumstances and in his own way. Yet Pompey's restoration of the tribunate appears in many ways to be self-serving, rather than a symptom of any carefully conceived political reform.

The year 78 also saw the revolt in Italy of the consul M. Aemilius Lepidus, an opponent of Sulla.[7] This very short-lived episode often gets scant attention, although Cicero may have considered it an important precedent for his own actions in suppressing Catiline in 63. Yet what could be less characteristic of a traditional republic than the revolt of a consul who was one of the resplendent Aemilii, a member of one of Rome's greatest patrician families? But should Lepidus be regarded as a rebel? That would suggest that the republic of Sulla should be classified as the legitimate and legal government of Rome. Lepidus, who had been duly elected as consul, had a different opinion and agitated for political change immediately after the former dictator's death. He had also opposed granting Sulla a special new kind of funeral, paid for at public expense, that marked him as a person above all others in Roman society. Lepidus then turned to violence after his consular colleague Q. Lutatius Catulus (son of the consul of 102) prevailed in blocking constitutional reform and in burying Sulla on the Campus Martius in grand style. Lepidus' military failures should not obscure his political point. Meanwhile, a dangerous precedent had been set, as these consuls battled each other in the third year after free elections had been restored. Sulla had ordained that the consuls should stay in Rome during their year of office, but soon a new civil war broke out between them.

At this time, Rome also faced other challenges, which raised more general questions of law and order than did the political opposition of leading Romans like Sertorius and Lepidus. The two principal threats came from piracy in the Mediterranean and from a large-scale slave revolt in Italy, which was led by a gladiator from Thrace named Spartacus. These pressures were not unrelated to the political chaos in Rome and the lack of stable government over many years. Two previous slave re-

[7]See Christ 2002, 141–42, for the revolt in the years 78–77.

volts in Sicily in the later second century had been costly to deal with, but they had not caused major unrest in Italy itself. Now the situation was very different and Crassus struggled in Italy to defeat Spartacus and a slave army that was said to number as many as seventy thousand.[8] Although Spartacus' aim seems simply to have been to escape from Italy, his success would have encouraged other slaves to rebel and would have left a trail of destruction in its wake. Piracy was also a recurring problem, and another Antonius was sent out to try to restore safe travel, just as his ancestor had attempted to do in 102–100.[9] Political instability had a marked effect on the general condition of law and order, making the Italian countryside unsafe until the time of the principate. Reduced safety inevitably translated into more weapons being carried and more armed retainers for all sorts of travelers with the means to afford protection. Piracy also threatened the food supply of the city of Rome, as well as the ability of even the most elite Romans to travel overseas. In sum, the general level of violence in the city and the countryside was high, despite the restoration of a constitutional government.

Meanwhile, a new war with Mithridates was looming on the horizon.[10] Here again the message was clear: Sulla had failed. Despite his splendid triumph and the image of victory and world empire Sulla had promoted, the Pontic king still posed a threat to Rome, and it would take another decade of fighting to defeat him. The feeling that the New Republic was a failure was hard to escape. Continued violence and civil war, both at home and abroad, in combination with persistent calls for political reform and restoration, fostered the career and influence of Pompey, a man seen as powerful enough to bring resolution to Rome's problems.[11] His consulate with Crassus in 70 saw the restoration of the full powers of the tribunes of the plebs and an adjustment of the jury system, with the result that senators now shared the juries with other elite men,

[8]Shaw 2001 gives sources and discussion.
[9]Kallet-Marx 1995, 304–11.
[10]Sherwin-White 1984, 186–234.
[11]Gelzer 1984 remains the classic treatment, but see also Seager 2002 and Christ 2004. Further bibliography at Bleicken 2004, 311.

of equestrian and almost-equestrian status.[12] These individual reforms, however, did not address many basic questions, particularly the issue of how political power was to be distributed and exercised in Rome under a system that conformed neither to Sulla's model nor to an earlier one. The problems are especially evident in the subsequent turbulent history of the law courts and the tribunate, both of which contributed to the instability of republican politics rather than to a new level of civic concord and cooperation. Interestingly, both the tribunate and the law courts had originally been designed as watchdogs of republican government and of its civic values.

The Sixties

From a political point of view the 60s were a decade of increasing insecurities that ended with a powerful alliance between Pompey, Crassus, and Caesar, a political alliance that preempted and compromised the operation of a republican system of government.[13] Unrest at the consular elections was evident in 66, 65, 64 and 63, culminating in the revolt of Catiline.[14] This has been described as the decade of Pompey, and it was his career and aspirations that put an end to what was left of the Sullan system. He had already emerged as victor in the civil war in Spain in the 70s. That made him, de facto, the restorer of peaceful civic government, after so many years of fighting between Romans in different contexts since the early 80s. It was for him that an exception had been made to all of Sulla's rules about age, priority, and career patterns in holding high office. As consul he had had the courage and influence to adapt Sulla's republic, although he did not present a politically

[12]Cicero *Pro Cluent.* 130 is critical of the senatorial juries of the 70s. Meier (1980, 267) sees the reforms of the 70s as decisive in getting rid of Sulla's most important ideas. By contrast, Hantos (1988, 88–89) stresses Sulla's continuing influence, both on political theory and everyday practice.

[13]Gruen (1974) provides a classic discussion of this richly documented period. Wiseman (1994b) sees Pompey's reforms as harking back to the old republic. See also Baltrusch 2004. This was perhaps the time when Licinius Macer published his history of early Rome.

[14]*MRR*: in 68 Marcius was left alone as consul after the deaths of two colleagues.

sound or fully coherent alternative vision. Over the next several years it was to him that Romans of varying backgrounds and political persuasions turned as they confronted the major challenges their city faced.

Pompey received extraordinary powers to control piracy in the Mediterranean and his rapid success made him the obvious candidate to face Mithridates.[15] Consequently, he was away from Rome from 66 to the end of 62, during which time he eliminated Mithridates and put Rome on a new and much more powerful footing in the eastern Mediterranean. His exercise of enormous powers and his wide-ranging military activities from the Caucasus to Jerusalem stood in sharp contrast to Sulla's orderly model of constrained and standardized provincial government, dependent on precise instructions from Rome.[16] Pompey played the role of a warlord in the East, but one much more successful in the field than Sulla had been. Roman foreign policy, therefore, became more aggressive and expansionist after Sulla, especially with the campaigns of Pompey in the East and of Caesar in Gaul, both of whom added vast provinces to the Roman empire. This militaristic and imperialistic policy was also fundamentally out of tune with the more traditional and hegemonic approach of the *nobiles*. Meanwhile, long and aggressive campaigns leading to significant expansions of the empire inevitably created the kinds of powerful generals Sulla had tried to avoid. In addition, the number of magistrates was not adjusted to provide governors on a regular basis for the new provinces, and leading Romans were able to refuse the assignment of a province in defiance of the pattern of public service mandated by Sulla.[17]

At the same time, Pompey's career is more reminiscent of Marius' than of Sulla's. The Romans of the late second century had turned to Marius as the only man who could save

[15]Cicero *Leg. Man.*; Livy *Per.* 99; Appian *Mithr.* 99.
[16]See Kallet-Marx 1995, 291–334, on the East from Sulla to Pompey. For the Romans in Syria, see Sartre 2005, 37–53, with full bibliography.
[17]Mackay (2004) stresses this point throughout his account. For Sulla's arrangement of provincial administration, see Hantos 1988, 89–120. The following provinces were added to the ten in existence under Sulla: Cyrenaica, Crete, Syria, Bithynia and Pontus, Cyprus, Illyricum, and then the extensive Gallic territory conquered by Caesar in the 50s.

them from the Cimbri and Teutoni. Marius' repeated consulships and extraordinary prestige were a decisive factor in the
fall of the last republic of the *nobiles*. Now Romans again
turned to a single strong man, although at the suggestion of
various tribunes they voted him a multiyear command rather
than continuous consulships. Perhaps power abroad would be
less threatening, if it was to be exercised by a man who was
not at the same time chief executive at home year after year (or
so some Romans may have thought). Nevertheless, significant
riots and violence accompanied the voting of Pompey's command in 67.[18] As it turned out, Pompey's personal prestige and
vast influence could not be accommodated within a republic
he had by now done so much to shape. Fears about his return,
already strong in 63, soon became self-fulfilling prophecies.
Senators were unable to negotiate a compromise that would
allow Pompey to be reintegrated into Roman life with due
recognition of his achievements, nor could they find a way to
send him off again on another mission, as if in an orbit of his
own, which would have removed him from city politics. Whatever conclusions are drawn about Pompey's personal motives
and ambitions, which were notoriously hard to read even for
contemporaries, his position outside the republican system,
combined with his extraordinary military success, created a
volatile situation that the senate and the magistrates at home
could not control. In political terms, however, there was much
more at stake than mere personal jealousy and pettiness.

The 60s also saw the rise to prominence of Cicero and Cato,
two famous Romans who would play their own roles in destabilizing what was left of republican politics, although each
claimed to be defending a traditional system. Cato came from
a famous political family and had a grand heritage of public
service to live up to.[19] Yet his politics of constant obstruction
and provocation made any kind of negotiation or compromise
significantly harder to achieve, and was at variance with everything that was most traditional about the republic that his

18Wiseman 1994b, 331–39.
19Meier (1980, 275) describes his prominence as bad for republican politics.
Fehrle 1983 provides a full discussion. Mackay 2004, 144: "It was the Republic's misfortune that its most prominent defender was an uncompromising
man whose inflexibility would result in civil war."

great-grandfather and namesake, the famous censor, had been such a vital part of. Cato was a man of his age in insisting on narrow family tradition over constructive dialogue or innovation (unlike the elder Cato) and in focusing on appearances at the expense of reality (again, unlike his ancestor). The younger Cato's antiquarianism was essentially artificial and involved a complete denial of the real consequences of Sulla's reform program and of subsequent events. Cato's personal fantasy that he was living in the same kind of traditional republic as his ancestors had was not simply a delusion or a silly game.[20] It was a dangerous political stance that prevented both him and others from addressing the actual problems Rome faced and from finding solutions that could have created a more stable and less contested republic.

Cicero, by contrast, was a "new man" from Arpinum, a countryman and relative of Marius.[21] It is difficult to assess his role objectively because so much of what we know about this whole period comes from his decidedly personal perspective. Thus he is both the invaluable witness and emblem of the age and also something of a liability. Despite his protests that he stood for all that was most Roman and republican in city politics, his views cannot be taken as representative either of a majority of senators or (especially) of the most powerful and aristocratic inner circle. From the perspective of the present discussion he contributed to a sense of insecurity in Rome, especially in his consulship of 63, which was a crucial time of destabilization and fierce partisanship. The last vestiges of republican life disintegrated soon thereafter into the pact of the Big Three and the subsequent political chaos of the 50s.

---

[20]Cicero *Att.* 2.1.8 (21.8 Shackleton Bailey), of June 60: *nam Catonem nostrum non tu amas plus quam ego; sed tamen ille optimo animo utens et summa fide nocet interdum rei publicae; dicit enim tamquam in Platonis politeia, non tamquam in Romuli faece, sententiam* ("For you are not more fond of our mutual friend Cato than I am. Nevertheless, he is meanwhile doing damage to our government, albeit with the best intentions and complete loyalty. He makes his policy statements as if he was in Plato's republic rather than among Romulus' dregs").

[21]Biographies: Gelzer 1969; Stockton 1971; Rawson 1975; Habicht 1990; Bleicken 1999.

We are very well informed about the events of 63 from Cicero's consular speeches, his subsequent correspondence, Sallust's monograph *De coniuratione Catilinae*, and other historical narratives.[22] Yet the later viewer's assessment of Cicero's consulship clearly depends on whether we interpret republican collapse as coming in the immediate aftermath of Cicero's execution of the Catilinarian conspirators, or twenty years later (in 43, around the time when Sallust was writing his first historical monograph). Cicero went into exile in 58 in order to avoid the odium he had incurred by putting Roman citizens to death without a trial. Opinions have differed as to the level of threat that Catiline really posed to the state. Cicero was certainly exaggerating some elements and was motivated by his personal desire to be seen as the savior of Rome within the short space of his consular year. Yet the army of rebels in Etruria was fairly easily defeated the following year.

On the one hand, Catiline and his followers raised issues that were endemic to some of the most pressing social problems of the time: debt, dispossession on the land, and the unwillingness of an aristocrat like Catiline to accept defeat at the polls. It also brought back haunting memories of Marius, one of whose eagles Catiline (who had himself sided with Sulla) used to rally his troops.[23] On the other hand, an argument can be made that it was Cicero who was responsible for a dangerous undermining of republican values when he declared an emergency, executed Roman citizens and even a fellow magistrate without a trial, and raised the specter of civil war and arson in the city.[24] It was a sign of things to come when many called for Pompey to return and save Rome from Catiline, just as he had intervened to help defeat Spartacus a decade before and would be called upon to be sole consul a decade later, after the murder of Clodius.

Cicero argued that his republic was intact because the consuls in office had dealt with the threat to the commonwealth. However, they had done so only by circumventing due process

[22]Ungern Sternberg von Pürkel 1970, 86–129; Nippel 1988, 94–107; Wiseman 1994b, 346–60.
[23]For the debt issue, see Wiseman 1994b, 346–47; Giovannini 1995. For the eagles of Marius, see Cicero *Cat.* 2.13 and Sallust *BC* 59.3.
[24]Further discussion in Flower 2006, 99–102.

and the civil rights of citizens, and by introducing the death penalty in a completely unrepublican way. The execution of the conspirators was doubly ominous because it also revealed the consul's complete lack of confidence in the court system on which the New Republic of Sulla was supposed to be based. When Cicero declared *salus rei publicae suprema lex* ("The safety of the *res publica* is the supreme/most important law"), this was no more than a hollow political slogan that portended the end of constitutional government.[25]

Meanwhile, nothing had been done during 63 to address the social ills and divisions that had allowed Catiline and others to raise an army: agrarian reform had been prevented, the sons of the proscribed were still excluded from political life, and Rome was full of the bitter and divisive commemorations of Marius, Saturninus, and Sulla himself. In the event, however, obstruction and illegal violence were no substitute for political dialogue and constructive legislation. A republican government had not even been able to deal with a Catiline by legal means. How, then, could a Pompey be accommodated when he returned and asked for the ratification of all that he had done in the East? The leading senators were simply unable to place him within their existing framework, and apparently could not think of any more workable solution than to oppose him completely. Pompey's great (third) triumph over Mithridates on September 29, 61, can be read as the potent symbol of the end of republicanism and the beginning of a new age of warlords.[26] Meanwhile, it is essential to note that the zero-sum game that was being played out in the late 60s, marked by bitter political divisions and few compromises even on essential issues, was in no way equivalent to the political strategies that the *nobiles* had employed in more traditional republican times.

There is every reason to believe, then, that the events of 63 tended toward the creation of an extralegal political alliance between Pompey, Crassus, and Caesar. Too much effort has been expended on what to call this private arrangement

---

[25]Gotter 1996, esp. 248–49, 253.
[26]Beard (2007, 7–41) gives a detailed reading entitled "Pompey's Finest Hour?"

that was to overshadow politics from Caesar's consulship in 59 until Crassus' death in Syria in 53. The commonly used label of "First Triumvirate" is misleading in equating the position of the 50s with the official triumvirate of Antony, Lepidus, and Octavian, which lasted from 43 to 33.[27] However, it would also be unrealistic to say that the two groups of three had nothing at all in common, or that the later triumvirs never gave a thought to their powerful antecedents of only a decade before. In fact, the alliance between Pompey, Crassus, and Caesar is all the more significant in that it did *not* have an official title or any basis in law or custom. It can be compared with the kind of political deal that Saturninus and Glaucia were trying but failed to organize in 100. Both examples consisted of an arrangement that was based on the control of election results, continual office holding, and the consequent power that could be exercised by groups of men who were cooperating with each other over several years, while also being free from prosecution through the immunity afforded by political office.

At the same time, a comparison with Saturninus also brings out the huge changes in Rome over the forty years of turbulent politics since 100. The partners in power in the year 60 were enormously more influential and wealthy than their predecessors. They also exercised their control with the help of special multiyear commands, which by definition went against the most basic concepts of republican political office according to Sulla (collegiality, annuity, gaps between office, standardized career patterns, repeated accountability in a court of law). A man like Crassus had enough ready funds to pay for his own army and had many influential men in Rome in his pocket because they owed him money.[28] Pompey's career had been completely unusual and he had recently doubled the size of Rome's overseas empire. Naturally most ordinary citizens stood in awe of him. Meanwhile, Caesar now had access to almost limitless resources through his command in Gaul and Illyricum (including northern Italy), which made him enor-

[27]Meier 1980, 270–80. Mackay 2004, 142, 144: the triumvirs achieved "complete domination of the state [for the years 59–53]." Suetonius (*Jul.* 19.4) calls this alliance *societas*; Velleius Paterculus (2.44.1) *potentiae societas*.
[28]See Ward 1977 (in detail) and Burckhardt 2000 (for a brief overview).

mously wealthy, gave him the opportunity to create a client army of seasoned veterans, and made him the natural patron of all who served under him during a command that would stretch out over a ten-year period.[29] The conditions under which these three men operated and the resources available to them, in and of themselves, made traditional republican politics a thing of the past. Meanwhile, the attempt by some leading Romans to pretend that business could still go on as usual was certainly a crucial part of the problem, rather than a possible solution or a form of heroic resistance.

The Fifties

According to the scheme proposed here, the 50s no longer belong to a period of republican history.[30] Despite the ability of the Big Three to get their own legislation passed and to prevent political actions that they did not consider to be in their interests, they did not restore order to Rome or to her public life.[31] In this case, therefore, political domination did not bring the orderliness so often associated with totalitarian regimes. The grain crisis of 56 may serve as an example of difficulties in the city: the decision to call on Pompey to solve

[29]Caesar gives his own account in *De bello Gallico*. See Wiseman 1994a, 381–91; Lieberg 1998; and Canfora 2007, 88–123. For archaeological evidence, see Goudineau 1990.

[30]Cicero *Rep.* 5.2 speaks of the loss of the Republic in his generation (writing in the late 50s: see the epigraph for this section). Meier (1980, 280–300) gives a very interesting account. Mackay (2004, 147–52) stresses violence. Wiseman 1994b, 367: "... the very structure of the Republic itself was strained beyond its capacity for survival. The census of 70–69 doubled the size of the citizen body; the conquests of Pompey doubled the size of Rome's empire. With three new kingdoms to rule as provinces, and the unprecedented glory of Pompey's achievement as a goal for emulous ambition, the prizes of success in the political competition could not be allowed to depend on the free vote of an electorate too big to control by legitimate means. The constant bribery scandals of the sixties show all too clearly that the Republican constitution was fast becoming unworkable."

[31]Suetonius *Jul.* 19.2: *ne quid ageretur in re publica quod displicuisset ulli e tribus* ("that nothing should be done in politics that was displeasing to any of the three"). The negative quality should be stressed in any discussion of this political arrangement.

this problem only exacerbated the existing political issues.[32] Meanwhile, city life during these years was characterized by the violence of rival armed groups, which culminated early in 52 with the assassination of the leading popular politician Clodius in a seemingly random act of gang violence on the Via Appia, one of the main roads leading to the city.[33] Armed groups such as the one that killed Clodius might be called militias in another setting, and their leaders should not be classified simply as politicians in the traditional sense of the word. Men like Clodius and his archrival and eventual assassin Milo may sometimes have cooperated with one of the Big Three or with other politicians, but they were essentially independent agents in an increasingly fragmented political landscape. Any realistic analysis of the character of politics by this date needs to take seriously the corrosiveness and extent of the violence, both as a symptom and as a consequence of political disintegration.

For these reasons, an analysis of these years in terms of "party politics" inevitably misses the sheer degree of destabilization and the loss of coherent political identity that created a highly volatile situation leading to open civil war between Caesar and Pompey in 49.[34] The Romans had not had political parties in the second century, nor did anything like such clearly identifiable groups emerge after the period of the Gracchi. Party politics may have been in the air in 100, and later Cinna may briefly have had a party of sorts, but his political group had been destroyed and no one was eager to revive his memory. The lesson of the 60s seems to have been that at the end of the day only the most powerful generals could form a political alliance that mattered, an alliance backed by military might. Meanwhile, Pompey's use of legates to govern Spain granted him a power the others did not have, namely, the authority to delegate *imperium*, even in an overseas province.[35] His refusal to leave the outskirts of the city raised the question

[32]Cicero *Att.* 4.1 and Plutarch *Pomp.* 49.7, with Kolb 2002, 304–5.

[33]Tatum 1999, 214–42, with full bibliography. See also the perceptive remarks of Lintott (1999b, xiii–xv) beginning the introduction to the second edition of his book on violence.

[34]Taylor 1949 remains the classic treatment of "party politics."

[35]Mackay 2004, 138.

of what he was doing there and inevitably set the stage for his confrontation with Caesar in 49.

At the same time, a clear sign of the absence of a republican type of structure was the disruption in the cycle of elections.[36] Roman politics had always been characterized by annual elections, especially for the highest executive offices, the consuls who gave their names to the civic year. Many elections in the 50s were prevented from taking place, were marked by violence, or were subject to political arrangements. This pattern is especially noticeable after the pact between the Big Three was renewed at Luca in 56. Several years began without any consuls having been elected to office. This phase of destabilization can be associated with the time when Pompey and Crassus had also received great commands abroad, like Caesar's in Gaul. The system of elections seems to have broken down completely by 54 and elections were held only in 53, when Pompey returned to the city. But again no magistrates were chosen, and the year 52 also started without consuls. Violence culminated in the murder of Clodius and the subsequent burning of Sulla's senate house, which was deliberately used as Clodius' funeral pyre by the angry urban mob.[37] As a result, Pompey was chosen by the senate as sole consul, giving him the authority to take control of a situation that had clearly become completely lawless and anarchic.

Pompey's sole consulship in 52 needs to be recognized as the turning point that it was for Rome. Another man would have used this opportunity to restore republican politics; Pompey was not that reformer.[38] The alliance between the Big Three had dissolved with the death of Crassus and the disastrous defeat of the Romans in Syria during the previous year. Meanwhile, resistance to Roman rule in Gaul had been much fiercer than Caesar had anticipated. Once the balance of power between the three men had been destroyed, a faceoff between Caesar and Pompey may, therefore, have seemed inevitable to many. Moreover, Julia, Caesar's daughter who had been married to Pompey, had died in 54. When the consuls

---

[36]*MRR*: problems with elections are recorded in 55, 54, 53, and 52.

[37]Dio 40.49–50 and Asconius *Mil.* 33, 42, with Coarelli in *LTUR* 1993 (*Curia Hostilia*).

[38]See Gotter 1996, 257, on his attempt to restore order through the courts.

turned to Pompey to save the state in January of 49, that tactic represented a replay of the situation in 52 and an effective
acknowledgement that even the shadow of republican government had passed away since Clodius' death.[39]

After the year 52, politics was dominated by the question
of when and under what circumstances Caesar should return
from Gaul. This issue in and of itself presupposes the end of
a functional republican system that would have regulated
such a transfer of power in an accepted manner according
to precedent.[40] How could there be a question about what
would happen after the end of a command abroad or a term
as provincial governor? Roman governors had been returning
in regular ways from provinces abroad since the mid-third
century. Within living memory, Sulla had laid down explicit
guidelines for provincial commands and for the replacement
of one governor with another in orderly succession. The only
excuse Caesar had was the one that the law of the ten tribunes
had apparently sanctioned.[41] In effect, Pompey and others had
allowed Caesar to write his own rules in 52. Now they were
no longer in a position to pretend that an existing set of norms
was actually still in place and that Caesar ought to comply
with them, when others clearly were not doing so. Nor did
Caesar or others believe that there was an impartial system
of justice administered by regular courts, which could have
adjudicated issues of dispute between Caesar and his political
rivals.[42] In addition, one may take note of a further type of
novel political pact that allowed three Claudii Marcelli to hold
the consulship in succession in 51, 50 and 49, at the expense
of other qualified plebeian candidates, including Cato.[43]

---

[39]*MRR* for 49: Caesar *BC* 1.6.

[40]This issue has traditionally and somewhat misleadingly been referred to by
modern scholars as *die Rechtsfrage* (the legal question/the question of law).

[41]Gruen (1974, 455) offers a particularly clear picture of this special dispensa-
tion for Caesar.

[42]Suetonius *Jul.* 30.4 is the classic statement, put into the mouth of Caesar
after Pharsalus by Asinius Pollio: *hoc voluerunt: tantis rebus gestis Caius
Caesar condemnatus essem, nisi ab exercitu auxilium petissem* ("This is what
they wanted: I, Gaius Caesar, would have been found guilty in court, even
after my great achievements, if I had not sought help from my army").

[43]See Gruen 1974, 155. One may wonder whether Cato agreed to yield to
these Marcelli, since he does not even seem to have run again after an initial

My reconstruction has, therefore, argued that we should take seriously Cicero's feeling of a lost republic in the year 60, especially when taken with the later decision of C. Asinius Pollio. An ally of Caesar who was a generation younger than Cicero and held very different views from the orator, Pollio decided to start his history with that year.[44] As Cicero's own career and writings attest, the politics of the 50s was a no-man's land in which even the most powerful players feared political disgrace and oblivion. The remnants of Sulla's republic had been destroyed by the domination of the Big Three and the spreading violence, both organized and random, that not even they could control. Meanwhile, the "restored" tribunate had only served to weaken due process in politics and to create exceptional multiyear commands.

Caesar himself stopped writing his commentary on his own activities in Gaul and their relationship to Roman politics with the events of 52, and, therefore, did not discuss the last two years of campaigning in 51 and 50.[45] This decision has been taken to reflect the changed situation on the ground in Gaul, but it may equally demonstrate that politics in Rome had moved into a completely new phase: it was difficult now for Caesar himself to address the changed political circumstances and his accustomed audience in Rome.

---

halfhearted attempt. Their patrician colleagues for each year (Ser. Sulpicius Rufus, L. Aemilius Lepidus Paullus, L. Cornelius Lentulus Crus) also appear to have been part of their political group.

[44]Syme 1939, 5–8, 484–86, and now Morgan 2000.

[45]Welch (1998, 86) argues for a political reason, claiming that the *De bello Gallico* had become "inconvenient" for Caesar. *Contra* Gruen 1974, 454: "Julius Caesar made no secret of his admiration for Pompey's accomplishment [as sole consul in 52]." For the situation in Gaul during Caesar's last two years, see Wiseman 1994a, 408–17.

══ IX ══

IMPLICATIONS

etiam senes plerique inter bella civium nati: quotus quisque
reliquus qui rem publicam vidisset?
Even among the old men most had been born in the time of
the civil wars: who was left who had seen a republic?
  Tacitus (*Annales* 1.3), speaking of those who were alive in AD
  14, at the death of Augustus, the first Roman emperor

The arguments presented above have proposed a new model
for understanding the evolution of republican politics in
Rome, with a special emphasis on how and why it finally
came to an end in the first century. Needless to say, if this
interpretation were to be accepted, it would have a multitude
of implications for our interpretations of Roman civic life and
culture. The political landscape looks significantly different to
the observer who thinks that Marius and Sulla put an end to
traditional republican politics and ushered in a lengthy and
unstable era of transition to a type of monarchy. This final
section will offer a brief overview of just some of the implications that may come to mind: many others could and should
also be discussed beyond the six outlined below.

Even within a periodization scheme that recognizes multiple Roman republics, many different emphases and perspectives are possible. The relative weight given to different issues
remains a matter of focus and priority. Meanwhile, the resolution of some old questions raises new ones for consideration.
Far from imposing a new orthodoxy, a more nuanced and
complex periodization opens up many areas for fresh discussion and evaluation. The overall conclusion will inevitably

be that flexible periodization makes an enormous difference to any analysis, especially of contested events. Periodization forms the basis of any interpretation and commentary in a historical context: it should never be simply taken for granted, but should be regularly reevaluated as the foundation of historical analysis.

Nobilis and Nobiles

The most characteristic and successful republics were the ones that belonged to the *nobiles*. These elected office holders, both patricians and plebeians, had traditionally been the real Roman heroes, the men who built Rome's empire in Italy and abroad, who gave their names to the years of her history, who oversaw the public production of art and literature, and who first wrote her history in prose. It was their status as the leaders of society and as the definers of Rome's values that was threatened by the rise of the new man Marius and of the new patrician Sulla, both men with nontraditional political careers, military power bases composed of many disenfranchised soldiers, and ambitions outside the framework of republican values. The whole point of a republic had been that it was not dominated by bloody wars between rival warlords and their client armies. Civil war, therefore, signaled the basic failure of republican politics, far more than the failure of any system based on a narrower group of power sharers. In this sense, civil war was the antithesis of republican political culture, with its basis in cooperation, compromise, and the deliberate limitation of individual ambition.

The definition of the *nobiles* was, consequently, closely tied to the definition of the particular republics they had shaped. Their type of "nobility" was linked to the holding of high political office, and was identified with the wax mask (*imago*) of the office holder that his relatives could display at home and in their funeral processions after his death.[1] In order to earn the right to be represented by such a mask, a man had to

[1]Flower 1996.

hold a curule office, that is, a political office that entitled him to a special type of chair of office that he used as magistrate.[2] The curule offices were the aedileship, the praetorship, and the consulship.[3] In other words, simply becoming quaestor, or even gaining admission to the senate, did not make a man a *nobilis*. Similarly, those who had held only the office of tribune of the plebs did not qualify. Moreover, since not every praetor or consul had been an aedile, a man might gain the right designated by the mask at a different stage in his career from his peers. It was the mask and the chair that traditionally identified a man, and his family, as part of the political elite.

However, as has often been noted, in the time when Cicero was composing most of his works, the Latin word *nobilis* was often used in a much narrower sense to designate former consuls or their relatives, especially direct descendants in the male line.[4] There are, therefore, two rather different definitions of the Latin word *nobilis*. The richness and importance of Cicero's testimony has led many scholars to argue that Roman nobility was always linked closely to the consulate, despite the fact that there had been a time when the political offices had not been arranged in a strictly fixed hierarchical order.[5] In fact it was the aediles, so closely connected to the city of Rome and its everyday life, who really represented the most basic function of the mask and the chair as badges of status and rank.

Be that as it may, the periodization suggested here can help to indicate how and why the term *nobilis* came increasingly, as far as we can see, to be used in a much more specific sense during the course of the first century. Sulla's New Republic featured a much larger senate with a proportionately smaller circle of elite senators who had been elected to the highest offices. Given the many new Italians in the Sullan senate, and the increased number of praetors, it was logical that the old

[2]For curule chairs, see Bleicken 1981; Schäfer 1989; Flower 1996, 77–79.
[3]The plebeian aediles (whose office is traditionally thought of as being much older than that of the curule aediles) also seem to have been represented by *imagines*, at least in the time of Cicero, who held the office in 69.
[4]Afzelius 1938 and 1945; Brunt 1982; Flower 1996, 61–70.
[5]Brennan 2000, vol. 1; Beck 2005a.

political families should seek ways to preserve and enhance their status as Rome's real leaders. It was precisely in order to impress a parvenu from an Italian town, like Cicero, that the traditional office-holding families were closing ranks. The narrower focus on those who had previously held one of the two annual consulships (in what had been a different republic), together with the relative devaluation of the other political offices, was the product of a new type of republican politics.[6] The new and more exclusive definition of *nobilis* can be directly related to the many other displays of pedigree and family heritage that became increasingly common after Sulla, on coins, in art, in antiquarian tastes of all kinds, and on monuments throughout the city.[7]

Generals, Soldiers, and Voters

The "Late Republic" of received accounts is dominated by repetitive but complex patterns of interaction between powerful generals, their client armies, and the citizen voters at home (and eventually throughout Italy). The result has often been represented as a type of stalemate, whether ultimate blame is fixed on the ambitions of the generals, the greed of the soldiers, the weakness or obstructionism of the leading senators,

[6]Hantos 1988, 163; Wiseman 1994b, 328–29. The pressure of the new Italian senators was combined with Sulla's more competitive system of offices. Each year twenty men were elected as quaestors, but only eight as praetors. Meanwhile, there were still only four aediles and two consuls. That is, fewer than half the quaestors would be elected praetor, and then only a quarter of praetors would become consul. Very many would remain at the rank of ex-quaestor and would never be entitled to an *imago* mask after death.

[7]Beck 2005b, 690: "Was in dieser mittleren beziehungsweise 'klassischen' Republik als klassisch erscheinen mag, ist ja großenteils aus späten und idealistierenden Quellen bekannt, in denen das vergiftete Klima der Gegenwart nicht selten mit einer (vermeintlich) besseren Vergangenheit vorbildlichen Helden und ihren exemplarischen *virtutes* kontrastiert wurde" ("The traits that may appear classical in this middle or 'classical' Republic are mostly known to us from late sources that idealize. These sources often tend to contrast the poisonous climate of their own day with a [supposedly] better past of model heroes and their exemplary virtues").

or the fickle and violent behavior of the mob in the city.[8] The model proposed here offers a more varied picture of rapid change and direct political consequences resulting from novel behavior patterns. A quick review of some implications for the traditional categories of Roman citizens mentioned in my subheading seems appropriate.

The last republic of the *nobiles* was destroyed by the first clash between rival generals, which was set up in 88 by the reforming tribune Sulpicius. Traditional republican culture had been based on the principles of equality between colleagues in office and short terms of office holding, followed by an immediate return to private life. During the last decade of the second century, Marius decisively and repeatedly broke these rules in his career pattern, a career pattern that was created by outside pressures and eventually by the invasion of Italy. However, the inherited republic could not survive Marius and his ambitions, nor was he able to play the role of political savior in 100, as the crisis of city politics required. Meanwhile, it is no coincidence that Sulla, the man who would twice lead a Roman army on the city, was both an old officer and a new political rival of Marius. Marius' excessive ambitions, revealed by his bid for power in 88 at the age of nearly 70, were the result of his previous career and were all the more intolerable because of the six consulships he had already held. While Sulla expected to be ruined by Marius' ruthless tactics, he realized that a solution to his own political dilemma could be found in the insecurity, brutality, and material expectations of his own soldiers.

Marius' army reforms and the type of soldier he trained as a professional to serve the needs of Rome's imperial ambitions have been closely associated with political crisis.[9] If Sulla's army had been unwilling to march on Rome, which all but one of the officers had in fact refused to do, then the outcome

---

[8]Meier 1980, 300: "Die alte *res publica* bewies also nach Sulla noch eine erstaunliche Zähigkeit und Haltbarkeit. Das Fehlen einer Alternative machte die Lösung der Krise unsagbar schwer" ("After Sulla the old *res publica* still demonstrated amazing toughness and durability. The lack of an alternative made solving the crisis unspeakably difficult").

[9]Gabba 1976, 1–69; De Blois 1987; Keppie 1998, 57–79; Bleicken 2004, 308; and Keaveney 2007, esp. 93–102.

would obviously have been completely different, no matter how power-hungry Marius or Sulla were as individuals. The fact that the army destroyed the republic within twenty years of Marius' army reforms reveals something of the connection between Rome's republican political culture and her system of compulsory military service by small landowners, who served both as citizen soldiers and as voters. However, the issue in 88 was not the veterans' benefits, which were to loom so large for a later generation of soldiers. Marius' first veterans from the Jugurthine War seem to have received land grants, which indicates that a pattern of refusal by the senate to accommodate veterans had not yet been clearly established.[10] In the end, it appears to have been the Social War that created both Sulla the consul and Sulla's own particular kind of client army that was willing to march on Rome at his bidding, for the first time in Roman history.[11]

According to the ancient sources, Sulla persuaded the men to march on Rome by telling them that if he were to be replaced as commander they would miss the opportunity to fight Mithridates and to come home laden with the booty of the East.[12] The truth of this assertion is not immediately self-evident, but the soldiers chose to believe Sulla. It seems that they feared Marius and *his* close connection with *his* veterans, thinking that he would prefer to take his own soldiers East with him. No ancient source relays the thoughts of the soldiers themselves, but it seems that their ambitions and expectations were closely tied to immediate booty, especially from a campaign in the East, rather than to future benefits provided by the state upon discharge or to the particular political ambitions and career goals of their commander. No doubt Sulla was a charismatic figure and an excellent public speaker, but

---

[10]Cicero *Off.* 2.73; *Bell. Afr.* 56; *Vir ill.* 73; *II* 13.3 no. 7; *ILS* 1334 (Uchi Maius), 6790 (Thibari); *AE* 1951.81 (Thuburnica), with Brunt 1971, 577–81; Lintott 1994, 95; and Gabba 1994, 109–10.

[11]Keaveney (2007, 71–92) brings out the importance of mutinies during the Social War.

[12]See esp. Appian *BC* 1.57, with Caesar *BC* 1.7.5; Cicero *Phil.* 8.2.7; Sallust *Ep.* 2.6.1–4, Velleius Paterculus 2.18.6, with Dahlheim 1993, 100–104. One may note Sulla's own position as someone who had finally attained the consulship at the age of 50 as a result of the Social War.

soon Cinna, a man who would later be killed by his own soldiers, was to have similar success in leading troops on Rome.[13]
An argument can certainly be made that we should focus less
on the personal charisma of these leaders and more on the
specific political and economic conditions of the soldiers in
the aftermath of the Social War, men who increasingly did not
share the views of the voters (or senators) in Rome. It remains
unclear how many of Sulla's men in 88 were newly enfran-
chised Italians; perhaps not very many.

The republican culture of the *nobiles* foundered on the
question of extending the franchise in Italy, a political issue
that had first been raised in the 120s by problems relating to
Italian land and to the agrarian commission set up by Tiberius
Gracchus.[14] Even though Rome had managed to survive the
formidable military challenge posed by the Italians, her republic crumbled over the issue of enfranchisement. In many
ways this was the essential question: who was to be a Roman
citizen and how was that man to cast his ballot? In other
words, were there still to be different grades of civic status, or
should all Italians receive the same treatment and be equally
distributed among the existing tribal voting units? It is interesting that no new tribes seem to have been proposed. A
stark choice emerged: either the Italians were to be excluded
and marginalized, as had hitherto been the case for all but
the elites, or there would be a political revolution that would
open up the voting assemblies to all kinds of new pressures
and opinions. Clearly such assemblies would be much harder
to influence. Rome's identity as a city-state seemed to be at
stake, although the ideology of the nation-state had not yet
been developed as an alternative political option. It is telling
that the dispute of 88 was not one over ethnic identity, or
symbolic capital, or economic rights, but over the composition of the units in the voting assemblies: it was, therefore, a
truly political issue that reflected the importance of voting in
the Roman imagination.

[13]See Greenidge and Clay 1960, ad loc., for the sources.
[14]Gabba 1994 is a convenient summary of the traditional argument that the
Italians had wanted Roman citizenship all along. For a variety of new arguments, see Mouritsen 1998; Lomas 2004; and Jehne and Pfeilschifter 2006.

The "Last Generation" of the Roman Republic

The division of past history into generations has proved a powerful tool in modern historiography.[15] Whether the Romans themselves would have thought in exactly the same way is less clear. Sulla's more rigid career hierarchy presumably made age cohorts more of a factor in Roman political thinking than they had been before. Nevertheless, the concept of "the generation" remains one of the ways in which we think about both the past and the present. If, however, the last traditional republic ended in 88, as I have argued, then the 70s, 60s, and 50s come "after the Fall." In this case, the time of Caesar and Pompey belongs to a different chapter in Rome's story from the one to which it is usually assigned, and the "last generation" must also be displaced to the thirty years before the great Social War, which would be the generation after the death of Gaius Gracchus and the essential failure of the political revolution envisioned by the whole Gracchan political and economic initiative in 121. This time period corresponds to the adult experience of Sulla, who was probably about eighteen years old in 120 and fifty when he held the consulship of 88 and first marched on Rome. Marius, however, had been born in the early 150s, some twenty years before Sulla.

Unfortunately, we are very poorly informed about events in the 90s, the decade immediately before the collapse. In the new context that I have proposed, however, the last twenty years of the second century, and especially its final decade, take on a new significance in republican history. These years were dominated by a very different, much smaller, republican senate than the one that Cicero described, and by the equestrian juries established by Gaius Gracchus, rather than the senatorial juries of Sulla or shared jury courts of Aurelius Cotta. The law courts played a smaller and much more limited role than after Sulla. Many aspects of Roman life were in flux, including the system of education for Rome's political elite. According to Polybius, ten years of military service had been essential for

---

[15]The title of this subheading is from Gruen 1974, the classic discussion. Gotter 1996, 233–66, is insightful and complex. Nora 1996 discusses the generation as an historical and social category.

the aspiring politician in the third and earlier second centuries; by the 50s Cicero could describe a very different curriculum that offered choices, including a training focused mainly on oratory and the law, with very little emphasis on physical prowess or military service.[16] The story of these last years of the second century deserves close attention, or at least as close as we can give it without the speeches and letters of a Cicero or the yearly installments written from the front by a Caesar on campaign. Thinking in terms of generations can also bring out the differences between the milieu and experiences of Caesar and the world of his parents or grandparents.

Caesar Crosses the Rubicon

Caesar's crossing of the Rubicon River and his invasion of Italy in January 49 mark the earliest moment that is usually discussed as a possible date for the end of the Republic.[17] As discussed in section I, many scholars have proposed that a slightly later date is actually more meaningful and accurate in its reflection of political realities, or at least of the contemporary ways of thinking. According to the present proposal, by contrast, traditional republican civic life was already in serious political turmoil in 100, the year of Caesar's birth, and it collapsed in 88 when he was only twelve years old.[18] Accordingly, his experience of that collapse, followed by hardships suffered under a patrician dictator and as an exile, shaped his view of politics and of the limits of Sulla's New Republicanism. Caesar had never seen a fully functional republic of the traditional Roman kind in action. Like Sulla, he was in his fifties when he became dictator, but unlike his predecessor, he did not see clear possibilities for reform or for a continuation or revival of a republican system after the

---

[16]Polybius 6.19.1; Cicero *Pro Cael.* 11; Harris 1979, 11–15.
[17]See Jehne 2005.
[18]Caesar's birth has been put in either 102 or 100 (Macrobius *Sat.* 1.12.34; cf. Appian *BC* 2.106, 149; Suetonius *Jul.* 88; Plutarch *Caes.* 69). Canfora (2007, 349) opts for 100. For biographies, see Gelzer 1960; Meier 1982; and Jehne 2001.

political chaos of the 50s and the subsequent civil war. We have plenty of evidence for Caesar's own views about contemporary events, but not much indication of his opinion of the past or of his proposed solutions for the future of Rome. In this context, it may seem less surprising that he apparently questioned the whole meaning of *res publica*.[19] Similarly, the Liberators do not seem to have assessed the past accurately, nor had they laid a detailed plan for the shape of a future republic.

Another way to explain the implication of the new chronology for Caesar is to say that it makes his invasion in 49 appear more as a symptom of the republic's failure than as its cause.[20] This interpretation does not necessarily provide a justification or excuse for his behavior. It merely furnishes a different historical background to give context to the same events. Caesar still invaded and captured a defenseless Italy with his veteran legions. At no point afterward did he even try to restore republican politics, although he apparently paid lip service to it in some of his speeches and writings, at least in the early 40s.[21] He himself expected both exceptions to the remaining rules for career advancement and a freedom from accountability such as only Sulla and Pompey had enjoyed previously.

Caesar was the man who demonstrated how outdated and essentially meaningless the rhetoric of a republican continuity or restoration was by this time. The fact that he turned out to be right in the long run does not make his view morally superior or more laudable. However, given the political reality, his stance is actually more understandable, and to some extent more honest than those of many of his contemporaries: even the modified republic designed by Sulla had ended some ten years earlier, just before Caesar set out for Gaul. Caesar's personal fears must have been realized by political irregularities in Rome, especially after 56, and during the sole consulship

---

[19]Jehne (2001, 99–100) argues that the elite did not expect Caesar to restore a republic.

[20]A similar point is implied for the traditional watershed year of 133, the tribunate of Tiberius Gracchus, which was the result of societal tensions and the use of the secret ballot.

[21]Batstone and Damon (2006) offer a new analysis of the *De bello civili*.

of Pompey in 52. It is reasonable to imagine that the year 52 was just as much of a watershed for Caesar as for anyone experiencing the violence in Rome and the spectacle of the ordinary populace of Roman citizens setting fire to their senate house. In all these ways, it makes more sense to see Caesar as a man very much of his times rather than as a visionary outsider.[22]

Civil War and Literature

The golden age of Latin literature has traditionally been associated with the loss of republican politics, with the anxieties of the triumviral period, and with the establishment of the Augustan principate. Writers such as Virgil, Livy, Horace, and Propertius were shaped by their experiences of political turmoil and constitutional change. A different periodization will not bring back more literature from an earlier period for us to appreciate: almost all of the Latin literature of the third and second centuries is lost, and many authors can only be glimpsed in fragments.[23] However, if times of political change and insecurity tended to produce literary innovation and exploration, then a more realistic appreciation of the political and social turmoil of various moments in Roman history can help us to understand that new genres and leading authors had also emerged before, in patterns similar to those of the later first century. The generation that saw Caesar die and Octavian triumph was not the first to feel that a republic had been lost or that political change was worth commenting on in a variety of literary formats. A shift in the way we periodize history is bound to suggest possible effects for the way our study of Roman literature is articulated.[24]

In the context of "late republican/civil war literature," Lucilius emerges as perhaps the first who deserves to be noted

---

[22]*Contra* Meier 1982. See also Jehne 1986, for Caesar's dictatorship.
[23]Conte 1994; Suerbaum 2002; Goldberg 2005.
[24]Conte 1994 provides the following examples: "Oratory and Historiography in the Archaic Period," "Literature and Culture in the Period of the Conquests," "The Age of Caesar (78–44 BC)."

and appreciated.[25] He is credited with the invention of the developed genre of satire, a way of writing criticisms of society in both prose and verse that the Romans claimed as their own creation without any Greek inspiration. Lucilius seems to have died in 102, a time that Cicero would look back on as the peak of Hellenism in Rome. The writing of satire, apparently originally known as *sermones* (conversations) or *schedia* (improvisations), would be taken up by Horace in the unsettled times of the 30s, but it had been first developed by Lucilius in the 130s and 120s.

The later second century was rich in literary production, especially in historiography. The suspension of the priestly chronicles, whose annual installments had been publicly displayed for so many generations, surely changed traditional Roman conceptions of the past, whether or not the same time (around 120) saw the publication of the *Annales Maximi* in eighty books.[26] The 120s saw Coelius Antipater write the first historical monograph in Latin, a work focused on a single episode (the Second Punic War) that was written in an elaborate and adorned style.[27] Calpurnius Piso, the consul of 133, was perhaps the first to write prose history in a fully developed "annalistic" form, which is to say year by year.[28] Meanwhile, Sempronius Asellio, a veteran of the Numantine war, wrote contemporary history in Latin under the influence of Polybius.[29] The writing of history in several styles had, therefore, been developing in the two decades immediately before political autobiography first emerged.

Oratory also flourished at this time, and speeches were certainly circulated in written form. The loss of the speeches given by the Gracchi brothers and their opponents is particularly

---

[25]Astin (1967, 294–306) reconstructs the historical context. For more recent discussions, see Scholz 2000 and Manuwald 2001. For Lucilius' later influence, see Freudenburg 2001.

[26]Frier (1999) disputes this publication date.

[27]Chassignet 2003a, xli–xliv, 50–70; Suerbaum 2002, no. 167; Walter 2003b, 141–43; Beck and Walter 2004, 35–83.

[28]Forsythe 1994; Beck and Walter 2001, 282–329.

[29]Chassignet 2003a, liv–lvii, 84–89; Suerbaum 2002, no. 168; Beck and Walter 2004, 84–99.

regrettable. Gaius Gracchus has been considered the most influential and accomplished Latin orator between Cato the Censor and Cicero. The fragments of the orators are so meager that their context and tone is often impossible to recover.[30] Yet we should have no doubt that rhetoric evolved, especially in the speeches given before the people. It can be no coincidence that Sulla tried to put an end to the *contiones* that had become such a feature of public discourse before his dictatorship and that would be so important again for politics in the 60s and 50s.[31] The attempt by the censors of 92 to close Plotius Gallus' rhetorical school suggests a struggle over oratory and education that mirrored the political issues surrounding Rome's relationship with her Italian allies.[32] The important and original treatise entitled *Rhetorica ad Herennium*, whether or not it should be associated with Gallus' school, is one of the very few extant pieces of literature from the 80s, and it suggests an innovation in both genre and style, an attempt at a type of political and rhetorical theory before Cicero would (re)invent that genre in the 50s and 40s.

Meanwhile, republican drama in the form of newly written tragedy seems to have come to an end with the republic of the *nobiles*, and some would assign Lucilius a role in its demise. But the Atellan farce and mime still flourished, and theater was obviously a very popular form of entertainment to be seen on many days of the year in Rome.[33] Other generic innovations came in the areas of philology, with the work of L. Aelius Stilo Praeconinus, and of antiquarianism, as represented by the research of Junius Gracchanus and C. Sempronius Tuditanus.[34] The generation of Cicero and Varro relied heavily on such teachers and mentors for oratory and many other forms of literary production.

---

[30] *ORF*[4].

[31] Cicero *Pro Cluent*. 40.110.

[32] Cicero *De Or*. 3.24.93; Suetonius *De Gramm. et Rhet.* 25.2 (with Kaster 1995, ad loc.); Tacitus *Dial.* 35. Gabba (1994, 109) connects this Latin school of rhetoric with Italians who appeared before courts in Rome.

[33] Fantham 1988–89.

[34] See Conte 1994, 124, 572–73; Sehlmeyer 2003, for discussion of the emergence of antiquarian literature in a late republican context.

Perhaps most striking and significant of all, however, was the emergence of political autobiography and memoirs, a literary genre that can be directly linked to the divisive political climate and to the related need to publish one's own account beyond what was contained in the more customary speeches and political pamphlets.[35] It was no longer enough for leading politicians to wait for the eulogy that they would expect to receive from the *rostra* on the day of their funeral. There is every reason to believe that these autobiographical writings were a vital part of political debate at the time, as it developed immediately before and after Sulla's dictatorship, the most important watershed in the age. The first publication of such political memoirs seems to come at the very end of the second century, a time of flourishing Hellenism but also of significant political unrest in Rome. This development was foreshadowed by Gaius Gracchus' biography of his brother Tiberius, which seems to have been an influential text in shaping positive traditions about the Gracchi and the watershed year of 133.[36]

Of the known authors of such texts, the first one to publish seems to have been Q. Lutatius Catulus, the well-known orator and author of epigrams in the Greek style, who wrote a single volume account of his consulship in 102, apparently immediately after his term of office and the subsequent Roman victory at Vercellae in 101.[37] This first attempt at self-justification was written in epistolary form and was addressed to his friend A. Furius. It makes most sense as part of Catulus' reaction to the enormous prestige of his consular colleague Marius, with whom he also competed in building a temple on the Campus

[35]See Chassignet 2003c for an overview. Her new edition that includes the autobiographical fragments (2004) puts them in the traditional order but treats them as a group, on the assumption that there would have been many more such works that do not survive. See also Suerbaum 2002, 437–56; Walter 2003a.

[36]The only two fragments are Cicero *Div.* 1.36 and Plutarch *TGracch.* 8.9. See also Badian 1966, 13.

[37]*RE* 7 Münzer, with Meier 1980, 268–69; Suerbaum 2002, no. 172. See Chassignet 2004, xcvii–xcix, 170–71 (fragments are all from Plut. *Mar.* 25–27). For Catulus' philhellenism, see McDonnell 2006, 281–84. Catulus also wrote Hellenistic-style epigrams.

Martius (to Fortuna Huiusce Diei) and a victory monument in the form of a portico on the Palatine.[38] It had been Marius who had gained the main credit for the defeat of the northern invaders, although he had celebrated a triumph together with Catulus. Meanwhile, the emergence of a personal, often critical, voice in autobiography should also be related to the precedent set by Lucilius, who died while Catulus was consul.

Consequently, we can see that it was precisely the increasingly bitter political competition, best symbolized by Marius' repeated election to the consulate in successive years, that caused both a sharpening in traditional practices of self-advertisement and the development of new forms of recording one's achievements. Catulus was also the man who first accorded an aristocratic-style funeral (with ancestor masks, procession, and public eulogy) to a woman, his mother Popilia.[39] During these years, Catulus was the commanding officer of Sulla, who seems to have learned useful lessons from his example. Sulla's memoirs in twenty-two books put their stamp on the whole age and were enormously influential in representing the dictator's point of view, both of his own actions and of all the events that led up to his seizure of power.[40] Sulla's position in Roman society was symbolized and enacted in his written account, just as much as in his monuments, portraits, coins, and the public funeral he had specifically requested. Literary expression was a tool in political conflict, as well as being itself a symptom of societal change.

Religion in an Age of Anxiety

The succinct character and political focus of this essay has not afforded an opportunity to explore a variety of perspectives on the Roman experience, of which religion is one of the most vital and informative. A number of patterns in religious behavior

---

[38]Fortuna Huiusce Diei (Fortune of This Day, presumed to be Largo Argentina temple B): Hinard 1987; Gros in *LTUR* 1995; McDonnell 2006, 269–70, 280–85. Portico on the Palatine: Berg 1997, 127; Papi in *LTUR* 1999.

[39]Cicero *De Or.* 2.11.44, with Flower 1996, 122.

[40]See the fragments (mostly from Plutarch's biography) in Chassignet 2004. Sulla also wrote Atellan farce and Greek epigrams.

support and shed light upon the new periodization being proposed here. The religious fears and anxieties of the later second century provide a reliable indication of the perceived loss of traditional values and societal norms that corresponded to the many political and social changes taking place during these years.[41] The death of Tiberius Gracchus can be clearly seen in terms of sacrilege and religious pollution, as the sacrosanct tribune was subjected to a *consecratio* (a deadly type of religious curse) by the *pontifex maximus*.[42] Opimius' decision to purify the city through the ritual of a *lustrum* and to build a temple of Concord next to the Forum by the senate house sought a religious solution to political dissension and violence in 121. The Romans' fear of the threat posed by the Cimbri and Teutoni is indicated both by their decision to bury alive a pair of Gauls and Greeks in the Forum Boarium in 114 and by their suspicions about the chastity of the Vestal Virgins in that same year and the next.[43] Roman interest in voting and its practices is reflected in the law of 104 that instituted a form of election with a secret ballot for the office of *pontifex maximus*.

Amid all these religious events, two distinct themes stand out as particularly significant: the developing cult of personality accorded to exceptional leaders, and the devastating destruction of the temple of Jupiter Optimus Maximus on the Capitol in 83. While much attention has naturally been paid to Divus Julius, the first of the Caesars to rule Rome, there is ample evidence that divine honors accorded to Roman politicians, whether in their lifetimes or after death, were both a factor in and a symptom of the political changes that Rome experienced from the time of the Gracchi onwards.[44] Plutarch clearly attests to spontaneous divine cult offered to the memory of the Gracchi (probably around 120), both at the sites where they had died and throughout the city.[45] In this way ordinary people in Rome expressed their feelings about the Gracchi and the roles that they had played in Roman life.

[41]Rawson 1974; Bergemann 1992. For the Social War, see Schultz 2006.
[42]Linderski 2002.
[43]Greenidge and Clay 1960, ad loc.
[44]In general, see Gradel 2002, 27–53.
[45]Plutarch *CGracch.* 18.3, with Simón and Pina Polo 2000; Flower 2006, 79–81.

Twenty years later, Marius received libations at the evening meal on the part of citizens after his victory at Vercellae.[46] In other words, he was hailed as a savior of Rome, whose deeds far surpassed the ordinary achievements of Roman republican generals. Similarly, his kinsman Marius Gratidianus, who took credit for a stabilization of Roman coinage, received statues and ritual offerings of wine, incense, and candles at the neighborhood shrines throughout the city.[47] There is good reason to believe that Sulla also received honors at these same local shrines, and his statues would have stayed in place longer than those of Marius Gratidianus, just as his statue at the *rostra* was still to be seen at the time of Caesar's dictatorship.[48]

Most telling of all, in the present context, is the unprecedented funeral at public expense that was granted Sulla in 78.[49] This honor may be connected with his role as the lawgiver in the New Republic he had founded. His veterans staged a huge show of strength, emphasizing the victory themes that were associated with his memory. There was, for the first time, a suspension of public business (*iustitium*) to mark his death, and all the women of Rome were called upon to wear mourning dress for a year, as if their own fathers had died. The women also made an image of Sulla composed of precious spices.[50] The exalted position of Sulla at the time of his death, and the types of recognition he received, provide clear evidence for the fact that any type of old republic, based on a group of *nobiles* who were essentially peers, was now gone and that a new age had been inaugurated.

In a similar way, continuity with a long republican history was decisively broken by the huge and unexplained fire that destroyed the Temple of Jupiter Optimus Maximus on the Capitol on July 6, 83, after Sulla had invaded Italy but well before he reached Rome.[51] This temple, whose original construction was attributed to the regal period, had come to be a symbol of Rome's republican politics and her position in the world. It

[46]Flower 2006, 88–89.
[47]Flower 2006, 94–95.
[48]*CIL* 6.1297 = *ILS* 872 = *ILLRP* 352.
[49]Wesch-Klein 1993, 11, 92; Flower 1996, 123–24; Thein 2002, 313–35.
[50]Plutarch *Sulla* 38.
[51]Flower 2008 provides a detailed discussion.

was the oldest monumental temple in Rome and had stood un-
damaged as a sign of Rome's destiny and in defiance of attack-
ers, such as the Gauls in the fourth century or Hannibal in the
third. Its sudden and complete destruction was surely a fearful
sign for the inhabitants of the city, as they waited for Sulla to
reach Rome and exact the vengeance he had promised his political enemies. Consequently, it was the conscious mark of a
new beginning when Sulla chose the ruins of the great temple
as the setting for his official assumption of the name Felix, the
sign of his own personal destiny as the founder who intended
to establish a new and better Republic in Rome.[52]

[52]Plutarch *Sulla* 24, 34; cf. Velleius Paterculus 2.27; Frontinus *Strat.* 1.11.11;
Appian *BC* 1.97; *Vir. ill.* 75.

⟢ APPENDIX ⟣

I: An Assortment of Timelines

A. Traditional Timeline

This traditional timeline has long, loosely defined periods and is more descriptive of our surviving evidence than of events in history. It lacks precision and tends to be teleological. The triumvirate of the 40s BC is included in the republican era. This scheme uses a dynastic pattern for the imperial period.

B. Roman Republics Timeline

This new time map, which reflects the arguments made in this book, is more precise but consequently also more complex. It delineates multiple republics and includes transition periods between them. It is focused sharply on internal politics, to the exclusion of other possible criteria of definition. As a result, it is consistent but specific.

C. Alternative (and Simpler) Traditional Timeline

This alternative timeline takes a longer view of Roman history beyond the Republic. It is also simple. According to this scheme Julius Caesar and Vespasian are the two most significant founder figures, as big breaks are envisaged in 49 BC and AD 69/70. The Caesarian and Julio-Claudian period is described as distinct from the High Empire, which was a political system no longer based on the influence of republican elites and their family groups. The extended patrician family group of the Julio-Claudians kills off the republican system of government, which emerged from the Conflict of the Orders some three hundred years earlier.

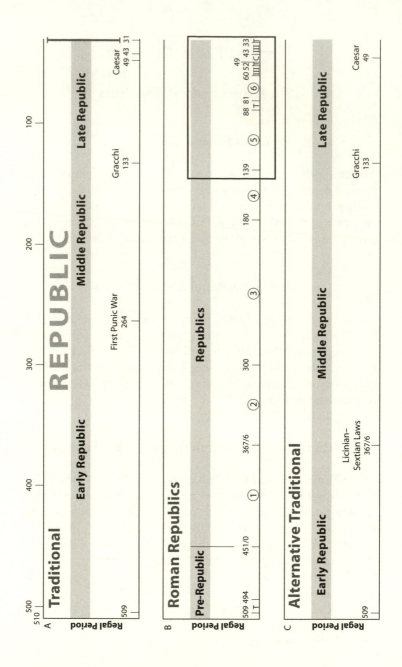

A Traditional

REPUBLIC

510	500	400	300	200	100	

Regal Period | 509 | Early Republic | Middle Republic | Late Republic

First Punic War 264 | Gracchi 133 | Caesar 49 43 31

B Roman Republics

Pre-Republic | Republics

Regal Period | 509 494 | 451/0 | 367/6 | 300 | 180 | 139 | 88 81 | 49 | 60 52 | 43 33 | IIIIIIICIIIIII

① ② ③ ④ ⑤ ⑥

C Alternative Traditional

Regal Period | 509 | Early Republic | Middle Republic | Late Republic

Licinian–Sextian Laws 367/6 | Gracchi 133 | Caesar 49

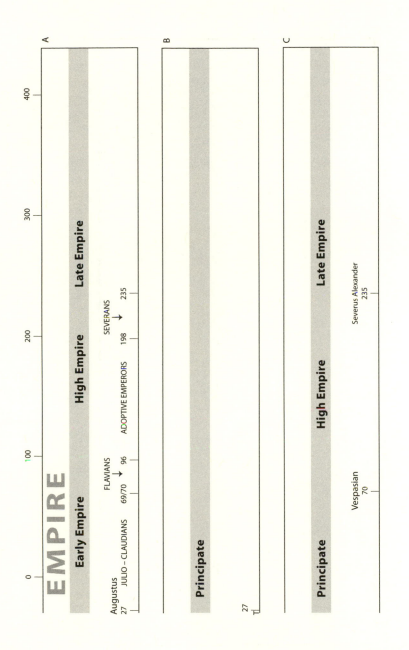

EMPIRE

| Early Empire | High Empire | Late Empire |

| Augustus | FLAVIANS | ADOPTIVE EMPERORS | SEVERANS |
| 27 JULIO – CLAUDIANS | 69/70 → 96 | 198 → 235 |

0   100   200   300   400

A

| Principate |

27

B

| Principate | High Empire | Late Empire |

Vespasian
70

Severus Alexander
235

C

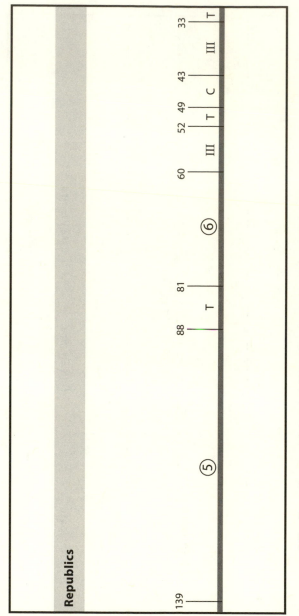

Assortment of Timelines. T = transition period, III = triumvirate, C = Caesar's dictatorship.

II: The Hellenistic Age and Republican Time

Republican times at Rome overlapped to a significant degree with the period of Greek history known as the Hellenistic Age (323–31 BC).[1] This synchronism is significant in a number of ways, most obviously perhaps because the Roman conquest of Egypt after the battle of Actium in 31 BC is generally agreed to have marked the end of the Hellenistic Age, the period defined by modern historians of the Greek world as the era from the death of Alexander the Great in 323 BC, when his vast conquests were divided among his generals, who became the founders of hereditary monarchies in various kingdoms, to the death of Cleopatra VII of Egypt, the last monarch in the several lines of successors to Alexander. The Hellenistic Age is interesting as a time period not least because most historians have agreed on its parameters. The term "Hellenistic" has also been borrowed to describe time periods in other cultures, such as that of the Etruscans.[2]

Meanwhile, the Romans, and in particular their supreme leader, who would soon call himself by the new name of Augustus, can be represented as the heirs to Greek political life in the eastern Mediterranean, even as they also appear to replace Greek time with their own new age. Many modern historians, therefore, place the end of a single long era called "the Republic" at essentially the same time as the end of the Hellenistic Age.

In the generation of Appius Claudius Caecus (born around 340 BC), the first Roman whose life and career we can reconstruct in any detail, a new type of Greek culture was spread throughout the eastern Mediterranean and beyond, first by Alexander and then by his companions and heirs. The developed forms of republicanism at Rome, then, emerged at about the same time as the Hellenistic monarchies, even as both types of political system (whether led by elected *nobiles* or by

---

[1]For a convenient discussion of the Hellenistic Age as an epoch, see Green 2007, xv–xx. The term was invented by Johann Gustav Droysen in 1878.
[2]See, e.g., Steingräber 1985, 58–68, for a Hellenistic period in Etruscan wall painting.

hereditary Hellenistic kings) behaved much more aggressively in war and diplomacy than the earlier city-states had, both in Italy and in the Greek-speaking eastern Mediterranean. In other words, both Roman *nobiles* and Hellenistic kings acquired empires close to home and abroad.

Rome's complex interactions with the dynamic political and intellectual culture of this "Hellenistic world" have tended to support the traditional chronological framework of a single republic. A distinct new beginning in the late fourth century played a decisive role in both political spheres. In fact, the Romans had learned much from various groups of Greeks well before this time, both directly and indirectly from others such as the Etruscans. But it is worth noting that it was the radical hellenization of many areas of Roman life toward the end of the second century, which accompanied and was a by-product of the Romans' striking military successes against Hellenistic kings, that helped to shape the reform movements in republican political culture, whether violent or nonviolent. Like the Romans themselves, we should keep an eye on Greek time and Hellenistic politics in our study of Roman republicanism.

III: Temple Time

During their long history the Romans put a violent end to many eras that belonged to others, of which one of the most famous must surely be that named for the "Second Temple" in Jerusalem (in fact, this temple was actually the third building on the same hallowed site and had been built by king Herod the Great quite recently). The Roman commander Titus' stark decision to raze the famous Jewish Temple in AD 70 (August 28), after he had carefully removed all its treasures for transport to Rome, has had a lasting impact on the Jews, whose relationship with the Romans was forever changed by this aggressive erasure.[3] The rhetoric of this gesture, which has had effects far beyond what Titus could have planned or imagined at the time, serves to remind us of the importance in antiquity of eras attached to temples. We may tend to consider such eras "religious," but they were often used to label times in a much more general sense.

In Rome also, temple time was ancient and integral to city life. The urban landscape was full of temples whose annual birthdays and life spans recalled Roman conquests and the self-representation of generals, who wanted to be remembered both for their victories and for their piety. The most conspicuous and well-known temple of all was that dedicated to the Capitoline triad, Jupiter Optimus Maximus, Juno, and Minerva, a shrine that became closely identified first with the republican form of government and eventually with Rome's overseas empire. Its foundation date was ascribed to the first year of republican government (traditionally 509 BC), and its destruction by an (apparently) accidental fire in 83 BC marked the end of an era in many ways.

Similarly, a second devastating fire in AD 69 that destroyed the second Capitoline temple built by Q. Lutatius Catulus, part of the extensive damage to the city caused by the civil war between the supporters of Vitellius and those of the Flavians, marked the violent end of the Julio-Claudian dynasty and the rise of new emperors, who did not come from the

---

[3]For the destruction of the Jewish Temple, see Barnes 2005; Rives 2005.

republican nobility. The new temple, built carefully according to republican precedents by Vespasian, burned soon after in AD 80. Vespasian's younger son Domitian then erected a quite different kind of temple, all clothed in white marble from the Greek island of Paros, which dominated the Capitoline hill throughout the High Empire and well into Late Antiquity.

Just as was the case for other great cities in antiquity, Rome's principal temples reflected and shaped the times and major changes in the community's story. To build or restore such a temple was a great ambition, narrowly missed by Tarquinius Superbus and Sulla, and boasted of by Catulus and Augustus. The history of the city could, therefore, be conceived of and written in terms of temple time, a time that was familiar to the many citizens who never read history in a literary form.

Titus was surely aware of this way of thinking, and even acknowledged it openly in his brazen act of destroying the great Jerusalem temple, a violent choice that can presumably be related to recollections of the destruction of the first Jewish Temple by king Nebuchadnezzar and his army of Neo-Babylonians in 586 BC. Yet one should not overlook the significance of the complete destruction of the Capitoline temple in Rome only a few months before (late in AD 69), during the civil war that had brought Vespasian and his sons to power. An era had ended in Rome, and Titus chose to carry out a similar destruction in Jerusalem. Henceforth, the annual tax that Jews had paid to the Jerusalem Temple was to be contributed to Jupiter on the Capitol, and these proceeds helped to rebuild and maintain the Romans' principal temple.

BIBLIOGRAPHY

Abbreviations of journal titles follow the conventions adopted by *L'Année philologique*.

Afzelius, A. 1938. "Zur Definition der römischen Nobilität in der Zeit Ciceros." *C&M* 2: 40–94.

———. 1945. "Zur Definition der römischen Nobilität vor der Zeit Ciceros." *C&M* 7: 150–200.

Alexander, M. C. 1990. *Trials in the Late Roman Republic 149–50 BC*. Toronto.

———. 2006. "Law in the Roman Republic." In Rosenstein and Morstein-Marx 2006, 236–55.

Astin, A. E. 1967. *Scipio Aemilianus*. Oxford.

Badian, E. 1966. "The Early Historians." In *Latin Historians*, ed. T. A. Dorey, 1–38. London.

———. 1970. *Lucius Sulla: The Deadly Reformer*. Todd Memorial Lecture 7. Sydney.

———. 1972. "Tiberius Gracchus and the Beginning of the Roman Revolution." *ANRW* I.1: 668–731.

———. 1983. *Publicans and Sinners: Private Enterprise in the Service of the Roman Republic*. Ithaca, NY.

———. 1984. "The Death of Saturninus: Studies in Chronology and Prosopography," *Chiron* 14: 101–47.

———. 1990. "The Consuls, 179–49 BC." *Chiron* 20: 371–413.

———. 1996. "*Tribuni Plebis* and *Res Publica*." In *Imperium sine fine: T. Robert S. Broughton and the Roman Republic*, ed. J. Linderski, 187–213. Stuttgart.

Baltrusch, E. 2004. *Caesar und Pompeius*. Darmstadt.

Bargagli, B., and C. Grosso, 1997. *I Fasti Ostienses: documento della storia di Ostia*. Rome.

Barnes, T. D. 2005. "The Sack of the Temple in Josephus and Tacitus." In *Flavius Josephus and Flavian Rome*, ed. J. Edmondson, S. Mason, and J. Rives, 129–44. Oxford.

Batstone, W. W., and C. Damon. 2006. *Caesar's Civil War*. Oxford.

Bauman, R. 1967. *The Crimen Maiestatis in the Roman Republic and the Augustan Principate*. Johannesburg.

Beard, M. 2007. *The Roman Triumph*. Cambridge, MA.

Beard, M., and M. Crawford. 1999. *Rome in the Late Republic: Problems and Interpretations*[2]. London.

Beck, H. 2003. "'Den Ruhm nicht teilen wollen': Fabius Pictor und die Anfänge des römischen Nobilitätsdiskurses." In Eigler et al. 2003, 73–92.

———. 2005a. *Karriere und Hierarchie: Die römische Aristokratie und die Anfänge des cursus honorum in der Mittleren Republik*. Berlin.

———. 2005b. Review of Bleckmann 2002. *Gnomon* 77: 689–93.

———. 2007. "The Early Roman Tradition." In *A Companion to Greek and Roman Historiography*, ed. J. Marincola, 259–65. Oxford.

Beck, H., and U. Walter. 2001. *Die frühen römischen Historiker* 1. Darmstadt.

———. 2004. *Die frühen römischen Historiker* 2. Darmstadt.

Behr, H. 1993. *Die Selbstdarstellung Sullas: Ein aristokratischer Politiker zwischen persönlichem Führungsanspruch und Standessolidarität*. Frankfurt.

Berg, B. 1997. "Cicero's Palatine House and Clodius' Shrine of Liberty: Alternative Emblems of the Republic in Cicero's *de domo sua*." In *Studies in Latin Literature and Roman History* 8, ed. C. Deroux, 122–43. Brussels.

Bergemann, C. 1992. *Politik und Religion im spätrepublikanischen Rom*. Stuttgart.

Blackburn, B., and L. Holford-Strevens. 1999. *The Oxford Companion to the Year: An Exploration of Calendar Customs and Time-Reckoning*. Oxford.

Bleckmann, B. 2002. *Die römische Nobilität im Ersten Punischen Kreig: Untersuchungen zur aristokratischen Konkurrenz in der Republik*. Berlin.

Bleicken, J. 1968. *Das Volkstribunat der klassischen Republik: Studien zu seiner Entwicklung zwischen 287 und 133 v. Chr.*[2] Munich.

———. 1981. "Das Volkstribunat: Versuch einer Analyse seiner politischen Funktion in republikanischer Zeit." *Chiron* 11: 87–108.

———. 1995a. *Gedanken zum Untergang der römischen Republik*. Stuttgart.

———. 1995b. *Die Verfassung der römischen Republik: Grundlage und Entwicklung*. Paderborn.

———. 1999. *Cicero und die Ritter*. Göttingen.

————. 2004. *Geschichte der römischen Republik*[6]. Munich.

Bonnefond-Coudry, M. 1989. *Le Sénat de la république romaine de la guerre d'Hannibal à Auguste: pratiques délibératives et prise de décision*. Rome.

Bradley, K. R. 1994. *Slavery and Society at Rome*. Cambridge.

Braun, M., A. Haltenhoff, and F.-H. Mutschler, eds. 2000. *Moribus antiquis stat res romana: Römische Werte und römische Literatur im 3. und 2. Jahrhundert v. Chr.* Munich.

Brennan, T. C. 1992. "Sulla's Career in the Nineties: Some Reconsiderations." *Chiron* 22: 102–58.

————. 1995. "Notes on Praetors in Spain in the Mid-Second Century BC." *Emerita* 63: 47–76.

————. 2000. *The Praetorship in the Roman Republic*. 2 vols. Oxford.

————. 2004. "Power and Process under the Republican 'Constitution.'" In Flower 2004, 31–65.

Brind'amour, P. 1983. *Le calendrier romain*. Ottawa.

Bringmann, K. 2003. *Krise und Ende der römischen Republik 133–42 v. Chr.* Berlin.

————. 2007. *A History of the Roman Republic*. Cambridge.

Brunt, P. A. 1971. *Italian Manpower*. Oxford.

————. 1982. "*Nobilitas* and *novitas*." *JRS* 72: 1–17.

————. 1988. *The Fall of the Roman Republic and Related Essays*. Oxford.

Burckhardt, L. A. 1988. *Politische Strategien der Optimaten in der späten römischen Republik*. Stuttgart.

————. 2000. "M. Licinius Crassus—Geld allein macht nicht glücklich." In Hölkeskamp and Stein-Hölkeskamp 2000, 219–29.

Burnett, A. M. 1977. "The Authority to Coin in the Late Republic and Early Empire." *NC*[7] 17: 37–63.

Canfora, L. 2007. *Julius Caesar: The People's Dictator*. Edinburgh.

Carandini, A. 1997. *Nascita di Roma: dei, Lari, eroi e uomini all'alba di una civiltà*. Turin.

————. 2006. *Remo e Romolo: dai rioni dei Quiriti alla città dei Romani: 775/750–700/675 a. C. circa*. Turin.

Carandini, A., with D. Bruno. 2008. *La Casa di Augusto: dai "Lupercalia" al Natale*. Bari.

Chassignet, M. 2002. *Caton, "Les origines" (fragments)*[2]. Paris.

————. 2003a. *L'annalistique romaine* 1[2]. Paris.

————. 2003b. *L'annalistique romaine* 2. Paris

————. 2003c. "La naissance de l'autobiographie à Rome: *laus sui* ou *apologia de vita sua?*" *REL* 81: 65–78.

————. 2004. *L'annalistique romaine* 3. Paris.

Christ, K. 1994. *Caesar: Annäherungen an einen Diktator.* Munich.

————. 2000. *Krise und Untergang der römischen Republik*[4]. Darmstadt.

————. 2002. *Sulla: Eine römische Karriere.* Munich.

————. 2004. *Pompeius: Der Feldherr Roms: Eine Biographie.* Munich.

Classen, A. J. 1963. "Gottmenschentum in der römischen Republik." *Gymnasium* 70: 313–38.

Connolly, J. 2007. *The State of Speech: Rhetoric and Political Thought in Ancient Rome.* Princeton, NJ.

Conte, G. B. 1994. *Latin Literature: A History.* Baltimore.

Corfield, P. J. 2007. *Time and the Shape of History.* New Haven, CT.

Cornell, T. J. 1995. *The Beginnings of Rome: Italy and Rome from the Bronze Age to the Punic Wars.* London.

————. 2005. "The Value of the Literary Tradition Concerning Archaic Rome." In *Social Struggles in Archaic Rome: New Perspectives on the Conflict of the Orders*[2], ed. K. A. Raaflaub, 47–74. Oxford.

Crawford, M. 1974. *Roman Republican Coinage.* 2 vols. Cambridge.

————. 1996. *Roman Statutes.* London.

Dahlheim, W. 1993. "Der Staatsstreich des Konsuls Sulla und die römische Italienpolitik der achtziger Jahre." In *Colloquium aus Anlaß des 80. Geburtstages von Alfred Heuß*, ed. J. Bleicken, 97–116. Kallmünz.

David, J.-M. 1996. *The Roman Conquest of Italy.* Oxford.

Davis, K. 2008. *Periodization and Sovereignty: How Ideas about Feudalism and Secularization Govern the Politics of Time.* Philadelphia.

De Blois, L. 1987. *The Roman Army and Politics in the First Century BC.* Amsterdam.

————. 2000. "Army and Society in the Late Roman Republic: Professionalism and the Role of the Military Middle Cadre." In *Kaiser, Herr, und Gesellschaft in der römischen Kaiserzeit*, ed. G. Alföldy et al., 11–31. Stuttgart.

De Libero, L. 1992. *Obstruktion: Politische Praktiken im Senat und in der Volksversammlung der ausgehenden römischen Republik (70–49 v. Chr.).* Stuttgart.

De Ligt, L. 2006. "The Economy: Agricultural Change during the Second Century." In Rosenstein and Morstein-Marx 2006, 590–605.

De Souza, P. 2000. *Piracy in the Greco-Roman World*. Cambridge.

Dillery, J. 2002. "Q. Fabius Pictor and Greco-Roman Historiography at Rome." In *Vertis in Unum: Studies in Honor of Edward Courtney*, ed. J. F. Miller, C. Damon, K. S. Myers, 1–23. Munich.

Doblhofer, G. 1990. *Die Popularen der Jahre 11 bis 99 v. Chr.* Vienna.

Dumont, J. C. 1987. *Servus: Rome et l'esclavage sous la République*. Rome.

Eck, W. 2007. *The Age of Augustus²*. Oxford.

Eckstein, A. M. 1987. *Senate and General: Individual Decision Making and Foreign Relations 264–194 BC*. Berkeley, CA.

———. 2006. *Mediterranean Anarchy, Interstate War, and the Rise of Rome*. Berkeley, CA.

Eigler, U., U. Gotter, N. Luraghi, and U. Walter, eds. 2003. *Formen römischer Geschichtsschreibung von den Anfängen bis Livius: Gattungen—Autoren—Kontexte*. Darmstadt.

Evans, R. J. 1994. *Gaius Marius: A Political Biography*. Pretoria.

Fantham, E. 1988–89. "Mime: The Missing Link in Roman Literary History." *CW* 82: 153–63.

Feeney, D. 2007. *Caesar's Calendar: Ancient Time and the Beginnings of History*. Berkeley, CA.

Fehrle, R. 1983. *Cato Uticensis*. Darmstadt.

Flaig, E. 1995. "Die *Pompa funebris*: Adlige Konkurrenz und annalistische Erinnerung in der römischen Republik." In *Memoria als Kultur*, ed. O. G. Oexle, 115–48. Göttingen.

Flower, H. I. 1996. *Ancestor Masks and Aristocratic Power in Roman Culture*. Oxford.

———, ed. 2004. *The Cambridge Companion to the Roman Republic*. Cambridge.

———. 2006. *The Art of Forgetting: Disgrace and Oblivion in Roman Political Culture*. Chapel Hill, NC.

———. 2008. "Remembering and Forgetting Temple Destruction: The Destruction of the Temple of Jupiter Optimus Maximus in 83 BC." In *Antiquity in Antiquity: Jewish and Christian Pasts in the Greco-Roman World*, ed. G. Gardner and K. L. Osterloh, 74–92. Tübingen.

Flower, H. I. Forthcoming. "Alternatives to Written History." In *The Cambridge Companion to Roman Historians*, ed. A Feldherr. Cambridge.

Forsythe, G. 1994. *The Historian L. Calpurnius Piso Frugi and the Roman Annalistic Tradition*. Lanham, MD.

———. 2005. *A Critical History of Early Rome: From Prehistory to the First Punic War*. Berkeley, CA.

Fraschetti, A. 1994. *Rome et le prince*. Paris.

Freudenburg, K. 2001. *Satires in Rome: Threatening Poses from Lucilius to Juvenal*. Cambridge.

Frier, B. 1971. "Sulla's Propaganda and the Collapse of the Cinnan Republic." *AJP* 92: 585-604.

———. 1999. *Libri Annales Pontificum Maximorum: The Origins of the Annalistic Tradition*[2]. Ann Arbor, MI.

Gabba, E. 1976. *Republican Rome: The Army and the Allies*. Trans. C. J. Cuff. Oxford.

———. 1994. "Rome and Italy: The Social War." In *The Cambridge Ancient History*[2] 9, 104–28. Cambridge.

Galinsky, K. 1996. *Augustan Culture: An Interpretative Introduction*. Princeton, NJ.

Galsterer, H. 2000. "Gaius Iulius Caesar—der Aristokrat als Alleinherrscher." In Hölkeskamp and Stein-Hölkeskamp 2000, 307–26.

Gargola, D. 1995. *Lands, Laws, and Gods: Magistrates and Ceremony in the Regulation of Public Lands in Republican Rome*. Chapel Hill, NC.

Geary, P. J. 1994. *Phantoms of Remembrance: Memory and Oblivion at the End of the First Millennium*. Princeton, NJ.

Gehrke, H.-J. 1999. *Kleine Geschichte der Antike*. Munich.

———. 2004. "Die 'klassische' Antike als Kulturepoche—soziokulturelle Milieus und Deutungsmuster in der griechisch-römischen Welt." In *Handbuch der Kulturwissenschaften 1: Grundlagen und Schlüsselbegriffe*, ed. F. Jaeger and B. Liebsch, 471–89. Stuttgart.

Gelzer, M. 1960. *Caesar, der Politiker und Staatsmann*[6]. Wiesbaden.

———. 1969. *Cicero: Ein biographischer Versuch*. Wiesbaden.

———. 1984. *Pompeius*[2]. Munich.

Giardina, A., ed. 2000. *Roma antica*. Rome.

———. 1999. "Esplosione di tardoantico." In *Prospettive sul tardoantico*, ed. G. Mazzoli and F. Gasti, 9–30. Como.

———. 2008. "*Metis* in Rome: A Greek Dream of Sulla." In *East and West: Papers in Ancient History Presented to Glen W. Bower-*

sock (Loeb Classical Monographs 14), ed. T. Corey Brennan and H. I. Flower, 61–83. Cambridge, MA.

Giovannini, A. 1995. "Catilina et le problème des dettes." In *Leaders and Masses in the Roman World: Studies in Honor of Zvi Yavetz*, ed. I. Malkin and Z. W. Rubinsohn, 15–32. Leiden.

Goetz, H.-W., and K. W. Welwei, eds. 1995. *Altes Germanien 1*. Darmstadt.

Goldberg, S. 1995. *Epic in Republican Rome*. Oxford.

———. 2005. *Constructing Literature in the Roman Republic*. Cambridge.

Goldmann, F. 2002. "*Nobilitas* als Status und Gruppe—Überlegungen zum Nobilitätsbegriff der römischen Republik." In *Res publica reperta: Zur Verfassung und Gesellschaft der römischen Republik und des frühen Prinzipats. Festschrift für Jochen Bleicken zum 75. Geburtstag*, ed. J. Spielvogel, 45–66. Stuttgart.

Gotter, U. 1996. *Der Diktator ist Tot! Politik in Rom zwischen den Iden des März und der Begründung des Zweiten Triumvirats*. Stuttgart.

———. 2000. "Marcus Iunius Brutus—oder: Die Nemesis des Namens." In Hölkeskamp and Stein-Hölkeskamp 2000, 328–39.

Goudineau, C. 1990. *César et la Gaule*. Paris.

Gowing, A. 2005. *Empire and Memory: The Representation of the Roman Republic in Imperial Culture*. Cambridge.

Gradel, I. 2002. *Emperor Worship and Roman Religion*. Oxford.

Green, P. 2007. *The Hellenistic Age: A Short History*. New York.

Greenidge, A. H. J., and E. W. Clay. 1960. *Sources for Roman History 133–70 BC²*. Oxford.

Griffin, M. T. 2008. "*Iure plectimur*: The Roman Critique of Roman Imperialism." In *East and West: Papers in Ancient History Presented to Glen W. Bowersock* (Loeb Classical Monographs 14), ed. T. Corey Brennan and H. I. Flower, 85–111. Cambridge, MA.

Gruen, E. S. 1968. *Roman Politics and the Criminal Courts 149–78 BC*. Cambridge, MA.

———. 1974. *The Last Generation of the Roman Republic*. Berkeley, CA.

———. 1984. *The Hellenistic World and the Coming of Rome*. 2 vols. Berkeley, CA.

———. 1990. *Studies in Greek Culture and Roman Policy*. Leiden.

———. 1992. *Culture and National Identity in Republican Rome.* London.

Habicht, C. 1990. *Cicero the Politician.* Baltimore.

Haltenhoff, A., A. Heil, and F.-H. Mutschler, eds. 2003. *O tempora, o mores! Römische Werte und römische Literatur in den letzten Jahrzehnten der Republik.* Munich.

Hamilton, C. D. 1969. "The *Tresviri Monetales* and the Republican *Cursus Honorum.*" *TAPA* 100:181–99.

Hantos, T. 1988. *Res publica constituta: Die Verfassung des Dictators Sulla.* Wiesbaden.

Harris, W. 1979. *War and Imperialism in Republican Rome, 327–70 BC.* Oxford.

Hinard, F. 1985. *Les proscriptions de la Rome républicaine.* Paris.

———. 1987. "Sur une autre forme de l'opposition entre *virtus* et *fortuna.*" *Kentron* 3: 17–20.

Hinds, S. 1998. *Allusion and Intertext: Dynamics of Appropriation in Roman Poetry.* Cambridge.

Holford-Strevens, L. 2005. *The History of Time: A Very Short Introduction.* Oxford.

Hölkeskamp, K.-J. 1987. *Die Entstehung der Nobilität: Studien zur sozialen und politischen Geschichte der Römischen Republik im 4. Jhdt. v. Chr.* Stuttgart.

———. 1988a. "Die Entstehung der Nobilität und der Funktionswandel des Volkstribunats: Die historische Bedeutung der *Lex Hortensia de plebiscitis.*" *Archiv für Kulturgeschichte* 70: 271–312.

———. 1988b. "Das *Plebescitum Ogulnium de Sacerdotibus*: Überlegungen zu Authentizität und Interpretation der livianischen Überlieferung im Jahre 300 v. Chr." *RM* 131: 51–67.

———. 1996. "*Exempla* und *mos maiorum*: Überlegungen zum kollektiven Gedächtnis der Nobilität." In *Vergangenheit und Lebenswelt: Soziale Kommunikation, Traditionsbildung und historisches Bewußtsein,* ed. H.-J. Gehrke and A. Möller, 301–38. Tübingen.

———. 1999. *Schiedsrichter, Gesetzgeber und Gesetzgebung im archaischen Griechenland.* Stuttgart.

———. 2000a. "Lucius Cornelius Sulla—Revolutionär und restaurativer Reformer." In Hölkeskamp and Stein-Hölkeskamp 2000, 199–218.

———. 2000b. "Senat und Volk von Rome—Kurzbiographie einer Republik." In Hölkeskamp and Stein-Hölkeskamp 2000, 11–35.

———. 2001. "Capitol, Comitium und Forum: Öffentliche Räume, sakrale Topographie und Erinnerungslandschaften der römischen Republik." In *Studien zu antiken Identitäten*, ed. S. Faller, 97–132. Würzburg.

———. 2004a. *Rekonstruktionen einer Republik: Die politische Kultur des antiken Rom und die Forschung der letzten Jahrzehnte.* Munich.

———. 2004b. *Senatus populusque romanus: Die politische Kultur der Republik: Dimensionen und Deutungen.* Stuttgart.

———. 2004c. "Under Roman Roofs: Family, House, and Household." In Flower 2004, 113–38.

———. 2006a. "Konsens und Konkurrenz: Die politische Kultur der römischen Republik in neuer Sicht." *Klio* 88: 360–96.

———. 2006b. "Pomp und Prozessionen: Rituale und Zeremonien in der politischen Kultur der römischen Republik." *Jahrbuch des Historischen Kollegs*, 35–72.

———. 2007. Review of Forsythe 2005. *Gnomon* 79: 50–56.

Hölkeskamp, K.-J., and E. Stein-Hölkeskamp, eds. 2000. *Von Romulus zu Augustus: Große Gestalten der römischen Republik.* Munich.

Hölscher, T. 1978. "Die Anfänge der römischen Repräsentationskunst." *MDAI(R)* 85: 315–57.

———. 1980. "Die Geschichtsauffassung in der römischen Repräsentationskunst." *JDAI* 95: 265–321.

———. 1990. "Römische Nobiles und hellenistische Herrscher." In *Akten des XIII. Internationalen Kongresses für Klassische Archäologie, Berlin 1988*, 73–84. Mainz.

———. 2001. "Die Alten vor Augen: Politische Denkmäler und öffentliches Gedächtnis im republikanischen Rom." In *Institutionalität und Symbolisierung: Verstetigung kultureller Ordnungsmuster in Vergangenheit und Gegenwart*, ed. G. Melville, 183–211. Cologne.

Humm, M. 2005. *Appius Claudius Caecus: la république accomplie.* Rome.

Hurlet, F. 1993. *La dictature de Sylla: monarchie ou magistrature républicaine? Essai d'histoire constitutionelle.* Brussels.

Itgenshorst, T. 2005. *Tota illa pompa: Der Triumph in der römischen Republik.* Göttingen.

———. 2006. "Roman Commanders and Hellenistic Kings: On the Hellenization of the Republican Triumph." *AncSoc* 36: 51–68.

Jehne, M. 1986. *Der Staat des Diktators Caesar*. Cologne.

——. 1993. "Geheime Abstimmung und Bindungswesen in der römischen Republik." *HZ* 257: 593–613.

——. 2001. *Caesar*. Munich.

——. 2005. "Über den Rubicon: Die Eröffnung des römischen Bürgerkriegs am 10. Januar 49 v. Chr." In *Und keine Schlacht bei Marathon: Große Ereignisse und Mythen der europäischen Geschichte*, ed. W. Kreiger, 25–49. Stuttgart.

——. 2006a. "Methods, Models, and Historiography." In Rosenstein and Morstein-Marx 2006, 3–28.

——. 2006b. *Die römische Republik von der Gründung bis Caesar*. Munich.

Jehne, M., and R. Pfeilschifter, eds. 2006. *Herrschaft ohne Integration? Rom und Italien in republikanischer Zeit*. Frankfurt.

Johnston, D. 1999. *Roman Law in Context*. Cambridge.

Jolowicz, H. F., and B. Nicholas. 1972. *Historical Introduction to the Study of Roman Law*[3]. Cambridge.

Kallet-Marx, R. M. 1995. *Hegemony to Empire: The Development of the Roman Imperium in the East from 148 to 62 BC*. Berkeley, CA.

Kaster, R. A. 1995. *Suetonius: "De Grammaticis et Rhetoribus."* Oxford.

Keaveney, A. 1983. "What Happened in 88?" *Eirene* 10: 53–86.

——. 2005a. *Rome and the Unification of Italy*[2]. Bristol.

——. 2005b. *Sulla, the Last Republican*[2]. London.

——. 2005c. "The Terminal Date of Sulla's Dictatorship." *Athenaeum* 93: 423–38.

——. 2007. *The Army and the Roman Revolution*. London.

Kelly, G. P. 2006. *A History of Exile in the Roman Republic*. Cambridge.

Keppie, L. 1998. *The Making of the Roman Army: From Republic to Empire*[2]. Norman, OK.

Kierdorf, W. 1980. *Laudatio Funebris: Interpretationen und Untersuchungen zur Entwicklung der römischen Leichenrede*. Meisenheim am Glan.

——. 2003. *Römische Geschichtsschreibung der republikanischen Zeit*. Heidelberg.

Kolb, F. 2002. *Rom: Die Geschichte der Stadt in der Antike*[2]. Munich.

Kondratieff, E. 2003. "Popular Power in Action: Tribunes of the Plebs in the Later Republic." Ph.D. Diss., Univ. of Pennsylvania.

Konrad, C. F. 1994. *Plutarch Sertorius: A Historical Commentary.* Chapel Hill, NC.

Kunkel, W. 1962. *Untersuchungen zur Entwicklung des römischen Kriminalverfahrens in vorsullanischer Zeit.* Abhandlungen der Bayerischen Akademie der Wissenschaften, Philosophisch-historische Klasse, n.F. 56. Munich.

La mémoire perdue 1 = *La mémoire perdue: à la recherche des archives oubliées, publiques et privées de la Rome antique.* Paris, 1987.

Levick, B. M. 1982. "Sulla's March on Rome in 88 BC." *Historia* 31: 503–8.

Levy, E. 1963. "Die römische Kapitalstrafe." *Gesammelte Schriften* 2: 911–44.

Lewis, R. G. 1991. "Sulla's Autobiography: Scope and Economy." *Athenaeum* 79: 509–19.

Lieberg, G. 1998. *Caesars Politik in Gallien: Interpretationen zum Bellum Gallicum.* Bochum.

Linderski, J. 1986. "The Augural Law." *ANRW* II.16.3: 2146–312.

———. 2002. "The Pontiff and the Tribune: The Death of Tiberius Gracchus." *Athenaeum* 90: 339–66.

Linke, B. 2005. *Die römische Republik von den Gracchen bis Sulla.* Darmstadt.

Linke, B., and M. Stemmler, eds. 2000. *Mos maiorum: Untersuchungen zu Formen der Identitätsstiftung und Stabilisierung in der römischen Republik.* Stuttgart.

Lintott, A. 1992. *Judicial Reform and Land Reform in the Roman Republic.* Cambridge.

———. 1994. "The Crisis of the Republic: Sources and Source-Problems." In *The Cambridge Ancient History*[2] 9, 1–15. Cambridge.

———. 1999a. The Constitution of the Roman Republic. Oxford.

———. 1999b. *Violence in Republican Rome*[2]. Oxford.

Lomas, K. 2004. "Italy during the Roman Republic 338–31 BC." In Flower 2004, 199–224.

Lott, J. B. 2004. *The Neighborhoods of Augustan Rome.* Cambridge.

Lovano, M. 2002. *The Age of Cinna: Crucible of the Late Republic.* Stuttgart.

Mackay, C. S. 2000. "Sulla and the Monuments: Studies in His Public Persona." *Historia* 49: 161–210.

———. 2004. *Ancient Rome: A Military and Political History.* Cambridge.

Manuwald, G., ed. 2001. *Der Satiriker Lucilius und seine Zeit.* Munich.

Martin, P. M. 1994. *L'idée de royauté à Rome 2: Haine de la royauté et séductions monarchiques (du IVe siècle av. J.-C. au principat augustéen).* Clérmont-Ferrand.

McDonnell, M. 2006. *Roman Manliness: Virtus and the Roman Republic.* Cambridge.

McGing, B. C. 1986. *The Foreign Policy of Mithridates VI Eupator, King of Pontus.* Leiden.

Meier, C. 1980. *Res publica amissa: Eine Studie zu Verfassung und Geschichte der späten römischen Republik*[2]. Wiesbaden.

———. 1982. *Caesar.* Berlin.

Michels, A. G. 1967. *The Calendar of the Roman Republic.* Princeton, NJ.

Millar, F.G.B. 1989. "Political Power in Mid-Republican Rome: Curia or Comitium?" *JRS* 79: 138–50.

———. 2002. *The Roman Republic in Political Thought.* Hanover, NH.

Mommsen, T. 1859. *Die römische Chronologie bis auf Caesar*[2]. Berlin.

———. 1899. *Römisches Strafrecht.* Repr., Graz 1955.

Montesquieu, Charles de Secondat, Baron de. 1734. *Considerations sur les causes de la grandeur des romains et de leur decadence.* Facsimile, ed. B. Hemmerdinger, Naples 1995.

Morgan, L. 1997. "'*Levi quidem de re...*': Julius Caesar as Tyrant and Pedant." *JRS* 87: 23–40.

———. 2000. "The Autopsy of C. Asinius Pollio." *JRS* 90: 51–69.

Morris, I. 1997. "Periodization and the Heroes: Inventing the Dark Age." In *Inventing Ancient Culture: Historicism, Periodization, and the Ancient World,* ed. M. Golden and P. Toohey, 96–131. London.

Morstein-Marx, R. 2004. *Mass Oratory and Political Power in the Late Roman Republic.* Cambridge.

Morstein-Marx, R. and N. S. Rosenstein, 2006. "The Transformation of the Republic." In Rosenstein and Morstein-Marx 2006, 625–37.

Mouritsen, H. 1998. *Italian Unification: A Study in Ancient and Modern Historiography.* London.

Nicolet, C. 1976. *Le métier de citoyen dans la Rome républicaine.* Paris.

Nippel, W. 1988. *Aufruhr und "Polizei" in der römischen Republik.* Stuttgart.

——. 1995. *Public Order in Ancient Rome.* Cambridge.

Nora, P. 1996. "Generation." In *Realms of Memory* 1: *Rethinking the French Past: Conflicts and Divisions,* English edition ed. L. D. Kritzman, trans. A. Goldhammer, 499–531. New York.

Oakley, S. P. 1997. *A Commentary on Livy Books VI–X.* Oxford.

——. 2004. "The Early Republic." In Flower 2004, 15–30.

Ormerod, H. A. 1924. *Piracy in the Ancient World: An Essay in Mediterranean History.* London.

Osgood, J. 2006. *Caesar's Legacy: Civil War and the Emergence of the Roman Empire.* Cambridge.

Ostwald, M. 1986. *From Popular Sovereignty to the Sovereignty of Law: Law, Society and Politics in Fifth Century Athens.* Berkeley, CA.

Palmer, R.E.A. 1970. *The Archaic Community of the Romans.* Cambridge.

Pappalardo, U. 2004. "The *Domus Romana*: Pictorial Decorations and Cultural Values." In *Domus: Wall Painting in the Roman House,* ed. D. Mazzoleni, 41–52. Los Angeles.

Patterson, J. 2006a. "The City of Rome." In Rosenstein and Morstein-Marx 2006, 345–64.

——. 2006b. "Colonization and Historiography: The Roman Republic." In *Greek and Roman Colonization: Origins, Ideologies, and Interactions,* ed. G. Bradley and J. P. Wilson, 189–218. Swansea.

——. 2006c. "Rome and Italy." In Rosenstein and Morstein-Marx 2006, 606–24.

Paul, G. M. 1984. *A Historical Commentary on Sallust's "Bellum Iugurthinum."* Liverpool.

Pina Polo, F. 1996. *Contra arma verbis: Der Redner vor dem Volk in der späten römischen Republik.* Stuttgart.

——. 2004. "Die nützliche Erinnerung: Geschichtsschreibung, *mos maiorum* und die römische Identität." *Historia* 53: 147–72.

Pohl, H. 1993. *Die römische Politik und die Piraterie im östlichen Mittelmeer vom 3. Bis 1. Jhdt. v. Chr.* Berlin.

Porter, J. I. 2006. *Classical Pasts: The Classical Traditions of Greece and Rome.* Princeton, NJ.

Potter, D. S. 2004. "The Roman Army and Navy." In Flower 2004, 66–88.

Powell, J.G.F., ed. 2006. *M. Tulli Ciceronis: "De re publica," "De legibus," "Cato maior de senectute," "Laelius de amicitia."* Oxford.

Purcell, N. 1995. "On the Sacking of Carthage and Corinth." In *Ethics and Rhetoric. Classical Essays for Donald Russell on his 75th Birthday*, ed. D. Innes, H. Hine, and C. Pelling, 133–48. Oxford.

———. 2003. "Becoming Historical: The Roman Case." In *Myth, History, and Culture in Republican Rome*, ed. D. Braund and C. Gill, 12–40. Exeter.

Raaflaub, K. A. 1996. "Born To Be Wolves? Origins of Roman Imperialism." In *Transitions to Empire: Essays in Greco-Roman History 360–146 BC in Honor of E. Badian*, ed. R. W. Wallace and E. M. Harris, 273–314. Norman, OK.

———, ed. 2005. *Social Struggles in Archaic Rome: New Perspectives on the Conflict of the Orders*[2]. Oxford.

———. 2006. "Between Myth and History: Rome's Rise from Village to Empire (the Eighth Century to 264)." In Rosenstein and Morstein-Marx 2006, 125–46. Oxford.

Raditsa, L. 1973. "Julius Caesar and His Writings." *ANRW* I.3: 417–56.

Ramage, E. S. 1991. "Sulla's Propaganda." *Klio* 73: 93–121.

Rawson, E. 1974. "Religion and Politics in the Late Second Century BC at Rome." *Phoenix* 28: 193–212 (repr. in *Roman Culture and Society* [Oxford, 1991], 149–68).

———. 1975. *Cicero*. London.

———. 1985. *Intellectual Life in the Late Roman Republic*. Baltimore.

———. 1994a. "The Aftermath of the Ides." In *The Cambridge Ancient History*[2] 9, 468–90. Cambridge.

———. 1994b. "Caesar: Civil War and Dictatorship." In *The Cambridge Ancient History*[2] 9, 424–67. Cambridge.

Rich, J. 1983. "The Supposed Manpower Shortage of the Later Second Century BC." *Historia* 32: 287–31.

———. 1997. "Structuring Roman History: The Consular Year and the Roman Historical Tradition." *Histos* 1 (http://www.dur.ac.uk/Classics/histos/1997/rich1.html, accessed September 5, 2008).

Richardson, J. S. 1986. *Hispaniae: Spain and the Development of Roman Imperialism 218–82 BC*. Cambridge.

———. 1996. *The Romans in Spain*. Oxford.

Rickman, G. 1980. *The Corn Supply of Ancient Rome*. Oxford.

Riggsby, A. M. 1999. *Crime and Community in Ciceronian Rome*. Austin, TX.

Rives, J. 2005. "Flavian Religious Policy and the Destruction of the Jerusalem Temple." In *Flavius Josephus and Flavian Rome*, ed. J. Edmondson, S. Mason, and J. Rives, 145–66. Oxford.

Rosenstein, N. S. 1986. "*Imperatores victi*: The Case of C. Hostilius Mancinus." *CA* 5: 230–52.

———. 1990. *Imperatores Victi: Military Defeat and Aristocratic Competition in the Middle and Late Republic*. Berkeley, CA.

———. 1993. "Competition and Crisis in Mid-Republican Rome." *Phoenix* 47: 313–38.

———. 2004. *Rome at War: Farms, Families, and Death in the Middle Republic*. Chapel Hill, NC.

Rosenstein, N. S., and R. Morstein-Marx, eds. 2006. *A Companion to the Roman Republic*. Oxford.

Rüpke, J. 1995. *Kalender und Öffentlichkeit: Die Geschichte der Repräsentation und religiösen Qualifikation von Zeit in Rom*. Berlin.

———. 2006. *Zeit und Fest: Eine Kulturgeschichte des Kalenders*. Munich.

Ryan, F. X. 1998. *Rank and Participation in the Republican Senate*. Stuttgart.

Salerno, F. 1999. *Tacita libertas: l'introduzione del voto segreto nella Roma repubblicana*. Naples.

Santangelo, F. 2007. *Sulla, the Elites and the Empire: A Study of Roman Politics in Italy and the Greek East*. Leiden.

Sartre, M. 2005. *The Middle East under Rome*. Cambridge, MA.

Schäfer, T. 1989. *Imperii insignia, sella curulis und fasces: Zur Repräsentation römischer Magistrate*. Mainz.

Scheidel, W. 2001. "Progress and Problems in Roman Demography." In *Debating Roman Demography* (*Mnemosyne* Suppl. 211), ed. W. Scheidel, 1–81. Leiden.

———. 2004. "Human Mobility in Roman Italy: The Free Population." *JRS* 94: 1–26.

Scholz, P. 2003. "Sullas commentarii—eine literarische Rechtfertigung: Zu Wesen und Funktion der autobiographischen Schriften in der späten römischen Republik." In Eigler et al. 2003, 172–95.

Scholz, U. W. 2000. "Die Sermones des Lucilius." In *Moribus antiquis res stat romana: römische Werte und römische Literatur im 3. und 2. Jhdt. v. Chr.*, ed. M. Braun, A. Haltenhoff, and F.-H. Mutschler, 217–34. Leipzig.

Schultz, C. E. 2006. "Juno Sospita and Roman Insecurity in the Social War." *YCS* 33: 207–27.

Scullard, H. H. 1980. *A History of the Roman World 753–146 BC*[4]. London.

Seager, R. 2002. *Pompey the Great: A Political Biography*[2]. Oxford.

Sehlmeyer, M. 1999. *Stadtrömische Ehrenstatuen der republikanischen Zeit: Historizität und Kontext von Symbolen nobilitären Standesbewußtseins*. Stuttgart.

———. 2003. "Die Anfänge der antiquarischen Literatur in Rom: Motivation und Bezug zur Historiographie bis in die Zeit von Tuditanus und Gracchanus." In Eigler et al. 2003, 157–71.

Shaw, B. D. 2001. *Spartacus and the Roman Slave Wars: A Brief History with Documents*. Boston, MA.

Sherwin-White, A. N. 1973. *The Roman Citizenship*[2]. Oxford.

———. 1984. *Roman Foreign Policy in the East 168 BC to AD 1*. London.

Simón, F. M. 1996. *Flamen Dialis: el sacerdote de Júpiter en la religion romana*. Madrid.

Simón, F. M., and F. Pina Polo. 2000. "Mario Gratidiano, los compita y la religiosidad popular a fines de la republica." *Klio* 82: 154–70.

Smith, C. J. 2006. *The Roman Clan: The Gens from Ancient Ideology to Modern Anthropology*. Cambridge.

Sonnenschein, E. A. 1904. "The Plural of *Res Publica*." *CR* 18: 37–38.

Spaeth, B. 1990. "The Goddess Ceres and the Death of Tiberius Gracchus." *Historia* 39: 182–95.

Spann, P. O. 1987. *Sertorius and the Legacy of Sulla*. Fayetteville, AR.

Spielvogel, J. 1993. *Amicitia und res publica: Ciceros Maxime während der innenpolitischen Auseinanderstzung der Jahren 59–50 v. Chr.* Stuttgart.

Steingräber, S. 1985. *Etruscan Painting*. New York.

Stockton, D. 1971. *Cicero: A Political Biography*. Oxford.

———. 1979. *The Gracchi*. Oxford.

Strauss, B. 1997. "The Problem of Periodization: The Case of the Peloponnesian War." In *Inventing Ancient Culture: Historicism,*

Periodization, and the Ancient World, ed. M. Golden and P. Toohey, 165–75. London.

Suerbaum, W., ed. 2002. *Handbuch der lateinischen Literatur der Antike* 1: *Die archaische Literature*. Munich.

Sumi, G. S. 2005. *Ceremony and Power: Performing Politics in Rome between Republic and Empire*. Ann Arbor, MI.

Suolahti, J. 1963. *The Roman Censors: A Study on Social Structure*. Helsinki.

Syme, R. 1939. *The Roman Revolution*. Oxford.

———. 1964. *Sallust*. Berkeley, CA.

Tatum, W. J. 1999. *The Patrician Tribune: P. Clodius Pulcher*. Chapel Hill, NC.

Taylor, L. R. 1949. *Party Politics in the Age of Caesar*. Berkeley, CA.

———. 1960. *Voting Districts of the Roman Republic: The Thirty-Five Urban and Rural Tribes*. Rome.

———. 1962. "Forerunners of the Gracchi." *JRS* 52: 19–27.

———. 1966. *Roman Voting Assemblies from the Hannibalic War to the Dictatorship of Caesar*. Ann Arbor, MI.

Thein, A. G. 2002. "Sulla's Public Image and the Politics of Civic Renewal." Ph.D. Diss., Univ. of Pennsylvania.

———. Forthcoming. "Roman World Rule and the Late Republican Capitolium." *AJAH* n.s. 6 (2007).

Thommen, L. 1989. *Das Volkstribunat der späten römischen Republik*. Stuttgart.

Timpe, D. 1994. "Kimbrertraditionen und Kimbrermythos." In *Germani in Italia*, ed. B. Scardigli and P. Scardigli, 23–60. Rome.

Torelli, M. 2006. "The Topography and Archaeology of Republican Rome." In Rosenstein and Morstein-Marx 2006, 81–101.

Trzaska-Richter, C. 1991. *Furor Teutonicus*. Trier.

Tucci, P. L. 2005. "Where High Moneta Leads Her Steps Sublime: The 'Tabularium' and the Temple of Juno Moneta." *JRA* 18: 6–33.

Ungern Sternberg von Pürkel, J. Baron. 1970. *Untersuchungen zum spätrepublikanischen Notstandsrecht: senatus consultum ultimum und hostis-Erklärung*. Munich.

Vansina, J. 1985. *Oral Tradition as History*. Madison, WI.

Vedaldi Iasbez, V. 1981. "I figli dei proscritti sillani." *Labeo* 27: 163–213.

Virlouvet, C. 1985. *Famines et émeutes des origines de la République à la mort de Néron*. Rome.

————. 1995. *Tessera frumentaria: les procédures de la distribution du blé public à Rome*. Rome.

Volkmann, H. 1958. *Sullas Marsch auf Rom*. Munich.

Von Ungern-Sternberg, J. 1982. "Weltreich und Krise: Äussere Bedingungen für den Niedergang der römischen Republik." *MH* 39: 263–65.

————. 1988. "Überlegungen zur frühen römischen Überlieferung im Lichte der Oral-Tradition-Forschung." In *Vergangenheit in mündlicher Überlieferung*, ed. J. von Ungern-Sternberg and H. Reinau, 237–65. Stuttgart.

————. 1990. "Die Wahrnehmung des 'Standeskampfes' in der römischen Geschichtsschreibung." In *Staat und Staatlichkeit in der frühen römischen Republik*, ed. W. Eder, 92–102. Stuttgart.

————. 1991. "Die politische und soziale Bedeutung der spätrepublikanischen leges *frumentariae*." In *Nourir la plèbe: Actes en hommage à Denis van Berchem*, ed. A. Giovannini, 19–42. Basel.

————. 1998. "Die Legitimätskrise der römischen Republik." *HZ* 266: 607–24.

————. 2000. "Eine Katastrophe wird verarbeitet: Die Gallier in Rom." In *The Roman Middle Republic*, ed. C. Bruun, 207–22. Rome.

————. 2004. "The Crisis of the Republic." In Flower 2004, 89–109.

————. 2005. "The End of the Conflict of the Orders." In *Social Struggles in Archaic Rome: New Perspectives on the Conflict of the Orders*[2], ed. K. A. Raaflaub, 312–32. Oxford.

————, ed. 2006. *Römische Studien: Geschichtsbewußtsein, Zeitalter der Gracchen, Krise der Republik*. Leipzig.

Walter, U. 2003a. "*Natam me consule Romam*: Historisch-politische Autobiographien in republikanischer Zeit: Ein Überblick." *AU* 46: 36–42.

————. 2003b. "Opfer ihrer Ungleichzeitigkeit: Die Gesamtgeschichten im ersten Jhdt. v. Chr. und die fortdauernde Attraktivität des 'annalistischen Schemas.'" In Eigler et al. 2003, 136–56.

————. 2004. *Memoria und res publica: Zur Geschichtskultur im republikanischen Rom*. Frankfurt am Main.

————. 2006. "The Classical Age as a Historical Epoch." In *A Companion to the Classical Greek World*, ed. K. H. Kinzl, 1–25. Oxford.

Ward, A. M. 1977. *Marcus Crassus and the Late Roman Republic.* Columbia, MO.

Watson, A. 1975. *Rome of the Twelve Tables.* Princeton, NJ.

Welch, K. 1998. "Caesar and his Officers in the Gallic War Commentaries." In *Julius Caesar as Artful Reporter: The War Commentaries as Political Instruments,* ed. K. Welch and A. Powell, 85–110. London.

Welch, K. E. 2006. "Art and Architecture in the Roman Republic." In Rosenstein and Morstein-Marx 2006, 496–542.

Welwei, K.-W. 2000. *Sub corona vendere: Quellenkritische Studien zu Kriegsgefangenschaft und Sklaverei in Rom bis zum Ende des Hannibalkrieges.* Stuttgart.

Wesch-Klein, G. 1993. *Funus publicum: Eine Studie zur öffentlichen Beisetzung und Gewährung von Ehrengräbern in Rom und den Westprovinzen.* Stuttgart.

Williamson, C. 2005. *The Laws of the Roman People: Public Law in the Expansion and Decline of the Roman Republic.* Ann Arbor, MI.

Wiseman, T. P. 1971. *New Men in the Roman Senate 139 BC to AD 14.* Oxford.

———. 1985. "Competition and Cooperation." In *Roman Political Life 90 BC–AD 69,* 3–19. Exeter.

———. 1994a. "Caesar, Pompey, and Rome 59–50 B.C." In *The Cambridge Ancient History*[2] 9, 368–423. Cambridge.

———. 1994b. "The Senate and the *Populares,* 69–60 B.C." In *The Cambridge Ancient History*[2] 9, 327–67. Cambridge.

———. 1998. "Roman Republic, Year 1." *G&R* 45: 19–26.

Yakobson, A. 1995. "The Secret Ballot and its Effects in the Late Roman Republic." *Hermes* 123: 426–42.

———. 1999. *Elections and Electioneering in Rome: A Study in the Political System of the Late Republic.* Stuttgart.

Yavetz, Z. 1979. *Caesar in der öffentlichen Meinung.* Düsseldorf.

Zanker, P. 1988. *The Power of Images in the Age of Augustus.* Ann Arbor, MI.

Zecchini, G. 2001. *Cesare e il mos maiorum.* Stuttgart.

Zerubavel, E. 2003. *Time Maps: Collective Memory and the Social Shape of the Past.* Chicago.

INDEX